I CAN 2

John 3:16

I Can 2

Art Lindsay, I Can 2

ISBN 1-887002-93-6

Cross Training Publishing
P.O. Box 1541
Grand Island, NE 68802
(800) 430-8588

This book is manufactured in the United States of America.

Library of Congress Cataloging in Publication Data in Progress.

Published by Cross Training Publishing
P.O. Box 1541
Grand Island, NE 68802
1-800-430-8588

Photo Credit:
Gordon Thiessen
University of Nebraska Photography

TABLE OF CONTENTS

DISCLAIMER

Though this story is based upon a true account of Ron Brown's life, it seemed prudent to change the actual names of certain individuals in order to protect their right to privacy.

Ron Brown's royalties from this book
will go to Mission Nebraska.

FOREWORD
By Tom Osborne

• •

Ron Brown is truly one of the most unusual and remarkable people that I have met. Ron possesses a very strong work ethic. This was clearly illustrated to me when he was hired at the University of Nebraska as an offensive coach even though all of his previous experience as a player and coach had been primarily with the defensive side of the football. Ron worked diligently to become a receivers coach on short notice and made a remarkable transition. He continues to do everything that he can to further his abilities as a coach. In addition to his coaching abilities, he is a tireless and thorough recruiter. He consistently covers a large part of the United States in a very efficient manner for us.

More importantly, Ron has a tremendous compassion for young people. He spends a large portion of his summer running camps for underprivileged young people on the East coast, here in Lincoln, and also in Macy, Nebraska, where he works primarily with Native American children. Ron has also been quite active in the Big Brothers/Big Sisters program and always has extra time for our players and their personal needs.

Ron has a very strong Christian commitment. He sincerely tries to present himself as a living sacrifice in his service to Christ and is one who leads consistently by example. His faith is clearly evident in everything that he does as a coach, as a husband, and as a friend.

This book traces Ron's life from its inception at a foundling home in New York City to his childhood years on Martha's Vineyard to his career at Brown University as a student-athlete through several pro football camps and concludes with events involving his decision to go into coaching, first at Brown University and later at the University of Nebraska.

This book is written in a way that enables the reader to really come to know Ron and, more importantly, the faith that motivates and inspires his life. Ron's efforts to become a professional football player provide insights into all that goes into a career in professional athletics that is not readily observable to the general public. Art

Lindsay has done a fine job of putting all the information together in a very concise and readable form. I hope that you enjoy reading this book about a truly fine human being who inspires all of those who know him well.

Tom Osborne
Former Head Football Coach
University of Nebraska

INTRODUCTION
WHY THIS BOOK?

• •

When Arthur Lindsay approached me with his desire to write a Christian biography based on my life after listening to me present my testimony, I was very apprehensive.

My nature has normally permitted me to think that biographies should only be based on the lives of people, past or present, who are important and influential by the world's standards. The same would hold true in Christian circles. To read about a "household" name, such as Tom Osborne, seems appropriate; therefore, I was initially very embarrassed about a book written on my life.

But this is where my "normal" nature has failed me. Arthur Lindsay convinced me that the book was about someone who, in fact, was important and influential: Jesus Christ, not Ron Brown.

Ron Brown is merely a "worm on a hook." I was searching for success in this life–like almost everyone else–in all the wrong places. Until one day I met the Savior. That was the turning point in the game for me.

So how dare a basically unknown college assistant football coach comply with having a book written about him? The answer is that it isn't really about him. Rather, it's about the Lord Jesus Christ and how He can take a weak, needy, insecure, fearful, and doubting person like me and transform that life into one filled with inspiration and purpose.

It is my desire that this book would inspire you to seek God's definition of success for your life. That is life's most thrilling victory!

As you read this book you might ask: "Why not more information about Ron's family?" My family has been such a delight to me. I thank the Lord for my wife, Molvina. She has been a tremendous companion to me through this topsy-turvy world of mine. She has a stability, consistency, and balance about her that helps keep our "family ground" on a level plane. With all of that–the bottom line is that I love her deeply and intimately.

There's also something about little girls that I so cherish. Perhaps it's the "let's spoil Daddy" complex, but my young daughters, Sojourner and Bronwyn, have me heart wrapped around their little pinkies. Yet, I realize that they will not remain as little girls. They're growing fast. This is why I have purposely desired that Molvina, Sojourner, and Bronwyn be kept to a bare minimum in this book. Privacy is crucial for my family and me. Privacy almost seems like an oxymoron when you're a Nebraska football coach, yet Molvina and I have done everything we can as a team to keep our home free as possible from the public world that I live in outside of my home. I have chosen to be somewhat transparent with my personal life simply in order to use the visible platform that God has given me to share my faith in Jesus Christ. Out of protection of this privacy, I do not want to add anymore visibility to my wife and children than what is normal. This is my way to preserve the privacy of my family whom I cherish and need so much.

Ron Brown
Assistant Football Coach
University of Nebraska

CHAPTER 1

THE RECRUIT
WHO MADE THE TEAM

S orrow etched itself deeply into the brow of Mike Stachmus. His nostrils objected to the terrible odor of hospital disinfectant. An awful awareness of his own limited ability and the despair of defeat flooded through his mind.

"How's the pain, son?" he asked, though he knew there was little he could do to relieve the discomfort of the weakened young man lying in the machine-shrouded bed next to him. Nor did he really expect an answer, for throughout the year-long physical ordeal, his son seldom complained. Young Victor Stachmus was made of tough stuff. Physical agony was no stranger to him. In previous circumstances, however, it had been of his own choosing. He had knowingly accepted pain through strain as a standard for his life when he bridged the gap from childhood into adolescence. When he decided to compete in football, he knew full well that pain was a necessary price to pay in order to excel.

Football was a natural decision for Victor. In his native Oklahoma, every other endeavor paled in comparison to the college gridiron glories of the Sooners or the Cowboys. His earliest memories were of the excitement that his father and others reveled in as they argued pigskin tactics and strategy. Even as a kid, to him the mention of a wishbone had little to do with chicken. Vic was thoroughly infected from his youth with every aspect of football.

Of course, his early football days were the simple joys of a sandlot game as his parents encouraged him without ever being pushy. However, as he entered his teens, he began to take seriously his personal responsibility. He rigorously disciplined his growing body with the goal of becoming a standout player. He drove himself to pay the price in order to be the best.

Nonetheless, success in football was not an easy prize. He hoisted tons of weights, watched a thousand gut-grinding miles pass slowly beneath his feet, and slammed his body through endless hours of perfecting drills on the practice field. No tobacco. No drugs. No booze. No backtalk. He gave instant obedience to his coaches. His goal was specific: he would be the best football player that McAlester, Oklahoma, had ever produced.

At the tender age of eighteen, he attained that first plateau in his dream for life. His 6'5" frame, muscled with 250 pounds of never-say-die energy, helped power his hometown to statewide prominence. He was a celebrated hero to all who knew him.

He was ready to begin the difficult climb to the next level of excellence: collegiate football. His prospects for an outstanding career were superb.

In football-crazed Oklahoma, such a young man, of course, was destined for notoriety in the university ranks as either an Oklahoma Sooner or an Oklahoma State Cowboy. That was a given. The choice was merely a decision between the two.

But it was impossible for the state to keep the youngster's talents hidden. His abilities attracted national media attention. Competition to sign him for a college football scholarship waged intense. Recruiters from across the nation took up residence on his doorstep. One such coach, Ron Brown from archrival Nebraska, even had the audacity to head south to try to steal the prize. It was an improbable gambit: no Oklahoma athlete had ever gone directly from high school to play football at Nebraska.

Yet, sometimes the unbelievable, the outrageous does happen.

Nearly everyone in Oklahoma who knew anything at all about football was in a state of shock when word got out that Vic had verbally committed to play college ball for the Big Red at the University of Nebraska. But Oklahoma State did not give up the battle. The tug-of-war continued. Papers had not yet been signed.

Pressures built on the young man from many directions to reverse field. Most of Victor's relatives were OSU fans. One high school teammate and close friend, Lee Keith, had committed to the in-state school.

College recruiters are fearless, resourceful, and forceful, or they don't last long, because competition for the best prospects is often fierce. Yet, behind Victor's gentle outward demeanor was a resolve equally as tough as that of any coach.

The February signing deadline drew near. Oklahoma State increased its persuasive thrust. Ron Brown was off in Seattle visiting another high school standout, Jon Bostick. But Victor kept his word and held to his principles. He had made a commitment. He spoke his final word and stayed with his original decision.

The excitement of the actual signing, with Coach Brown looking on, took place in February 1988. With that weighty matter behind him, Victor turned his attention to the carefree pleasures of his final high school semester, and beyond that to the enjoyable rigors of his college career. He was really hyped up to wear a Cornhusker red jersey and play football at Nebraska.

At the same time, however, he realized that the tiredness in his body was something other than the strain of physical exertion. The football season was long since over; he should have lots of pep. His strength always had been enormous; he could bench press 370 pounds five times consecutively and push away a half-ton on the hip sled. During the exhilarating days of his senior season, he had brushed aside the infrequent, momentary inner pain. He simply challenged himself to tough it out and push ahead whenever he felt the drag of being unusually tired. But as spring burst forth in all of its beauty across the Oklahoma landscape, he admitted to his parents that something must be wrong with him.

The shocking report after Victor's first visit to a doctor struck his family and friends a devastating blow. Nor could Ron Brown at first believe the distressing news he received from Victor's parents, Mike and Marianne. "Victor is gravely ill with acute lymphoblastic leukemia. His chance of living one year is one out of five. His chance of living five years is almost none."

Ron altered his schedule at once to fly to Tulsa to see Vic in the hospital. It would be but one of many such visits, for he considered commitment to be a two-way street. The boy had committed to Nebraska, but Nebraska also was committed to the boy.

"Vic made a tremendous impact on me by the way he faced his battle with cancer," Ron commented later. "Even through great physical pain and exhaustion, he displayed incredible unselfishness and courage. He was always considerate and concerned, often asking me from his hospital bed, 'Coach, did you have a safe trip? Are you comfortable?'"

Victor maintained his composure amazingly well for a teenager. He never grumbled of physical distress to those attending him. On a pain tolerance scale of 0 to 10, he was usually at 8 or 9. He bravely bore the unbearable. As nurses asked, "How are you doing?", his customary response was, "Fine. I'm OK. I'm ready to go home."

The young man's previous health and his extreme enthusiasm for life gave him an early edge in the battle with leukemia. His condition improved dramatically after the first onset of the illness and the initial treatments. He was out of the hospital in 23 days, a near record time. He was able to attend his high school graduation, receiving a standing ovation as he crossed the stage.

The doctors told his father that if Vic had a relapse, his chances of surviving a year would be only 1 in 20. "I'm not telling Victor this," Mike responded angrily. "I've got more faith than that."

Shortly, however, Vic was back in the hospital. Again he responded to the medical treatment and was out in 28 days. He felt great and was doing fine. He knew he was going to win this one and he was preparing for college. The cancer, though, stealthily built its forces for another onslaught. In September, when his blood count dropped again, he and his family were referred to specialists in Houston. Already he was missing what was to have been his first year of college football at Nebraska. In unfortunate contrast, however, he was playing the game of his life.

He was put on a new protocol with the hope that it would bring him back into remission for a bone marrow transplant, which was his final hope. Mike Stachmus searched nationwide for a possible donor; there was only a 3/4 sibling match and there was no perfect unrelated match in the donor banks in the United States, England, or the rest of Europe. No suitable match could be found. Victor, truly, was one of a kind.

The spirits of all concerned sank, but they refused to be beaten.

The Stachmus family was finally referred to the UCLA Medical Center in their determination to bring about a cure. New tests were conducted. The immediate results were most ominous. The cancer and the terrible side effects of the chemotherapy had devastated Victor's vital organs. He was very weak.

The doctor was gentle yet blunt: "It's your decision. You can stay off chemotherapy and likely die in three weeks. Or you can go on heavy doses of chemo, with a fair chance that it'll cause organ failure, but with an outside chance that you'll make it through."

Victor didn't hesitate. One of his strongest attributes was that of being a possibility thinker, gaining advantage through positive action. "Let's get started," he responded with as much twinkle in his blue eyes as he could muster. "It's my last chance."

Unfortunately, the new protocol proved to be but an agonizing stalling tactic against the advancing enemy. Step by step, the cancer marched forward throughout his system, claiming new ground with every passing hour. It was a monstrous war of attrition. Victor's strength continued to retreat noticeably day by day. His once robust body dwindled to, what was for him, a weak, tired, frail, and helpless shell of a mere 200 pounds.

Still, he made a tremendous effort to walk the halls twice a day to maintain his strength. But he had to stop. From the physical standpoint, it appeared that the final battle was about to be engaged.

Thankfully, Victor and his family were not alone in their bid for victory. The young athlete's condition had been reported nationally in the press. That, along with the organization of a "Go Big Vic Day" in the states of Nebraska and Oklahoma, initiated a veritable flood of cards and letters from across the land. Thousands were standing in support of Vic and his family.

As Victor's physical war was drawing toward a dismal conclusion, Ron Brown was attending the National Coaches Convention in Nashville, Tennessee. On the evening of January 8, 1989, about fifty coaches gathered together in a Fellowship of Christian Athletes prayer and share time during the convention.

Several, including Brown, raised petitions to God for Vic Stachmus, praying that God would have His way with Victor both spiritually and physically.

Little did they know that at that very moment, Victor was near death, fighting a debilitating battle, struggling fiercely with extensive internal disorders. The doctor, having done all he could, advised his parents, "There's a chance that Victor won't make it through the night. His blood pressure has dropped to 50 over zero."

Victor slept uneasily. He was afraid that he would soon lose his life. Because he didn't understand death, he feared it.

But as the coaches (and countless others across the nation) prayed for the youth, Vic eased into such a restful slumber that those attending him dreaded that he had fallen into a finalizing coma. His breathing was shallow and labored. His blood pressure and vital signs were dangerously low. Nurses checked him every 15 minutes, certain that he would not make it through the night. Suddenly, unexplainably, his condition improved. He awoke with a surprised smile on his face. Looking around the room and at his father and mother, he stated in a bewildered tone, "Dad, I'm still here." His blood pressure had returned to 120 over 80 and his vital signs were stable.

Returning to sleep that evening, he had an amazing dream which he related to his relieved parents when he awoke brightly the next morning. "I walked up this beautiful avenue to the gates of heaven. There were brilliant lights beyond the entrance, so bright you couldn't see in. The guard asked me if I wanted to go in now or if I wanted to stay. The sight was very inviting, but I told them I wanted to fight it out. So they sent me back."

His father said, "Vic, you just had a dream."

But with an expression of total confidence, Vic said, "No, Dad, I was actually there." He smiled lamely at his mother, "I guess you're stuck with me, Mom."

Marianne brushed her hand lovingly across his sunken cheek. "That's OK with me," she said as she choked back tears of comfort. Her son was still here.

So, contrary to the medical odds, Victor was yet alive as the sun broke brilliantly through the Los Angeles haze on January 10. Obviously, God's game plan for this star athlete was not quite finished.

Immediately after the conclusion of the convention in Nashville, Ron Brown flew to California to be with Victor. He marveled as to how quickly a potentially brilliant football career had screeched to a horrible halt. Expectations had been high. Not only that, but every contact with Victor had been a highlight for Ron in the previous year's recruiting effort. The muscular blond with the gentle blue eyes was on top of the world, the envy of all who knew him. Fame awaited. His powerful, disciplined body, his finely honed innate athletic ability, his hard-earned academic credentials, and his seemingly endless supply of energy all combined together to epitomize success to most Americans.

But Coach Brown wasn't going to UCLA to fret over what might have been. Rather, he was on a specific mission. He realized that the end of life might be near for his college recruit. In a year's time, the two had become closer than coach and athlete. They were good friends. Consequently, Ron ached in his heart that there was nothing he could do to ease the excruciating experience of misery through which Victor was going. Notwithstanding, he did have one resource of power to share: his personal faith in Jesus Christ as Lord and Savior.

The young coach had not walked long with Christ himself. But he had come to relish that relationship with the Lord above all else. On the long flight to Los Angeles, he meditated on an imaginary scene which most accurately illustrated to him his own decision for Christ.

He pictured himself at a three-ring circus. Looking high above the sawdust, he sat spellbound in the big top as a tightrope artist walked across a forty-foot stretch with just a pole for balance. Nothing but "death defying" empty space lay between the performer and the hard packed ground thirty feet below. The man accomplished the amazing feat, over and back again. Ron and everyone around him clapped exuberantly. He then laid aside the pole and walked across the expanse, without a balancing support, pushing a wheelbarrow.

As he returned to the safety of his platform, the applause rising from the stands was thunderous. "Fantastic! Unbelievable!" they roared.

The artist paused to look down upon his admirers in the audience. With a loud voice he asked, "Do you all believe that I can push this wheelbarrow across this narrow strand of wire with a person in it?"

Ron, along with everyone else, had seen him do so many great things that they all joined in a chorus of cheers. "Yeah, we believe that! We believe you can!"

The man's eyes swept slowly across the crowd. Suddenly, Ron was startled to realize that the piercing stare had stopped directly on him. The gaze was dazzling and at the same time powerful. The masterful artist pointed down from his lofty perch and challenged the sturdy youth. "You! Ron Brown! Come on up and get in my wheelbarrow!"

In a sense, that is exactly what happened with Christ. That concept had become the basic foundation for Ron's life. Nothing was more important to him than faith in Christ, entrusting himself continually to Jesus' care, getting in the Master's wheelbarrow. In doing so, he had experienced for himself the gigantic difference between knowledge about God and faith in God, between mental awareness and heart belief.

Ron realized that Victor mentally knew about Christ. But had he ever gotten into the wheelbarrow? From the age of seven, when his mother's mother taught him his first prayer, Victor always prayed about truly important matters. Certainly he had turned to God many times during his ten months of physical suffering. Yet what he yearned for most he could not find. He had no inner peace. He feared death.

As his flight arrived in Los Angeles, Ron had no plan as to how to talk to Victor about his relationship with the Lord. He wanted only that the young man know the satisfying thrill of being secure in Jesus' control.

On the ride from the airport to the Medical Center, Ron prayed for wisdom. "Lord, I just dedicate this time to you. I don't know where Victor stands spiritually even though we've talked a little about it. A lot of people are wondering whether or not Victor will play football again. Some are wondering if he will live. I am wondering as to where he will spend eternity. Please, Lord, just use me. I've been on a tight schedule. I'm too tired and frazzled to handle this on my own."

As he arrived at the hospital, Ron was greeted warmly by Victor's mother and father. They had been keeping vigil through the long nights when death was supposed to have come at any time, but somehow had been detained. Their spirits lifted noticeably at the sight of the man from Lincoln. Ron suggested that Vic's parents take a much-needed break. "I want to have a few minutes alone with Vic anyway."

The boy had been so sick that he had been totally inactive, barely alert. He had slept all day long. But when Ron walked into the room, he was awake, as if God had nudged him into consciousness for that very moment. He looked up in pleasant surprise, "Coach Brown!"

"Hey, Victor," Ron responded quietly, matching his somber tone with the hush that was upon the room. "Did you have a good trip?" Vic asked with a weak voice. "Are you comfortable?"

"Yes, I'm fine, Victor," the coach replied in admiration of the incredibly selfless attitude. Ron sat down next to the bed and took Vic's limp right hand in his. The boy's face was pale with a sick, greenish cast to it. He was quite apparently on death's doorstep, yet the door was still shut. The room was wrapped in stunned silence; the only sound came from a cart being wheeled down the hallway outside.

Searching for the right words, Ron finally asked, "Victor, what are you thinking right now?"

"Coach, I'm scared," he answered unashamedly, knowing he could trust the man beside him with such an intimate admission.

"Vic, there's not much I can do for you," Ron observed. "But would you like to pray?"

"Yeah, I sure do, Coach."

By the firm response, Ron understood at once that he didn't need to have any profound answers for Victor. God himself had prepared the boy's spirit for that particular instance. Ron opened the Bible he had carried into the room and said, "Vic, I want to read something to you from the Word of God first. I don't know where you stand with the Lord. But I do know what Jesus Christ accomplished in my life when I followed what it says here in Romans 10:9-13:

"If you confess with your mouth, 'Jesus is Lord' and believe in your heart that God raised him from the dead, you will be saved. For it is with your heart that you believe and are justified and it is with your mouth that you confess and are saved. As the Scripture says, 'Everyone who trusts in him will never be put to shame.' For there is no difference between Jew and Gentile–the same Lord is Lord of all and richly blesses all who call on him, for, 'Everyone who calls on the name of the Lord will be saved.'"

"That's beautiful, Coach," Vic responded.

Ron closed the Book and said, "Vic, I believe that Jesus wants to indwell your soul right now. Do you believe that too?"

"Yes, I do, Coach. I want to accept Christ."

Ron pressed the issue a step further to make sure Vic understood clearly. "Do you want to receive Jesus Christ as your Lord and Savior?"

"I sure do, Coach."

"Well then," Ron suggested, "let's pray."

The two closed their eyes and talked to God. Ron's words flowed freely. Frequent communication with his Heavenly Father had become a natural part of his life. Vic, although in a weakened condition, searched for sincere words as he breathed out his repentance with difficulty. Holding the boy's practically lifeless hand in his, Ron was not certain during intermittent instances of silence whether or not Vic had maintained consciousness. However, as Ron finished praying, he was stirred in his soul as he saw tears rolling down the young man's cheeks. God had truly touched his inner spirit.

Vic exerted himself to smile broadly at his mentor. He said, "Thanks, Coach! I feel great. I want you to know that I'm not afraid to die anymore. I'll never forget you." He paused for breath and continued, "I want a Bible. I want a whole Bible like yours."

"I'll go buy you one right away," Ron promised. He, too, felt great. He also was released into new strength. Just then Marianne came back into the room. Victor's voice seemed to pick up volume as he declared, "Mom, Coach Brown prayed with me!"

"I thought he probably would," his mother replied with an appreciative nod to Ron.

"And I asked Jesus to come into my heart–and I accepted Him as my Lord and Savior."

"That's wonderful," his mother said admiringly as she stepped close to her son's bed to take his left hand in hers. Her face beamed with joy in seeing him so radiantly happy. "I've never felt like this before in my life," Victor continued excitedly. "My whole body…I could just feel something go over my whole body. I feel better than I've ever felt."

Tears welled up in Marianne's eyes. On the one hand she heard her son's ecstatic words, but on the other she saw no physical change. She thought to herself, "Maybe he's being cured. It'll just be a slow steady process of getting well." She controlled her mounting excitement and kissed him on his cheek.

Later that afternoon, Coach Brown delivered Vic's Bible and prayed with him one last time before returning to his duties in Nebraska. His trip eastward, however, would not be with the uncertainty which had been his fretful foe on the trip west. By the gracious intervention of God, Vic had entrusted himself to Christ. He had boldly climbed into the wheelbarrow for a secure ride into the unknown beyond. Ron had written on the inside cover of the boy's Bible, "Victor accepted Jesus Christ as his Lord and Savior."

For ten months, Mike and Marianne had snatched at every possible solution to bring their son back to health. It had been an agonizing strain on their emotions and physical stamina.

Nonetheless, they had refused to give up hope, looking always to the prospects of the next day.

Victor's flush of excitement after receiving his assurance of peace in Christ brought renewed optimism to his parents. Marianne told her mother, "I want God to heal him!"

"I know you do, Marianne," her mother replied wisely, "but that may not happen. You're going to have to release him. All these people are praying for him, but you need to release him and let God do what He wants to do. I did that today," she confessed.

Making such a commitment of a son who had brought them nothing but pleasure for nearly two decades was not an easy decision for mother or father. They confessed to one another in a quiet moment, "It's just too hard to let him go."

On January 23, 1989, exactly one year from the day that she and her son had made his official visit to the University of Nebraska, Marianne let go. She drew up close to his bed and spoke in soft tones so as not to belie her underlying grief, "Victor, I've prayed for God to heal you. And I've asked God also to take you so you won't be in pain anymore. I've released you so that He can do whatever He wants to do." She bit hard into her lip to hold back the tears which wanted to flow.

"Victor," she concluded in resignation, "there's nothing else I can do. I've done everything I know." Victor's breathing was dry and shallow. "OK then," he said with difficulty. "I'm going to die. I have no fear of death."

His mother was heartbroken by his response. She put her head down on her arm on the edge of his bed and sobbed. With that resignation, Victor became exceedingly peaceful and closed his eyes to go to sleep. His parents' hearts began to spiral downward.

About fifteen minutes later, Vic's eyes popped wide open. Once again he was totally alert. "Just talk to me, Mom," he pleaded with slurred speech. "Dad, I don't want you to think I'm a quitter, but I'm getting so tired."

"You're not letting us down, son," his mother assured him.

"Hold my hand, Mom," he asked anxiously. "Don't leave."

"I won't, son, I'm right here."

Victor turned to his mother and said, "Mom, would you please ask Dad to leave?"

Marianne got up and went over to Michael and said, "Victor wants you to leave. Would you please go out in the hall?"

His father left the room and sat in a chair in the hall by the door, not questioning why.

Victor turned to his mother and said, "Dad's not going to let me go. He'll want me to fight and to stay. And I can't." Marianne said, "Talk to your father, Victor. He loves you so much. He'll understand."

Marianne went into the hall and asked Victor's father to return to his bedside. Victor was having great difficulty breathing and certainly in talking. He reached up with his large and gentle hands and put one on each side of his dad's head and pulled him within inches of his face. He looked at him and said, "Dad, we have fought too long. I'm tired, and I want to stop. I want to ask your permission to stop fighting and to go on. I love you, Dad."

His father's throat tightened. He gave permission with a nod of his head.

"Do you see heaven before you die?" Vic asked his mother.

"Some people do, some don't," she advised him as she brushed her reassuring hand across his brow.

Worriedly, he said, "I've been trying to see it again like I did two weeks ago. I haven't been able to."

"Are you afraid?" she asked him.

"No," he replied simply. "I'm going to know some people in heaven…grandpa's there…and…."

"And I promise you," his mother interrupted, "I'll come see you someday."

"Thank you, Mom," he responded as he once again closed his eyes peacefully.

The night wore on slowly. There was a gentle hush on the room. Victor's breathing became calm and clear.

Mike left the room. His heart was breaking with anguish. He

could not stand the pain of such uncertainty. He was not particularly thirsty but he drank again and again from the water fountain in the hallway near the nurses station–just a swallow at a time in nervous frustration.

Suddenly, after midnight he heard those feared words from Marianne, words which he had tried to push into oblivion. "Come quick!" she said. "Victor's calling you."

Mike rushed back into the room and sat at the foot of Victor's bed. A nurse held Vic's left wrist, monitoring his gradually ebbing pulse rate and then left, leaving Victor and his parents alone.

Victor was lying on his back and was having great difficulty breathing. His mother was exhausted and afraid and asked Victor in a quiet voice, "If you feel like you're leaving, let me know." He nodded in agreement. She laid her head on his chest and fell asleep with his arm across her back.

Suddenly, and very softly, with his eyes still closed, Victor started to gently rub his mother's head. He had done as promised. He woke her up.

Slowly, as if in recognition, with his eyes closed, his arms reached out to greet someone in an embrace. He raised slowly upward in bed, reaching out to someone who was coming to meet him. He stopped, then with a peaceful smile on his face, folded his arms across his chest and laid back down. With the Bible given to him by Ron Brown at his side, he made a quiet and graceful exit through the thin veil that separates this present life from the next.

It was 5:30 a.m. in Lincoln, Nebraska, when Ron Brown was awakened with the anticipated, yet startling news from Marianne. His recruit was dead. Victor would never fulfill his dream of playing football for the Cornhuskers. But thankfully, Ron had also recruited Victor Stachmus for God as well, and though he was a raw recruit of only a week, he had made the team!

CHAPTER 2

SNATCHED FROM THE DUMPSTER

Irene Chase enjoyed a life of wealth and luxury in the prestigious upper east side community of Grammercy Park in New York City. Through her husband's diligence and family fortune, she never experienced in her own life the sufferings of hunger and homelessness which is the sad lot of tens of thousands in that expansive metropolis. Easily she could have insulated herself from even the awareness of such needs. Her money and position could have been a buffer against life as it is.

This elegant lady, however, was not of that nature. She was not caught up with everything she had. She deeply cared to know the needs of others. She stretched herself beyond the confining security of her exquisite home. She didn't need to experience the humiliation of being fed in a South Bronx soup kitchen to empathize with hunger pangs. She didn't need to freeze in a gutter in the Bowery in order to know that she was blessed in having a warm bed of her own. In spite of her great wealth of privileges, she was sensitive to the pinch that others felt.

That very compassion, which was a driving force in her life, also created an inner strength which lent a particular grace to her already elegant beauty. In addition to her physical traits, the assurance by which she carried herself shined as a pure radiance, much as a rare diamond is admired when set in a particularly appropriate mounting.

Mrs. Chase chose never to flaunt her high position in the social register of New York's elite. For her, it was a springboard by which she could plunge in to do her part to help cure some of the hurts of an aching world.

She had many interests throughout the city and beyond, but one particular work to which she devoted great energy and time and the resources of her own wealth was with the New York Foundling Home, located downtown on Third Avenue. She was a staunch ally of Sister Bernadette, director of the home, who took a passionate stand against the abortion option which was widely practiced even before the approval of the Supreme Court. Sister Bernadette was dedicated to providing every mother of every unborn child an alternative to the willful termination of a pregnancy. As chairman of the board, Mrs. Chase followed a determined course in working with Sister Bernadette, who guided the day-to-day operation of the home.

The brownstone building, worn by decades of use and just as drab in appearance as all of its neighbors in the block, had served a host of occupants prior to becoming a refuge for unwanted children. The nuns had worked for years to get support and financing for their project of love, then invested nearly a whole year in renovating the facility. It was a happy occasion when the archbishop himself stood in the broad lobby to dedicate the home.

Yet, of far greater significance was the continuous line of frightened girls who, in time, entered the large oak door to gain sanctuary. They were the purpose, after all, for which the home was conceived. Though they came from varied walks of life, they all had one thing in common. Each was carrying a child she could not keep.

Typical of the thousands who found their way to that always open door was Margaret Pearce, a lovely dark-skinned music student from Tennessee. Her dream, in having come to the big city, was to become a success through study and serious effort. She intended to escape forever the difficulty of life in the South, which, for a black girl in 1956, was heavy with ugly uncertainty. True to her goal, Margaret applied herself stringently to the rigors of study and performance. Her professors at the Manhattan School of Music gave her constant encouragement. She was without hesitation on her way up the ladder. Perhaps even stardom rested in her future.

But even the best laid plans have a way of changing.

Arriving early one Sunday afternoon for a concert at the university, Margaret was impressed by the athletically built, well-mannered young man who opened the door for her. He, too, was instantly aware of a particular charm in the statuesque young beauty from Tennessee. They had arrived separately but left arm-in-arm: two lonely hearts brought together in a strange city.

In the following weeks, the two spent many happy times getting to know one another. He was fascinated by her carefree spirit, tempered by her strong dedication to a goal. She in turn loved the British tone of his deep-throated accent. Also, his gentle concern for her every need nurtured a growing bond of affection.

Varheem had come from his native India to study engineering. He, too, was driven by a forceful ambition to succeed: a degree from Columbia University would assure him of both prestige and position in his home country. Therefore, when Margaret told him that she was pregnant, he thought his whole world would crumble in on top of him. Instant fatherhood was not a part of his plan. He saw it as a tragedy. No way could a baby at this time fit into his future. Though he particularly loved the company of the beautiful young woman, taking on family responsibilities was out of the question.

"Sister," Margaret said hesitantly when she first arrived at the Third Avenue brownstone five months later, "I'm not Roman Catholic. But I have nowhere else to turn."

Sister Bernadette welcomed her warmly. "My dear girl, come in, come in! We are all God's children. He has many flocks." The thin, energetic nun had assisted hundreds of other young women through the particularly trying ordeal of being an unwed mother. As she observed Margaret, she was only sorry that this one had waited so long before seeking help. It was obvious that she would soon give birth.

It was a sad time for the expectant mother. Her lover had found cause not to return to the university for the fall term. His decision came at a time when she needed him the most. She had been able neither to work nor to continue her studies. But most distressing of all, she felt alienated from her family. That was not through their neglect or rejection. She simply had not possessed the courage to tell her mother of her plight. She dreaded to bring shame to those she loved so deeply. At the same time, she was afraid of being turned away by her family as she had been denied by Varheem. She could not face a hurt like that again. Better to suffer alone, she decided, than to face another rejection.

Bravely, Margaret had undertaken for herself until the burden within her became too great. But once established in the home, she sensed an immediate acceptance because everyone was engaged in fighting the same struggle as she. They understood the agony of bringing a new life into the world without a husband's support. They all shared the same sorrow of having no one who cared to press a loving hand against a stretched abdomen to feel the little kicking life on the inside. The nuns and other young women became Margaret's family, her consolation, as she was their's. With renewed determination, she knew she'd make it.

Nonetheless, it was a nostalgic time for all the young women in the home as Thanksgiving Day drew near. Friends may mean a lot, but holidays are a special time for family. Margaret longed to be with her mommy in Tennessee. To hear that tender voice. To eat her good cooking. But especially to feel the gentle caress of her consoling arms. Margaret felt she had little about which to be thankful that cold November Thursday. "I am too sick to eat," she complained to Sister Bernadette. "But worse, I'm afraid. This child is coming soon. I had my first real labor pain this morning."

"Now, don't you be afraid," Sister assured her. "We've been through this more times than I can possibly remember. We'll be right here with you through it all."

"No, you don't understand," Margaret said, with sorrow in her dark brown eyes. "I'm not afraid for myself. I'm afraid for the child. I won't be around when it needs me. Will it understand why its mother and father deserted it at birth? This child is a part of me. I love it! And I don't want it to be as alone as I've felt in the last six months."

The normally composed nun bit her lip to squelch a tear that wanted to respond to expressed sorrow.

"Now, my dear girl," Sister Bernadette said, with a strong tone of assurance she resurrected from her reserves. "I'll see to it that the baby is placed with just the right family. Through the adoptive parents it'll gain a double understanding of love. First, that you loved it enough to give him life rather than death. And second, that they loved it enough to choose it special."

Margaret was little comforted. She smiled only in humble submission.

On November 28, 1956, the solemn silence of the New York City Foundling Home was pierced by the loud wail of a new voice, announcing his traumatic arrival in God's world. A strong, energetic boy burst into life, delighted to be there. His mother had chosen not to interfere with God's plan for life. No oblivion in a rusty Dumpster for him.

Four days later, Margaret held her little boy for the last time. She was headed back to Tennessee, to her mother. "Son," she said to the bundle of potential cradled in her arms, "please always remember that I love you with all my heart."

Tears rolled down her cheeks as she walked along Third Avenue, suitcase in hand, to the subway. She never looked back. But she would never forget that little boy who would never know her. She would always celebrate November 28 as a day of joy; she had made the right decision.

Though Sister Bernadette had assured the young woman that she would see to it that the child would be placed in just the right home, she knew from the beginning that it would be difficult. Most of the potential adoptive parents in New York were white; in the mid-1950s few were looking to break the color barrier. There was little demand for black babies, even a little charmer like this one. And the sorry fact that he had been born with a clubbed foot complicated the case even more.

At the first meeting of the Board of Governors of the home after Christmas, Sister Bernadette drew attention to this particular problem. "More and more, the young ladies who come to us are from the black or Hispanic communities. Yet, rarely do we have a request for such a child. This darling little boy has been in our care now for six weeks, and I have no one looking to take on such a responsibility."

"I have an idea," Irene Chase said in immediate response. "My groundskeeper at my summer home on Martha's Vineyard would be a perfect father for the boy. He and his wife are childless. This would fill a great void in their lives as well."

"But, Madam, that's out of state," one man objected. "That's unheard of. We can't send children out of New York."

"Nonsense!" Mrs. Chase dismissed the disagreement authoritatively. "We have a child who needs a home, and Arthur and Pearl Brown have a home that needs a child. That sounds like a perfect match to me. We'll just have to find a way to change the rules."

"You say Mr. Brown is a groundskeeper?" another board member asked. "Can such an income support a family? Especially one with a growing, handicapped little boy?"

"Having the love of a hardworking father is more important than having a wealthy one," Mrs. Chase responded. "And I ought to know because my father was both. But I respected him far more for his diligence than for his riches.

"Arthur Brown is most certainly a worker. Besides gardening for me and others, he serves as a garage attendant, and does night jobs, sweeping out shops. His wife, Pearl, also works as a maid and a cook."

"I assure you, Madam, they sound like fine people," the vice chairman admitted. "But how do we convince them that they need a baby in their busy lives?"

"Mrs. Brown and I've talked about it a great deal," Mrs. Chase responded. "For years, she and her husband have longed to have children but couldn't. I believe if we advise them of this need and opportunity, they would be very happy to have an addition to their family at last."

On Mrs. Chase's strong recommendation and insistence, the board finally approved for her to contact the Browns. The couple was surprised by the suddenness of the opportunity and at first were a bit hesitant, at forty years of age, to take on a new lifestyle as parents. However, they quickly warmed to the idea and became eager to at last be able to satisfy the unfulfilled dream of their lives.

"We would love to have the boy," Arthur Brown informed Mrs. Chase, "if there is any way you can cut through the red tape for us to bring him to Massachusetts."

Irene Chase enjoyed the challenge of blazing a new trail. She took to the task with relish. Certainly setting a precedent is never easy. That is even more true when it involves the political and conflicting rights of two state governments. The system did not want to budge. But Mrs. Chase and others were not easily discouraged. They pushed on with relentless perseverance.

For Pearl and Arthur Brown, the waiting and uncertainty seemed as difficult as going through childbirth. Indeed, the process continued on through the winter, the spring, and into summer–eight months in all. But, as always, persistence won the victory.

In August, the Browns proudly carried their almost-ready-to-walk son out of the New York City foundling home and headed for the sun-bathed haven of Martha's Vineyard. The months of delay had given Pearl Brown many anxious thoughts as to whether she could ever genuinely feel that the child was hers. However, after only five seconds of holding the tiny, helpless life in her arms, all doubts were gone. She adored the little boy with all her heart. Lovingly, she touched the heavy, black, backward shoe on his left foot. It was awkward, but was intended to correct his problem. She was certain it would do just that. She wanted total health for her child. She was his mother.

It was a lofty day for the middle-aged couple when their son was christened Ronald Arthur Brown. Their expectations for him were high.

CHAPTER 3

DANCE ALL YOU WANT, BUT DON'T STOP TO SLEEP

Most people have no idea where Martha's Vineyard is. A few politically-minded individuals recall the questions, mystery, and controversy surrounding the bizarre incident of Ted Kennedy and the death of Mary Jo Kopeschne at Chappaquiddick. And movie buffs recall it as the picturesque location for the filming of the shock thriller "Jaws." But for Arthur and Pearl Brown and the pride of their lives, their newly adopted son, it was home.

Vineyard Haven, six miles directly across Vineyard Sound from the Massachusetts mainland, had been refuge to Pearl Brown's family for two generations. Her ancestors, seeking a new beginning, modestly settled in the village when they first emigrated to the United States from the Cape Verde Islands, off the northwest corner of Africa. Throughout the trials of establishing an identity in a strange land, her relatives had held together in a closely-knit bond. Consequently, within a four-block area from the house to which she and her husband brought their infant son were dozens of cousins and uncles and aunts.

The comparatively small, 120-square mile island of Martha's Vineyard stands as a calm guard against the raging Atlantic Ocean along Massachusetts' southern approach. Its quaint, quiet way serves as a permanent home to about 12,000 residents. But it also became a favored playground for rich and sometimes rowdy vacationers even before the turn of the century. Its normally tranquil population is overrun by five or six times as many vacationers during the gorgeous sunshine months of summer. The pristine, unspoiled waters are special attractions. In addition to other aquatic sports, they afford magnificent sailing opportunities which attract yachtsmen as surely as fish take to bait.

With no landbridge to the mainland, the island is somewhat isolated, accessible solely by air and boat. The ferries which ply the waters regularly for the tourist season taper off markedly during the long, unhurried winter months. Accordingly, the widespread communities of Martha's Vineyard have been able to maintain a considerable bit of their nineteenth century charm. It is a great place to live and do as you please, if you're not looking for grand cultural activities.

The people who live there all year are primarily vocational, blue collar workers. There is little hubbub of high powered business, no university crowd, and only one high school. Many of the kids who grow up on the island never leave it permanently. They stay, parenting another generation. In most respects, it was a great place for Arthur and Pearl Brown to rear their son (and daughter, Theresa, whom they adopted from the New York foundling home a year later). The quiet manner and slow pace of the island for nine months of the year was perfect in keeping with their own old-fashioned attitude of hard work matched with personal integrity.

It was at an early age, with parents old enough to be his grandparents, that Ron built an orderly attitude toward relationships. His first concern, insisted on by his father, was obedience to his parents. He saw it as a duty to live up to the high expectations his mother and father set for him. Their standard was simple: stay drug-free, alcohol-free, and do well in school. Though his parents never finished their own formal education, they expected their son to be an "A" student. To help keep his son on track, Arthur Brown enforced a strict curfew of no weeknights out and no weekend late nights.

Ron did not rebel. He recognized the love behind the plan and even took pride in it; many parents didn't care that much. Nonetheless, like any other action-oriented youth, he wanted desperately to hang out with the other kids and be their friend.

"Ronny, you're a square," his cousin Zachary said harshly as they were walking home from school one day. "You don't drink. You don't get high and hang out at night. You don't even have a steady girl."

"What would I do with a steady girl?" Ron thought sadly to himself as he turned his back and walked away without arguing. "Take her to church?" For church was the one other expectation that his parents insisted on for him. They saw to it that he never missed a week at mass.

To compensate for the great gulf that existed between what his mother and father demanded and what his peers enticed him toward, Ron developed a self-righteous attitude. "Hey, I'm on God's side," he thought. "I have it all together. I do well in school and I'm becoming a good athlete because I come from a disciplined home." He proudly looked down on the other children because their lives didn't reflect the same regulated lifestyle as his.

Nevertheless, he was lonely. He recoiled at being called a coach's pet or a teacher's pet. Such taunting is hard to take when you're in junior high. He insulated himself in two ways. Inwardly, where no one could see, he kept his emotions to himself. Outwardly, where most of the emphasis of success in this world was focused, he began to build an image by involving himself heavily in sports. It was a great way to escape the negative charge of being a square–and also, fortunately, he was good. He had outgrown the clubbed foot with which he had been born and was endowed by his Creator with definite agility and grace.

In addition to the peer pressures felt by any maturing young person, there were built-in difficulties for Ron in facing the underlying inequalities of the island's social fabric. Racism was not an often mentioned issue within the white community. They were comfortably in control. But the ugliness of prejudice was a continual menace to the black minority. That ignorant monster was always hovering just out of sight, waiting to pounce. His parents had learned to live above the verbal and nonverbal insinuations of inferiority; slights from whites did not bring them down. Instead, they concentrated on building self respect by adhering to their own high value system of doing their best in everyday work. Besides, they had seen dramatic improvement toward racial equality in their lifetime. Their northern community of the fifties was outwardly far advanced to what changes the Deep South was only beginning to experience.

But a new day was yearning to dawn, to shed new light in dark places. With it, Ron's generation began to stretch into maturity for itself. He and others his age had to make their own stand in life as it is and possibly push it into becoming life as it ought to be. In this regard, the struggle of young blacks for a wholesome identity always has been an intense battle because of the insensible prejudice so often blocking their path.

No matter how much encouragement and support he got at home, however, Ron realized early on that he had to make a place for himself in a subtly hostile world. Why did the color of his skin make a difference to so many people? He was a nice-looking kid, respectful of his elders, got good grades, was fast on his feet, and quick with his hands. But he learned from his earliest contacts outside the black community that he had to be much better than a white just to be taken seriously, to have an equal chance. Life at home, however, helped him overcome many of those harsh, negative realities of the world in which he lived. His parents were not influential people. They did not have a lot of money or earthly possessions. But they held high demands for their children always to do their best.

Arthur Brown did not have a philosophy of "let's reason together and talk this through." It was more like, "let's get it done!" No questions asked. Such a no-nonsense standard worked to Ron's favor. In following his dad's example, at an early age he developed a satisfying pride in doing a job right.

That kind of attitude was in striking contrast to the mentality of the two principle tourist types which flocked like migrating birds to the tiny island resort area during the high season months. First, there were those of the obvious wealthy, flashy, jet set breed. With too much easy money and too little incentive to expand their horizons or exert themselves unnecessarily in self-improvement, they tended to depend on others for effortless entertainment.

Also, the pleasures of the sand, sunshine, and surf of the Atlantic were a natural attraction for those who considered themselves to be upwardly mobile. These workers of the middle-class thought it necessary not only to drive a Mercedes and send their kids to the "right" schools, but also to vacation at the "right" spot. But at best, whatever reason either type had for coming, the magnificent scenic wonders of Martha's Vineyard satisfies such fast movers only in the daylight hours. The splendid quiet can become boring after a time. Consequently, along with carefree vacationers, a host of pros also flood in every summer to fill that dull, inert gap. They provide lively entertainment and enjoyment through the evening and into the wakeful night hours.

Eddie Heywood, well-acclaimed after World War II for his refreshing touch of jazz music, was one of the more popular of the performers who included the Martha's Vineyard night spots on his itinerary year after year. His outstanding rendition of his gold record signature song, "Canadian Sunset," kept him as a top draw for a decade. His mellow music was perfect in keeping with the laid-back pace of the seaside oasis. Everyone, regardless of race, was proud to call him friend. He was favored by countless name droppers. Eddie Heywood was a bridge between black and white.

After years of returning to the island for summer stints, Eddie decided that there was no other place in his wide travels which he liked more. He figured that it was time to establish roots. He searched diligently for days and finally found a house which suited his desires perfectly. He put down his deposit and began preparations to take possession. That's when the bottom fell out of the love affair between the entertainer and many of those he had entertained.

The house chosen by the popular black musician was smack dab in the middle of a well-to-do white section of town. The "boy" had overstepped his bounds. Whites were willing to dance to his music, but not when he piped a block-busting tune. "Sing all you want," they advised indirectly, "but don't think you can sleep in the house next door."

The white community was enraged. Tensions ran high. Though Heywood got his house, the long struggle rekindled strong emotions which had been hidden for years. The white majority gave in only grudgingly.

The confrontation had a lasting impact on Ron Brown, who was a good friend to Heywood's son, Robert. How do you explain color barriers to a growing boy with a zest for life? Were his opportunities in the world limited? He and his friends saw an evil and were angry. They were stuck on an isolated island, controlled by unwritten yet definite restrictions. They were filled with life's questions, and there were no intelligent answers in sight. So, while still in grade school, Ronny was fully aware of two facts: not only was he considered "different," but there were two distinct communities on his small island home. Though he experienced no physical violence, the insidiousness of prejudice was impossible for him to comprehend. He could not help but wonder if he would ever attain success in this world. Yet, that flame burned brightly in his heart.

Another factor which contributed heavily to the boy's early psychological development was the fact that he himself was not Cape Verdean. All of his adoptive cousins could boast of a pure, direct lineage across the expanse of the Atlantic to their roots. He could not. "Ma, they just don't accept me as part of the family because I'm different."

"Nonsense," his mother would assure him, "of course they do." However, she never convinced him.

Fortunately, he had other interests which kept him occupied. After outgrowing the awkwardness of the clubbed foot of his early childhood, his natural agility and athletic ability began to push him ahead of the competition. With that to his advantage, Ron built a strong comfort zone for himself where he was certain he could excel–in sports.

Though his greatest combination of talents added up to a promise of success in football, there was not much of an opportunity on the island. Martha's Vineyard Regional High School was too small to compete significantly with teams on the mainland. So basketball became the primary rallying point for the school's athletes and fans alike. At least that was true for the white end of town. They knew that their kids had a lock on the starting positions. In grade school, Ron and his friends contented themselves with perfecting their skills on the public playground. For hours on end, they played four-on-four half court, pausing only for an occasional shouting match about a rule infraction or elbowing one another for a turn to take gulps of refreshing water at the single pipe water fountain.

The summer before Ron's seventh grade year, however, circumstances in that small corner of the sporting world took a dramatic turn. A new coach, Jay Schofield, came to the island to take responsibility for the sport fortunes on Martha's Vineyard. The "good ole boys" days came to an end. Schofield, who was white, was a no-nonsense type of coach who looked for character and determination as well as skill in an athlete. He spent hours every day during that summer of 1970 both observing and occasionally competing with youngsters on the outdoor basketball courts. When school started, the coach singled Ron out. "I've been watching you play. You're good. I hope you'll try out for the team when you're a ninth grader because you have potential to be a very good athlete—and, from what I hear, a good student as well."

Those words naturally pricked the fancy of the thirteen-year-old kid, but his friends were not impressed. "You're not going to listen to that honky, are you? He's not interested in you. He doesn't care about you. He just wants to win games for his own hide."

Nonetheless, bursting with just as much desire to succeed in life as he was endowed with physical prowess, Ronny did listen. He showed up for tryouts at the start of the ninth grade basketball season. It was a significant first step for him on the long road of competitive sports. Fortunately, he was not a "token" black. In Schofield's first two seasons, the color barrier slowly faded and dissolved as the black guys dominated the court.

Again prejudice tried to rear its hideous head. "Why have you given the starting role to black boys and benched our sons?" some of the island's majority cried.

"Because they're better players," the coach answered matter-of-factly. "All summer long, while the whites were at the beaches trying to improve their tans, the black guys were busy improving their basketball skills on the practice courts. If you don't believe me, watch the progress of this team during the season."

His claim was prophetic. Martha's Vineyard High School ceased being considered an easy victory by schools on the mainland. Under a dedicated coach, the players, too, became dedicated. Consequently, the fans took the change of lineup without further whimper. The complaining stopped. Nothing like a positive win/loss record to undergird a coach's right to call the shots.

With guidance from Schofield, a man for whom he gained undying respect, Ron took to the rigors of organized sports with an unquenchable enthusiasm. His autumns were consumed with football, the winters followed with basketball, and he filled the intervals with more of the same. With only twenty-three players on the Martha's Vineyard football team, Ron was called on by Coach Gerry Gerolamo to play several positions: quarterback, receiver, safety. Though Ron had built-in strength, stamina, and skills, Coaches Schofield and Gerolamo stressed and insisted on mastering fundamentals–that, too, was an attraction to the teenager whose dad had always inspired him to aim for perfection.

Ron loved everything about athletics. There was the thrill of running a drill a hundredth time, then finally realizing that it had become almost second nature. The gasping for air and a burst of sweat when suddenly a second wind kicks into gear from out of nowhere. The joy of reversing field so expertly that the last defender between you and the goal is faked out of his socks as you speed on your way to score. The adoration of fans in the stands which spreads into instant recognition and status on the street. The sweet taste of success after snatching victory from the jaws of defeat, or after a loss making a promise, "We'll rock 'em next time." That love in Ron

Brown for anything related to sports produced results. The would-be athlete, although not physically the most talented in his high school, used the combination of character and talent to become an area star in both basketball and football.

Arthur and Pearl Brown followed the exploits of their son with devotion, making dozens of ferry crossings to the mainland season after season so as not to miss a single contest in which he competed. By the onset of his senior year in high school, he had earned a statewide reputation and was of definite collegiate material. Scouts from eastern seaboard universities began making overtures to recruit him for basketball and football. As the year progressed, he had two difficult choices to make: which sport and which school.

Though basketball had gotten him into competitive athletics, Ron realized that his greater natural talents were in rough and tumble football. It was a tough decision to lay aside the joys of one sport to concentrate on another, but with the final nod going to football, the selection of a college was easy. From the outset of the first recruiters pounding on his door, Ron had fancied one school above all the others. When commitment day rolled around, he signed with Brown University in the Ivy League.

Shortly before leaving home to start his college career, a respected lady of the community asked him to make one other commitment. "Ronny," Mrs. June Farmer said, "you have been such a good boy. Such a positive role model. You go to church every Sunday. You do all the right things. It seems we all want our kids to be just like you. I want you to make a promise to me."

"Sure, Mrs. Farmer," Ron replied seriously. "Anything. What would you like me to do? I'll do anything for the older people in the neighborhood."

She answered, "Well, I would like for you to go to church every Sunday when you get to college. You know, so many young boys go off to college or somewhere else and forget all about their upbringing."

A smile of relief creased the teenager's face. He had feared that the old friend of his mother was going to lay some heavy cause on him which would have hampered him in making a name for himself at Brown. But he could take church in stride and not miss a step in a triumphant march to college success.

He had big plans for himself once he escaped the island. He was on his way. College scouts had found him. Next it would be the pros. Ron Brown had been put down enough. He had seen too much racial suppression. He would help change things. He was going to succeed in this world. Church was the least of his concerns.

"Yes, Ma'am!" Ron replied with pleasure. "That's easy. I'll do that. I like going to church!"

CHAPTER 4

THE BIG SPLASH

Twin ambitions stirred excitement in the heart of the energetic, but as yet unproven young athlete as he headed for an unknown adventure on the campus of Brown University. Ron could not have defined or distinguished between those two desires, for they were part and parcel with one another. Football was what he intended to use to build prestige and gain success. But equally important to his famished spirit was the new freedom by which he could fashion a new image. In fact, the latter was such a driving force that it had priority. Even though athletics had been a key factor in helping lift him from a relatively poor home to a promising opportunity at a major academic institution, he was most anxious to gain popularity among people his own age. He longed to fill the empty void of loneliness which had overshadowed his teenage notoriety like a rain cloud at a summer's picnic. Even when he had been showered by praise and admiration he had felt unfulfilled, alone, and isolated.

It's true that Ron Brown had much for which he should have been thankful and satisfied. During four years of consistent effort in high school, he had achieved academic excellence: he applied his quick mind willingly, eagerly, to study. In athletics, he earned a statewide reputation as an outstanding competitor, zealously committing himself to tough training and giving heed to his coaches. And, if that were not enough, he was highly respected in his community for his moral lifestyle. Yet, it was not enough for Ron. He was not satisfied within himself.

By all normal standards for a high school graduate, he was a well qualified success. Nonetheless, Ron Brown was restless. He was bursting with pent-up desires to achieve unrealized adventure. His urge to expand his universe was ripe for anything, everything the world had to offer.

In reality, Ron was little more than a kid, eighteen years of age, when he first exploded onto the college scene in September 1975. Like most all other freshmen at a thousand different schools, he wanted people to think he was dynamic. However, within himself he felt more like a spent firecracker, which translated into initial shyness. He was still trying to come to grips with who he understood himself to be as a person.

The struggle, of course, had been going on for a long time. It was suddenly aggravated by transplantation two hours away from all the familiarities and securities of home. His emotions were in turmoil. In all his learning, no one had taught him, nor did he know how, to assess the conflicting aspirations and attitudes of the under-developed individual who inhabited his well-developed body. For years he had received high marks of praise from older people. Great! But he had never fit into the standards by which friends his own age lived. There was an awesome void between those two opinions, and he decided on a scheme by which he could straddle the chasm.

"The island is two hours away. I can still please those older people at home," he determined to himself. "I can still make them think that I'm such a good little boy who grew up and is a fine, upstanding man. But, now that I'm in a new place, I can develop a new identity, a new Ron Brown. So I can go ahead and be a class clown. And maybe I can try some of those devious things most of the other high school people did and I didn't. Maybe I can be popular among my friends and still be respected by people back home."

It was an impossible stretch: one foot firmly planted in the past on Martha's Vineyard, and the other attempting to find a secure foundation in the present in Providence, Rhode Island.

The first test of his resolve came within a few days of freedom away from the authority of home. He willingly had made a solemn vow to Mrs. Farmer never to succumb to the temptation to sleep in on the sabbath. Faithfully, self-righteously he slipped out of the slumbering dorm that first Sunday morning. He went to church, as had been his family's standard from his youth. Sitting there through the service, though, he realized that the guys he hung around with on the football team were nowhere to be seen. Others he had met were just as obvious by their absence. Scanning the congregation of strangers, he began to feel very out of place. "This isn't any fun," he said to himself. "My new friends aren't here. It was all right back home with Mom and Dad because it was good for my standing around town. But here I don't have a reputation. Not yet! And this isn't the image I want to develop."

What a splash! Not even a week had passed before the normally responsible youngster let one foot go kerplunk! It slipped off the familiar security of Martha's Vineyard and into the water nearer the mainland. Just a small step, insignificant by itself. Yet, who can gauge the value of even one broken promise? Would there be others?

For Ron that was it. He set a new course. No more wasted time in church for the newly emancipated Mr. Brown. True, there were no immediate disastrous consequences. Though the waves of the splash washed clear to the shores of heaven, no one in Providence either noticed or judged him harshly for his change of direction. Indeed, no one bothered even to know or care that he had tripped.

The great splash, however, that hundreds did observe and openly appreciate was in the succeeding days when the ambitious and friendly young man began to make his presence known across the breadth of the Brown University campus. He was free. Enthusiastically he extended himself into every possible opportunity for social exposure. From the football field to the dormitory to the parties–and even in the halls of learning–the kid from the quaint offshore island was sought after wildly and was welcome in the best cliques.

In high school, he had contented himself with the confining privilege of having one steady girl. After all, with the restrictions his parents had laid on him, his romantic options on Martha's Vineyard had been extremely limited. But with his sudden new freedom of choice, he determined to make up for lost time.

The response was an enormous boost to the young man's ego. There was no shortage of open doors for him. His apparent wholesomeness was an attraction, especially when matched with a sometimes wild dash of daring. He was clean-cut and handsome, with an angular face and lean athletic build. Some thought as well that they themselves gained status just being with him. All of that was a heady new experience for the formerly quiet kid from a sheltered background.

By all outward appearances, Ron handled the new variety of worship well. He managed to maintain his composure for public consumption. However, in times alone he worried that the days of adoration someday would escape him and he would be left only with his nagging fear of inadequacy. Often he was at cross purposes with his own emotions. Yet, he brushed aside the concerns in order to relish every minute. He had arrived.

Due to Ivy League rules, Ron's playing time was limited to the freshman team, and it was satisfying enough to him to be a starter. He gained invaluable experience, gearing himself for a varsity starting position as a sophomore.

His first semester in college consequently flew by him like a whirlwind. He was caught up happily in the frenzy of nonstop activities in which more often than not he was a central figure. The acclaim of his fellow students was such a boost to his ego that he freely allowed events and opinions to dictate his schedule and actions. Little by little, he surrendered control of his own course. New friends, and his own imperfect design of a new image, brought relentless demands upon him. Ron was under the impression that he was free just because things were different. In reality, he was allowing decisions to be made for him by the pressures and plans of others.

Temptations which had been held at bay by the strict standards of his parents exerted themselves against even his best instincts. The liberated teenager muddled along. He flowed compromisingly within the intensity of group dynamics. How much could a little bit of sin hurt?

Further, in conformity to the portrait of the new Ron Brown he was trying to paint, he also decided that he needed to slack up some in his efforts for the coaches and profs. In the university setting of the seventies, it was not in style to be the teacher's pet. No more front row seat in the classroom with an attentive look; slouching in the back with a whispered joke was more certain to gain the attention of classmates. Sure, he'd play hard on the gridiron because he enjoyed it, but extra laps and 110% stuff just to gain favor with a coach was taboo. He would get by on his ability.

Nevertheless, in spite of his experimentations, Ron somewhat imagined that he was deviating more from the strict standards of his past than was actual fact. The twig of his life had been so bent by the loving concern of his mom and dad that there was an inner safety mechanism which limited how far afield he could possibly let himself go. Certainly his folks would have been appalled to know he had allowed his guard to slip so low. But just as Ron had headed for college with two primary goals for himself (image and football), there were two far more powerful forces at work in his behalf. A divine plan had marked him, as it does every person in the world. And the hunger of his own spirit would keep him famished for truth until he found it.

Though new acquaintances, activities, and attitudes signaled a detour from his prior path, Ron's character was only marred, not destroyed. From his earliest years, there was a definite, obvious imprint on his spirit which demanded greatness. It would take more than a round of frat parties with the temptations of alcohol and too many girls to rend his heart from its foundation. He had seen too much degradation and senseless racial prejudice to lose sight of his heartfelt goal. He had within him from his youth a desire to make a difference in this world. That was a constant focus. Especially he sensed he was destined to be a witness of excellence both in and for the black community. That inner resource, raw and unrefined, withstood the storm.

More importantly, also, there was a divine scope for his life. Surely his birth mother had sensed something special within her when she determined to give him life rather than a brutal end in a hospital Dumpster. Pearl Brown also knew she was holding a child with purpose as she carried her little club-footed darling out of the foundling home. And though unseen, God was continually in control in spite of the fact Ron Brown was unaware of it. True, he had made a big splash when he landed on campus. Many would remember him for years. But the immersion of true importance was yet to come.

CHAPTER 5

TARGETED

Ron Brown was not unique. There were many other young men just like him, with similar traits of high energy, eagerness, and daring. Yet, not everyone at Brown University in the 1970s was in that mold. Not all were hung up on football, infatuated with girls, and determined to find instant personal gratification. In fact, a definite majority was dedicated to the Ivy League tradition of pursuing academic excellence. Regardless of the obvious sacrifice of temporary pleasures, they were determined above all else to gain knowledge. That keen awareness of purpose on the part of the faculty and most students was what kept Brown University near the top of the list of every high school guidance counselor in America as "highly competitive." Significantly, an education received there should qualify a graduate of the institution for further doors of opportunity.

Indeed, for the small army of academicians on the campus, learning was an end in itself. Dialoguing with one another within the bounds of the stately campus on the outskirts of the city was all the thrill they sought or thought. Pitting their minds in a good game of chess or quietly consuming the contents of a good book were to them more worthy challenges than competition in any sport, football included. They viewed such rugged endeavor at best as a mere physical venting of energy for those whose attention to more proper and essential pursuits was totally inadequate. Their most treasured enjoyment was in dedicating themselves to further insight by means of research and reasoning.

However, for the majority, the typical, run-of-the-mill student, long hours of study was not necessarily a pursuit of pleasure. It was a necessity in order to match the stiff test of minds at such a major center of learning. Yet, they also realized that academics had to be modified with some ordinary relief. Brown might be considered boring to a visitor from a "country club university," but pizza is still the campuswide food of preference and modern rock the concert of choice. The majority of students are identical to those found in any other college–a blend of youthful vitality from across the American landscape, with a healthy smattering of internationals to produce a true cosmopolitan influence.

Additionally, as in most other late-twentieth century universities, there was a vibrant minority which followed a different agenda. Though they attended Brown to get a first-rate education and ate pizza and liked football and enjoyed dating and social gatherings, they had an overriding allegiance to a Higher Power. They were convinced that the key to success was a truly well-rounded life, beginning with a vital spirit. Others might have been out of balance with too much emphasis on strain-training the brain at one extreme or excessive exercising of the body on the other. But these young people had found satisfaction by bringing both the physical and the intellectual into obedience to the spiritual force of life. A relationship with God, as they knew Him to be in Christ, was the most important focus of their lives.

There is an inner compulsion in such people, whether they are young college students or retired citizens: they can't keep their faith to themselves. They all readily identify with the testimony of the great missionary E. Stanley Jones, who said repeatedly, "The moment I had repented of my sins and knew that God had forgiven me for Christ's sake, I felt so loved that I wanted in turn to love the whole world to Jesus."

College-age believers, with their memory still fresh with the joy and zeal of their personal commitment to Christ, are often more persistent and more pervasive than those who have matured in their faith. For such young people, the "must" of being born again is not an option! Much in the same way as football fans pump themselves up at pep rallies, Christians on university campuses similarly meet in groups–large and small–to encourage and challenge one another. In prayer they find both guidance and power for their lives. They learn an intimate leadership from God, plot their purpose and strategies, and set their goals.

By choice, Ron Brown had wanted to have a high profile at Brown University. It was inevitable therefore, in the course of time, that he should sooner or later become an object of prayer and concern for those who care about the souls of other men and women. The would-be football hero had set his goal on establishing a flashy image for himself. While still a freshman, he attained a wide reputation. There was no mistaking who he was. He was a natural target for someone with evangelistic fervor.

Ron was sped through his freshman year by forces beyond his control. Quite instantly, it was gone. He hardly had time to enjoy it. The coaches wanted his body and brain to build into a bruising defensive back. Their demands were constant. He gave his all to their prescribed program.

The professors wanted his mind to mold into a mental marvel. He loved the academic challenge. He applied himself studiously.

Ron didn't pause to judge the motives of the young ladies. He thrilled in the notoriety and thirsted for more.

His days were consumed by the heady swirl of those three contending, and often conflicting, forces. He laughed and joked openly in obvious enjoyment. Yet, in none of them did he find satisfaction. He yearned for something which would give a sense of lasting fulfillment. But what? He was haunted with a sense of emptiness–sometimes even while still standing in the limelight.

Fortunately, there was yet another claim on his life. There was someone else, far more significant than all the others combined, who wanted him unselfishly. God had an eye on the boy whose bright face could so easily burst into a smile, whose dull heart bled with unrealized desires. God insightfully saw beyond the happy exterior to the sad interior wracked by uncertainty. God wanted Ron Brown's heart, mind, body, and soul. God loved the young man. He wanted to be able to release him into the full measure of the purpose for which he was born, for which he was spared from a fetal death. God had a scope of life planned which was far beyond anything young Mr. Brown had ever hoped or imagined.

Ron thought he had raised up a new image of himself so as to take hold of everything he had been missing in life. Quite to the contrary, God had given him free reign, knowing that such a prize would attract the best of his hunters. He was a marked man–by the grace of God.

One Tuesday night, a group of campus Christians were studying the Bible together and sharing mutual concerns. One of the men named Vance spoke up. "You know that freshman football player, Ron Brown?"

"Yeah, a star of the future," one pigskin enthusiast responded.

"He lives in my dormitory," Vance informed the group, "and I've been asking God to give me a chance to witness to him."

"Hey, man," another said, "just go up to the dude and nail him."

"Sure," Vance countered, "who do you think I am? Brown's a big stick on campus! And I'm a nobody."

"Introduce yourself," a girl encouraged. "As far as we know, you've got something–Someone–he doesn't. And he needs to hear it."

Vance took their advice, encouraged by their promises to pray for him. For two days, he tried to build up the courage just to go to the man's room, knock on the door, walk in and introduce himself, tell him about Jesus, and convert him. But he was afraid of rejection. He almost decided to give up on the whole idea. On the third day, however, as he rounded a corner of the dormitory building, there was his target walking directly toward him.

Wow! Brown looked bigger and more fearsome than Vance had imagined in his prayer time.

Boldly, with an inner resource not his own, the timid Christian stepped into the middle of the sidewalk, extended his hand, and introduced himself. "Hi, Ron. My name is Vance Watkins. I live in your dorm and just wanted to get to know you."

"Hey, man, how's it goin'?" Ron responded with his normal ready acceptance of others as he flashed his welcoming smile. "Yeah, I've seen you around a couple of times. It's good to meet you."

"Ron, I have an important question to ask you," the seemingly nobody blurted out while he had his momentum of courage. "Do you love the Lord?"

The simple question floored the macho athlete. He glanced around to see if anyone was looking. Had anyone else heard the question? Ron wished momentarily that he could roll up a corner of the sidewalk, crawl under it, and hide. He was totally, terribly embarrassed. He felt ill at ease. Although he had gone to church every Sunday of his life back home, he had never heard such a question. It was both confrontational and arrogant. How did any human being have the right to quiz another person in such a personal way?

Yet, strangely, Ron was not offended. Rather than being repulsed by the thrust, his heart was pierced by an understanding of love he had never before encountered.

It seemed as if an eternity passed in the brief pause before he found the words to assure his new acquaintance. "Yeah, sure I love the Lord," Ron mouthed the words. He was at once sorry for that. He knew he had been asked an all-important question and he had responded out of shock rather than from reason. He felt uncomfortable. He detested the all-too familiar sense of inadequacy which arose within him. But at least he had successfully repelled the attack. He had given the man the response that he assumed was wanted. So he wouldn't be bothered again.

"Praise God!" Vance followed with surprise; he hadn't expected an instant success in his quest. "Tell me, Ron, how did you come to know the Lord?"

"What are you talkin' about, man?" Ron asked, confused. Hadn't he given the right answer? "No one 'knows' the Lord. He's not around here anywhere. How can you 'know the Lord'?"

"Why, you repent of your sins and ask Jesus to come into your heart," Vance answered simply, matter-of-factly. He didn't employ fancy psychology or salesmanship, but at least his theology was to the point.

Ron was impressed by the man's straightforwardness, but he was not pleased that he was the object of the unexpected attack. "Hey," he responded with mounting anger in his voice. "I've been to church all my life. I've earned my stripes. I'm a pretty good guy. I don't need any more of this 'God' stuff."

Without worrying about tainting his image, Ron brushed passed the stalwart witness for Christ and ducked quickly into the dormitory. Vance was instantly shut out of his sight. But never again out of his mind. Never would he be able to forget the potent words that had come from the young man's lips. For that moment though, Ron was absorbed with anger. He tried not to appreciate the boldness of the young man. "Why did he come on so strong?" Ron wondered to himself. "Yeah, I'm going off a bit wild on this new image kick, and I know I probably shouldn't do that. But I'm cool with most people.

"I know one thing for sure: from now on I'm going to steer clear of people like Vance! I believe in God, and that's enough."

But that was not enough for God. The Lord who had created him desired an intimate relationship with the young man who had much to offer, the athlete who was looking only for personal gain, the seeker of a worldly success which would always elude him. God had plans for Ron Brown and was not about to quit just because he turned a cold shoulder to the first true witness who had been sent his way.

Ron thought he had ended the war and won the match by effecting his hasty retreat. That was far from accurate. Only the first shot had been fired. The battle was set. And God was not about to quit.

Though Vance never approached him again to talk about Jesus, it seemed to Ron that he encountered a "Vance" at every juncture of the campus. Surely that was an exaggerated feeling. But it was evidenced by the fact that in the ensuing months he ran into several others who called themselves Christians. It seemed to Ron that he was beset by a band of men and women who were constantly talking about God. Those who lived closest to his room in the dorm, next door and down the hall were Christians. Bold Christians! His head seemed to throb with the repeated inquiries: "Ron, do you love the Lord? Are you saved? Are you a Christian?"

He was becoming gun shy. It seemed he was the object of continual target practice.

One thing he had to admit in their favor, though. Their

questions were never taunting or demeaning. There was always a sense of sincerity in their approaches. Notwithstanding, he held them at bay and began lamely to retaliate. He refused to discuss with any of them the idea of a personal relationship with God. That was his defensive strategy. He knew that he had no knowledge with which to combat them. At first he tried simply to avoid them, but they turned up at the most inopportune, unexpected times and places. So he teamed up with his buddies, who were not Christians, to ridicule those they tagged as the "God Squad." They hung out together, doggedly taunting the believers when they came by.

Ron thought that would be a fatal blow to those whom he considered spiritual fanatics.

Spending the summer back home after his freshman year was a welcome release from college stress. Being again in the familiar surroundings, which he long had considered so restrictive, was a soothing balm to his soul. He obediently played church with his family and friends. In doing so, he was strangely reaffirmed in his confused conviction that the term "Christian" was a title that people who were too religious assumed for themselves.

But soon the weeks seemed to slow down to a snail's pace. Ron wanted back into the university swing. He was increasingly anxious to return to Providence, glad he could hit the campus early for the August football practices, back to the fast track, into the full swing of freedom from the home ties.

His first-year performance at Brown had attracted the approving attention of the coaching staff. There was no holding him back as a sophomore. The resulting new status as an acclaimed starter on defense for the varsity set him in even higher profile on campus. He wanted to savor every minute, to bask in the midst of the hype and glory. But he couldn't completely enjoy it. He was smart enough to know that in the glare of that limelight he was a constant mark for Campus Crusade people and other evangelical witnesses. They simply would not go away. He was amazed that they knew no fear. It actually seemed that the more he and his friends made fun of them, the more persistent they became.

But he held his ground. They would not get him.

One startling event did get his attention, however. As he headed off for class one morning, the whole campus was abuzz with the tragic news that a fellow student-athlete, Howard Lewis (an excellent cross country runner), had died in his sleep. The seemingly healthy young man had turned out the lights and gone to bed, but never got up again. He had choked in his sleep and had drowned in his own vomit. It was a sudden shock, and sweeping sadness blanketed even those who didn't know him. The uncertainty of death had struck very close at hand.

Ron sat down at lunch that day with Rachelle James, whom he had dated frequently. After a short greeting, their meeting slid into silence. Without confronting the tragedy, there was not much to talk about. But Ron didn't want to discuss death, and idle chatter seemed out of place at such a time.

Rachelle, however, shortly broke through the impasse. There was one primary thought in her head and she had to get it said. "You know, Ron," she spoke in a thoughtful drawl, "Howard was absolutely healthy. I can't get over that. There was absolutely nothing wrong with him."

She paused in her contemplation. "He was so alive and healthy just yesterday!"

Again she marveled silently before concluding, "You just don't know when you're going to die, do you?"

Ron made no response. He pretended to be concentrating on his food. Truth of the matter, he was doing his best to ignore the lurking enemy of death. He didn't even want to give voice to the possibility, edged in fact, that someday death would come knocking on his door.

Yes! He knew Howard Lewis was healthy!

Yes! He himself was an excellent specimen of healthy manhood!

No! He did not know when he was going to die!

No! He was not going to think about it!

CHAPTER 6

HEY, MAN! YOU'RE GREAT!

Summertime 1977 once again was a welcome rest for Ron Brown at the conclusion of his sophomore year. It had been a grueling, tough, unbelievably frustrating year. On the one hand, he had gloried in the steady acclaim as a rising star athlete in the Ivy League. But the grandeur was tempered by a realization that most of those friendships were extremely shallow and meaningless. This was boldly underscored as he battled a seemingly constant barrage of persistent Christian witness. Sports fans only sought him when he was hot. The Bible thumpers were after him continually.

He knew there was a significant difference. He could have savored the adoration and ignored the God Squad if it had not been for a gnawing doubt of insufficiency in his inner person. His desire for recognition was unending. But he masked it. By all means possible he sought to hide his own sense of inferiority which had plagued his every step from early childhood. He doubted himself and he knew it.

For the last several weeks of the spring term, he had looked forward to summer, wanting to distance himself from the extreme competition for top-dog status. He needed a break from the pressures of being sought after and being wanted just for the benefit of other people's pleasure.

The hoped-for-relief from stress promised to be better than ever before because he was headed for new surroundings. He was going to Los Angeles with Mike, one of his Brown University Bruin teammates. Within a week of his arrival in California, he shifted thankfully into the comfort zone of minimal demands and boundless relaxation. Then, however, he and Mike received similar letters from a group of those persistently concerned Christians back at the university.

"Am I safe nowhere?" he wondered. "How did they track me down, way out here?"

Dear Ronny:

We hope you are having a great summer away from the books and enjoying new sights and experiences.

We also wanted to encourage you that you're not forgotten here at good ol' Brown University. During this summer term, there are not many of us around and the pace is a lot slower. But that gives us more time to get together for fellowship, so our prayer and Bible study group meets five mornings a week to keep things going.

We want you to know that we pray for you regularly. We trust God to save your soul so that you can begin to apply all your great potential for the good of Christ's Kingdom.

Romans 3:23 says that "All have sinned and fallen short of the glory of God." That includes you and us.

Because of our sins, Romans 6:23 declares that "The wages of sin is death, but the gift of God is eternal life through our Lord Jesus Christ."

That gift of eternal life is God's provision for us all, as Jesus says in John 3:16, "For God so loved the world that he gave his one and only son so that whoever believes in him shall not perish but have eternal life." You can personalize that thought by inserting your own name—"If Ron Brown believes in Jesus he shall not perish but have eternal life."

All God asks of us is that we change our way and turn to Him. First John 1:9 promises, "If we confess our sins, he is faithful and just and will forgive us our sins and purify us from all unrighteousness."

We here at Brown are sincerely praying that you will open your heart to Jesus Christ even now.

We look forward to having you back on campus in August. In the meantime, if we can do anything for you, please let us know.

Love in Christ,

Ron was not pleased as he read the message. Indeed, he was greatly angered and offended. The Bible totin' crew at the university had gone too far. The two athletes agreed that the letter was all the more proof that the whole bunch were wild-eyed fanatics and were not to be taken seriously.

"How dare they intrude into my private life like this," Ron declared resentfully. "Just when I thought I was free from their nagging, they have to send a screwy letter about Jesus and sin and all that stuff."

"Aw, forget it," advised his friend, who wasn't so sensitive to religious issues and therefore not so easily pricked. "They're just a bunch of losers who need somebody to judge so that they won't feel so worthless."

However, Ron was not easily turned from his wrath. His anger burned hot. "Will they ever be sorry they wrote this letter. I will make their lives miserable when I get back to Providence," he vowed.

But his vow of revenge was idly made. He didn't have it within himself to willfully harm anyone. What he truly intended, or wanted, was just to be able to successfully avoid the whole lot of them.

The remaining days of vacation passed all too quickly, and Ron returned to Brown for the preseason practice sessions. In those intervening weeks, he had religiously, purposefully excluded all thought of Jesus Christ and His campus champions from his conscious mind. His attention was focused entirely on using the weeks of training to sharpen his skills which had earned him a starting position the previous season and which had extended his football notoriety beyond the campus.

Having kept active with physical activity while on the West Coast, his body quickly adjusted to the rigorous demands of the training regimen. He was anxious for the first day with pads and contact scrimmaging.

He was totally absorbed in football. Between the hours of physical training and the brain draining sessions of learning the details of the playbook, Ron gave little thought to God or the barrage of witnesses which had come his way the previous year. He had even forgotten about the summer letter until late one night after he'd gone to bed. Unable to go to sleep, it suddenly dawned on him that he'd been back in Providence for ten full days and no one had bothered him about his need of being "saved."

"Perhaps they finally got smart and gave up," he smiled sadly to himself.

Just as quickly, however, his smile turned upside down with an unexplainable fear that perhaps indeed they had given up on him. He did not sleep well that night.

Camaraderie began to build as composition of the team took form around the returning lettermen. Ron and the other veteran players took stock of the new batch of sophomores who served mostly as live practice targets. Harry Walls was one such player. He shared the locker next to Ron's. The two of them had not met the previous year for the simple reason that varsity jocks just don't spend much time watching freshmen play. Besides, as a first-year player, Harry had made no noteworthy contribution even to the freshman team. He had no special athletic ability to draw attention to himself. To Ron, the man seemed much too timid to be a gutsy football player. Yet, at the same time, Harry had a strength in his gentleness which was strangely attractive.

It was into the second week of practice before Ron and Harry finally had an occasion for more than a passing moment of greeting. They were just leaving the locker room when both stopped for a drink at the water fountain.

"Hey, Ron, you had a great practice today," Harry said enthusiastically.

"Thanks," Ron responded, wondering to himself, "What's this guy trying to say?" Certainly it wasn't unusual for someone to compliment him on having played an outstanding game. But never had another player made such a comment after a day of mere gut-grinding drills.

"I love the way you really put yourself into it," Harry continued as they walked up the ramp out of the fieldhouse. "It's just the way God made us," he added unapologetically, "you know, like it says in

1 Corinthians 10:31, '...Whatever you do, do it all for the glory of God.'"

Ron gaped at the man, speechless. Wasn't it enough that he'd have to try to get away from the fanatics in the dormitory and across the campus? Now he finds that one of these jokers had a football locker right next to his. He was about to tell the man to get lost before being confronted with the inevitable question, "Ron, do you love the Lord?" But before he could speak a negative word, Harry broke off the conversation. "Well, Ron, I've got to run. I'll see you in the morning at practice."

Ron was astounded as the lanky athlete turned and headed on his way. This was the first time he'd heard someone talk personally about God without being pushy. He no longer felt defensive. He dropped his guard as he watched the man go. Walking to his dorm, Ron could not help but ask himself, "How do you do something for the glory of God?"

Ron never got around to asking Harry the question. He didn't have to. He got an answer without even being aware of it.

Harry was one of those rare types of men who seemed to be able to handle everything in stride, no matter how difficult. Similar circumstances could possibly turn another individual inside out. But not Harry. The man seemed to have a smile painted on his slender face. At least by all outward appearance, he was always happy.

Notwithstanding, Ron kept a wary eye on the man. He had become gun shy from the persistence of other "Bible toters" on campus, and he was certain that Harry would pounce on him sooner or later. As he watched–always at arm's length–he was more and more confused by what he saw. He thought the man definitely was weird. Try as he may, he could not understand Harry's attitude.

Ron's primary definition of success at that juncture of his life was to be a starter on the football team. More than that, to be a truly good player, a standout, a star. He sought recognition. He sought popularity and its immediate gratification of status with the girls and the guys. Harry's manner, on the other hand, was in stark contrast to Ron's best laid plans through his two full years at Brown

University. Could Harry have a potent secret behind his cool demeanor? The thought began to gnaw away at Ron that perhaps there was something wrong with his own concept of success.

In the team's season opener against Yale, Ron played a spectacular game overall. But he blew a key assignment which led to Yale's only touchdown, which was, in turn, enough for their margin of victory. The Bruins wound up losing 10-9, which put them out of the driver's seat for the Ivy League championship.

The Brown locker room was a sullen place. No glad back slapping and high fives and congratulations. Ron soaked a long time in a hot shower. He was wound tight. In his mind he replayed the second quarter of the game over and over. But no matter how he tried to redo it, every time he failed. He missed the play. He blew it. It was a long, quiet ride back to Providence on the team bus.

Ron somehow survived a morbid weekend. No one had openly blamed him for the loss, but he was certain they must. He dreaded facing the team at practice on Monday. As soon as he stepped onto the field, however, Harry came running up to him with praise on his lips. He spoke vividly of everything right Ron had done in Saturday's game. There was no mention of the one mistake.

"Was this guy talking about the same game?" Ron wondered to himself. Since Harry was not on the traveling squad, perhaps he had missed some pertinent details in the radio account.

Ron, nonetheless, accepted the praise without complaint. He really needed the boost, and there was no doubting the warmth and obvious sincerity by which Harry spoke. It only bothered Ron that he was not able to return the compliment. There was nothing, in all honesty, for which he could applaud Harry, he thought, at least in regards to football prowess.

Ron was still thinking about Harry after practice as he stood a long time in the hot spray of the shower. Finally he stepped out of the shower, dried himself, and weaved his way around equipment and benches, slowly back to his locker. "Now, look at this guy," he thought to himself, as he studied Harry out of the corner of his eye. "He doesn't even get into the game. He doesn't play a down. He's a bench warmer. He doesn't even play much in practice. Yet he's always smiling. Always happy."

Ron shook his head in disbelief and started to dress, still deep in his own thoughts. "This guy is out of touch with reality. He just doesn't understand what is important in life. He's not pushing himself. He's not doing all he can. Yet, he's still happy. I just don't get it."

But Harry was applying himself and doing all he could. However, unlike Ron, his definition of success was based on process rather than results.

Harry had already dressed. He shut his locker and turned toward Ron with his hand extended for a final congratulatory shake. "I just want to tell you again what a great game you played on Saturday."

"Thanks," Ron said lamely.

With that, Harry walked away, leaving Ron more confused than ever.

The entire season progressed that way: Ron playing, Harry watching. Ron fearing a spiritual onslaught, Harry offering endless praise. It didn't matter to Harry whether it was practice or competition, his remarks of admiration were consistent and constant:

"Hey, man you made a great play on that last down in practice.

"That was a fantastic tackle on Jones.

"You must have leaped four feet on that interception.

"I love the way you run.

"I love the way you play."

Not one time did he express displeasure or resentment at not playing himself. His words of praise were always honest and tactically correct. Often he weaved a quote from the Bible into what he said, but never did he twist his words as a weapon against the more superior athlete.

Ron thought the guy was a little strange. Even so, he liked him and had an unspoken admiration for his zeal.

Late in the season, after a grueling, hard-fought win over

Harvard, Ron and his buddies celebrated late into the night. It was no fun getting up Sunday morning. He groaned as he rolled out of bed. It was after eleven o'clock when he strolled into the cafeteria to wait for the lunch line to open. He slouched in a chair, dressed in faded jeans and a sloppy sweatshirt. With a ball cap on backward, he was acting the clown for the entertainment of his friends.

In walked Harry. Fresh from church. He looked handsome in a suit and tie. His right hand grasped a Bible.

As Harry approached the cluster of men, his football teammates, they began a chorus of taunts:

"Hey, man, check out Harry!"

"Yeah, Harry the home boy."

"Don't he look cute with his Bible and suit."

Harry made no reply. He kept his focus straight ahead. He smiled thinly as he walked on by. Without comment, he took a place, all alone, in the growing line at the serving table. The insults faded into nothingness. The man's true bearing increased right before Ron's eyes.

As he watched Harry pass by, a sudden, intense sense of admiration for him swept over Ron. He whispered to himself, "Boy! You know there's something about this guy! Man, I respect him. It's not just the compliments he gives me, but there's something deep about this guy. I'm being tossed and turned like a leaf in the wind by my friends. Others are dictating my life by my sensitivity to what they say. They're making the moves in life–actually we're doing it to each other. Like puppets.

"But here's a guy who walks his own path. Here's a guy who doesn't care what other people think or say."

Of course, Ron didn't dare let his buddies know what he was really thinking. He only looked at them and chimed in, "Yeah, there's something about that guy."

"Someday," Ron affirmed to himself, "I'm going to tell Harry how much I appreciate him as a man."

CHAPTER 7

GOD'S ULTIMATE WEAPON

His junior year with the Brown University Bruins was a triumph for Ron Brown. The Ivy League football coaches and New England sportswriters had an opinion of him almost equal to that of the ever-praising Harry Walls. He was a unanimous selection to first team All-Ivy League. That, in turn, spurred his thinking and inflamed his vision beyond college to a professional career. Wasting little time, scouts from various pro teams began sending letters to him regarding their interest. They sought details to begin formulating their draft plans for the future. Without complaint, he was caught up in an ego-boosting whirlwind.

But the hype of athletic achievement is fleeting. With the end of the first semester, the glory of victories and the despair of failures during the football season faded into history. Ron had time finally to give himself to the pursuit of another interest.

He had first seen her in September as he and his buddies checked out the more than one hundred newcomers at the Minority Students Orientation. On that first occasion, she had smiled in recognition of his presence, and he had nodded in noble response. From that brief exposure, she had been indelibly etched into his mind.

He chided himself twice during the fall when he saw her on campus. "Man, get your act together. Just trot across the grass. Walk up, put on the charm, smile, and ask her out." But each time as he hesitated to build up his nerve, the opportunity vanished and he'd kick himself.

It was not until February that he, who was so brazen on the gridiron, overcame his timidity and fear of rejection to boldly ask her for a date.

Normally, he had no real apprehension in approaching anyone.

Though internally insecure, he had an outrageous compulsion to at least act with confidence. In this case, however, he also was unsure of whether or not he even wanted to commit himself. When he saw her, he also perceived a warning not to get involved. For he had inquired about her from others and learned that she was one of those "Jesus fanatics." That was enough to give him serious doubts as to whether or not anything worthwhile could come from such a relationship. Nonetheless, there was something so appealing about her that he decided that since he had been able to withstand the pressures to "convert" from all the other Bible thumpers that he could surely stand up against a single, slender young woman.

Not only was Audrey Dixon lovely to look at, she had quality on the inside as well. She was certain of what was important in life and why. She had solid goals set and was determined to reach them. None of that, however, had come her way with ease.

Audrey had been rescued from being a shameful product of one of the worst slums of the inner city of New York. Her mother had to double as a father since that man had not stayed around to shoulder any responsibility for Audrey, her sister, or her brother. In spite of the daily threatening push of drug dealers, constant reminders of violence, and insecurity from the street gangs, Audrey's mother succeeded in keeping at least one of her daughters safe from irreparable turmoil. She stayed in school, made good grades, and gained recognition at prestigious Stuyvesant High School.

At that point, one of the truly significant minority assistance programs, "A Better Chance," stepped in to offer Audrey a scholarship to attend Philip Exeter Boarding School. By sheer grit and determination, she had done well at Stuyvesant. But under the gentler atmosphere at Exeter, Audrey gracefully flowered into full bloom. Her keen mind propelled her through her studies successfully until, as a graduating senior, she was honored as salutatorian of the class. Just as importantly and significantly, however, at Exeter she was confronted with the Gospel of Jesus Christ and turned control of her life into His hands.

For their first date, Ron decided on the safety of a movie, for in such a situation a guy doesn't have to expend his efforts on detailed conversation in order to become intimate with a girl. Was he in for a surprise! Audrey was not impressed at being in the presence of a campus football star. If her date for the evening had been the "least likely to succeed" of the entire student body, her primary goal still would have been to get into serious communication.

Little wonder then that they did not make it to the theater that night. She was right on time when he called for her at the dormitory. It was easy for him to find something to say from the start–"Hey, you look nice!"–because that was the obvious truth. Beyond that, however, he had been searching desperately all the way to her dorm for a line to follow.

But not to worry. Audrey had an agenda. She had heard a lot about Ron Brown. Her goal for the evening was to get to know who he really was.

"Thank you," she responded as he helped her on with her coat. "You look nice yourself, sir."

Ron felt a surge of importance as she locked her arm in his as they stepped out the door into the brisk winter night. That simple gesture from her signaled an unspoken expression of "Please protect me!" And his instant reaction was positive. He would do just that.

They began to talk as they walked, and shortly they both were so caught up in conversation that by common consent they stopped in a coffee shop. Three hours later, having missed the movie, Ron walked her home. He was fascinated with the girl as he left her dormitory. Never had he opened up to any other person so freely.

Courting Audrey was a challenge for Ron like none other he had ever confronted. It was obvious from their first date that she was open to building a relationship with him, but not at just any price. In spite of the harsh background from which she came, her commitment to Jesus Christ two years earlier had revolutionized her life. She was a Christian with definite parameters. She knew who knew what was best for her, and she was determined not to stray from His plan for her life. If the budding friendship with Ron Brown was to be a significant part of that plan, fine. If not, that too would be fine.

Audrey was especially interesting to Ron because she was a multi-dimensional person. He had gained the impression from the first zealous witnesses for Christ on campus that they had only one goal in life–his heart for Jesus. Harry had altered his view somewhat, but Audrey was like a first chapter in a new book. She introduced him to a new concept of friendship, openness, and vitality which excited him about the prospect of getting beyond mere intro-ductions. However, that was no easy task. She was not a pushover for a varsity leather jacket. And even as a freshman, her time was consumed with the demands of countless friends, an intense program of study set toward a doctorate in psychology, and a loyalty to regular attendance at the "Romans 8:28 Bible Study" on campus.

"Ron, I truly did enjoy our time together the other night," Audrey said with a lilt in her voice as they walked across campus together a few days later. "And I don't want to push my convictions on you. But you can't expect me to fit my schedule to suit yours. You know that Jesus Christ is the most important part of my life and I spend a lot of time developing my relationship with Him through Bible study and prayer groups."

"I don't understand that much about religion, but I do know I want to…." Before he could finish his sentence, their conversation was interrupted by another couple who anxiously called Audrey over to them in front of the library. "Please excuse me for a second, Ron, I'll be right back," she said assuredly.

Ron did not follow her, but watched with resentment burning inside his chest. He was incensed. He knew what was up–and he was specifically excluded. The young man was a self-proclaimed leader of the "God Squad." He had attacked Ron with the Bible several times, but had never been able to break through his outer defenses.

"Audrey," the young man declared loudly enough for Ron to overhear, "that guy is not a good influence on you. He's not a believer. In fact, he's an outspoken critic of everything we do. He'll pull you down with him."

The young woman who was with them looked at Ron cautiously out of the corner of her eyes, as if she were peeking at the devil himself.

Ron complied with a sly smirk. The young woman anxiously turned her attention back to the teaching of the college guru.

"Listen," Audrey said without apology. "I like him. He's fun to be with."

"Don't get sucked in by all that charm and athletic mystique. We're not supposed to compromise our faith in Christ."

"I'm not compromising my faith," Audrey answered with a growing irritation evident in the tone of her voice.

"Well, did you tell him about Jesus and that he needs to be born again?" the woman demanded piously.

"Yeah!" her companion rejoined emphatically.

"He knows where I stand," Audrey responded flatly. "But beyond that, it's none of your business what Ron and I talk about."

"Oh, Audrey, 'Do not take lightly the instruction of a brother,'" the young lady coined a proverb.

"Yes, listen to the advice of Saint Paul," the young man said solemnly. "'Do not be yoked together with nonbelievers.'"

"We're certainly not 'yoked,'" Audrey assured them with a soft, secretive voice as she turned to go. "But you certainly have heightened my interest. Perhaps God intends to use me for Ron's benefit."

Undoubtedly God would use her. But how? In what way? The athlete intended to pursue a relationship with the lovely young woman from New York. But he was equally intent on avoiding the religious functions that consumed so much of her time. He had plenty to content himself with as he filled in those gaps. In no way was he interested in opening himself up to an interrogation on the status of his soul by other crusaders for Christ.

The understanding between the two of them broadened and deepened. They enjoyed being friends. Ron was thankful to have someone he could confide in without the fear of rebuke or rejection. She gave him a sense of confidence. Audrey assured him that it was all right just to be. To be who he truly was and not merely the happy-go-lucky clown he tried so hard to project.

For her part, Audrey also gained from the friendship. Though Ron could not share with her spiritually, what was of greatest significance to her, she knew that he respected her as a person, as someone of worth. And coming from a nonbeliever, she considered that to be quite a compliment. She frequently invited him to the many and varied special occasions of the Christian community, but Ron was not very responsive. He ducked into church with her twice, just because there had been too long a hiatus without seeing her. However, he fended off her gentle reminders that her primary goal in life was what should concern him as well: to perfect the purpose for which God brought us into life.

As the school year came to a close, Ron was not as keen as in previous years to get off campus and get home. He had learned to appreciate Audrey more than any female friend he had known. He began to miss her even before leaving campus. He wished there were an "understanding" between them, one that would insure their relationship for the summer. However, she had made it clear that they were just good friends.

After two weeks of slow summer fun, Ron could stand the separation no longer. He missed her terribly. He dialed her number in New York City. At the sound of her voice on the other end of the line, his face brightened.

"Hey! How're ya doin'? This is Ron Brown."

She laughed at the formality of identifying himself. His insecurity was showing. "Yes, Ron! I'd recognize that baritone voice anywhere. It's so good to hear from you. What are you doing?"

"Oh, I'm playin' a lot of b-ball and trying to keep up with the social life my mom has for me. Since I got home, she's had a constant parade of family and friends through the house."

Ron paused, wet his lips. His heart was thumping with a nervousness he'd never before experienced.

"Audrey!" he continued with determination. "I didn't call to talk about me. I just had to hear your voice. I miss you! I miss our walks and our talks."

"I miss you, too," she responded honestly.

The creased furrows of anxiety faded from his brow. An unfamiliar and unfathomable joy swept through him. He couldn't recall ever having been "missed" by anyone before.

"I sure wish I could see you today," Ron moaned. "September seems so far away–almost forever."

"I'll write you a long letter this afternoon," she promised in consolation. "And I'll write you often."

"I'm not so good at writing," Ron confessed, "but I've got your number and I'll be calling again–and again–and again."

She laughed.

He loved her laugh.

Was the pagan athlete, entrenched, unmoved, immovable by the barrage of persistent witnesses on campus, unknowingly caught in a tender trap of unadorned Christian love? Not by a long shot. He, of course, knew she was a Christian, a very dedicated believer. But his feelings for her had nothing to do with Jesus. This was between man and woman. Audrey and Ron. He gave no thought to Jesus Christ as being in the picture at all.

CHAPTER 8

WHATEVER HAPPENED TO HARRY?

Audrey, who never committed herself to anything lightly, held true to her promise: she wrote often during that summer. Of everything she mailed, however, her second letter was Ron's favorite. He read and re-read it almost daily.

My Dear Ronny,

I just returned from a quiet, wonderful time alone at Battery Park. To be by oneself in New York City is quite a feat with people, people everywhere. But I've found that it's not necessary to lock out the sounds and combustion of the day in order to be truly alone. In fact, I experience a beautiful assurance of peace as I observe all that is going on around me while at the same time, looking inward to all that God is accomplishing in my life. In moments like these I sense that I am alone in the presence of the Lord and that He has set aside all His other activities just to take notice of me.

As I sat on a wooden park bench, with the sun warm on my face, the Statue of Liberty standing majestic in the distance, and with the incessant blare of the tug boat horns beating on my ears, I thought of you.

I laughed at myself as I imagined you standing as tall and assured as Miss Liberty. In a way you are alike–immovable, and I like that about you. You, as she, offer hope to others with your determination to achieve, to succeed.

So, I prayed for you in a special way as I sat there. I thought of all the amazing potential God has wrapped up in your mind, body, and soul. I made no plea. I simply again entrusted you to His care. I'm confident that He will in His time enable you to accomplish all His purpose for your being.

Of course, one of those purposes is already being perfected. For the very thought of you brings joy into my life.

With love,

Audrey

Ron also kept his promise. He called often. Between those moments of special, but all too brief, communication, the summer passed with speed.

In addition to stoking the fires of love, however, Ron also had his days filled with his own hectic and rigorous patterning of physical training. He intended to arrive at the preseason training camp with the Bruins in the best possible condition. He had a shot at being a high draft choice by the pros and he intended to succeed beyond all measure in his senior season. The important eyes of scouts would be searching the stadiums of America every Saturday. He was determined that they would take notice of what he intended to be the most outstanding defensive back in the Ivy League and one of the best in America.

Heading back to Providence the second week of August, with Audrey not due to return from New York until after the first of September, Ron's thoughts of friendship centered on the other Christian he respected, Harry Walls. He had not seen the tall, lanky athlete much during the spring semester, but when he did the man always had a word of encouragement for him. He was looking forward to seeing the guy again. Especially, he began planning in his mind how he would tell Harry that he truly did appreciate him and valued his friendship. He wasn't very good at putting together "corny" words, but he wanted somehow to apologize. He sensed an urgency to erase from his memory the guilt of having stood silently by while others ridiculed the "Bible toter."

Ron enjoyed talking with other players that first night back in the dorm, but Harry wasn't there. Brown was not an inexpensive school, so Harry lived off campus in order to cut expenses. Ron realized, in the midst of the fun of the evening, that he wished Harry were present to put some meaning into the otherwise boring conversation. He began counting the hours to the warmup practice the next morning. He wanted to get on with the task of building a stronger relationship with the incomparable benchwarmer.

When Ron got to the locker room, there were a lot of other old friends to greet that he had not seen the night before. He kept looking beyond the milling players to catch a glimpse of Harry. The man was nowhere in sight. At last the talking and joking subsided, and Ron headed for his locker to change clothes. Only then did he realize that the locker next to his was empty. No sign of Harry.

Hurriedly, he put on his sweatsuit and tennis shoes and went directly to the equipment manager. "Hey, John, where's Harry Walls? His locker's empty."

"Harry's not comin' back," John replied flatly.

"What do you mean, 'he's not comin' back'?" Ron demanded with a sense of urgency.

"Well, he decided to transfer to another school," John answered.

"I'm really sorry to hear he transferred," Ron said sadly. "Maybe he finally came to his senses. Perhaps he went to a school where he can have a chance to play football."

Ron turned away from the equipment room and headed to the field. A gloom overrode his spirit. Why had he not grasped the relationship with Harry when it was in reach? He felt an inexpressible loneliness, yet there was something about Harry which would never leave him. His respect for the man was deep, though he doubted he'd ever see him again or have the opportunity to tell him the impact he'd had on his life.

Notwithstanding, Ron did not lament the lost opportunity for long. There was too much to accomplish. He plunged with intensity into the football program. He had arrived for the season with spirited determination and pushed the memory of the fourth-stringer out of conscious thought. He worked hard. He was ready from day one for the two-a-day sessions—even for pads on scrimmage. His own enthusiasm served to pump up the team morale to a fever pitch. Indeed! This last season of his collegiate career was going to be fantastic.

Then the schedule started. Perhaps it was due to the absence of Harry, with the man's constant and unsolicited compliments. Perhaps it was due to the pressure he put on himself to keep trying always to do even better, to break some of the standards he'd set as a junior. Perhaps it was the high expectations others expressed. Perhaps it was the inconsistency of the pro scouts: one day buddying up to him and another time ignoring him. Whatever it was, nothing he did on the football field satisfied Ron Brown.

It's a good thing Audrey arrived back on campus a few days early, ahead of the opening game of the season. Ron Brown, the brash, bold athlete, desperately needed someone to talk with, to confide in. To whom could he share his fears? Audrey listened as Ron poured out his frustrations.

"You know," he said with a disbelieving shake of his head, "probably the worst thing that can happen to a college athlete is to have a really good junior year, because then all of a sudden everybody has great expectations for your senior year.

"I just don't know what I can do more than I am doing now. I'm in top shape. I know the playbook both ways from Sunday. I give it my best effort. And nothin'! I feel nothin'! There's just no juice in it. Or somethin'."

"Ronny," Audrey suggested quietly, "I don't know a lot about football. In fact, I probably wouldn't go to a game except to watch you. But I do know that you're trying too hard. Let me read you something that just may give you a new slant on it.

"The Apostle Paul experienced many difficulties in his life and there was one problem he prayed and prayed about. It had him flustered. He loved and served God, but he never got the answer he wanted."

Without apology, she took a New Testament out of her purse, turned to 2 Corinthians 12:8-10, and read:

> "Three times I pleaded with the Lord to take it away from me. But he said to me, 'My grace is sufficient for you, for my power is made perfect in weakness.' Therefore I will boast all

the more gladly about my weaknesses, so that Christ's power may rest on me. That is why, for Christ's sake, I delight in weaknesses, in insults, in hardships, in persecutions, in difficulties. For when I am weak, then I am strong."

"Wow! That's heavy stuff," Ron observed. "What was the guy's problem?"

"No one knows for sure," Audrey answered simply. "But this Scripture has helped to assure me that the world doesn't rest on my shoulders. I don't have to be Miss Perfect for everyone. When I admit that I'm weak and can't handle something and turn it over to the Lord, He always comes through."

Ron felt an unusual calm in listening to her words. She didn't make it sound like she was preaching at him. She was sharing what had meaning for her. He liked that.

Throughout the season, he turned to Audrey frequently for consolation, and she was always there with a good word. Yet, he could not escape the loneliness, the insecurity that gripped him inwardly.

He tried constantly to please his friends. While they were around, the joking kept him pumped up. However, they weren't with him twenty-four hours a day. When they were gone, the "good times" went with them. But, even worse, eventually he had to try to go to sleep–alone.

In spite of the fact that his emotions performed erratic cartwheels in his soul, at least his relationship with Audrey blossomed. She encouraged him through the difficult times. Invariably, in such moments, she would open her Bible and read to him, in much the same way as young David sang Psalms to soothe the troubled spirit of King Saul. In time, he started going back to church on Sundays–not that he put much of himself into it–but it helped fill a void which he could not express.

Of course, no relationship could ever last if it were entirely one-sided. Audrey also had many insecurities; she had gone through many life-warping experiences before Christ came into her life. She too received from Ron. Mutually they shared the incredible encouragement of entrusting their soul burdens with one another. In a deepening friendship, Audrey and Ron wisely built on each other's strengths.

Amazingly, Ron continued to do well in his studies, though his mind was consumed with a desire to be a pro football player. He was shackled by that singleness of purpose. It was his passion. His goal. His first thought in the morning. His last thought at night.

As the season rolled around to mid-year, the Brown Bruins were having just a so-so season. One week up, the next week down. Holy Cross was to be the next game. The Crusaders were undefeated. They had beaten a couple of really good teams and were ranked number one in the New England area. It was a big game, a home game for the Bruins. ABC scheduled it for Eastern regional television coverage. A win would turn the entire season around for Brown University, but a loss would doom the team to a dismal season.

Going into the game, the Bruins were rated heavy underdogs even though they were playing in their own stadium. Of course, predicting is an inexact science. Any team can beat any other on a given day.

Ron and his teammates arrived at the locker room shortly before noon, having read all the dismal forecasts concerning their fate for the day. As they geared up for the game, they expressed their anger to each other at having been described so miserably by sportswriters—even in the local press. Slowly they began seething. As the coach entered into his pep talk, their anger was kindled into flame. By game time they burst onto the field like a great ball of fire.

Holy Cross didn't even think to get the license number from the truck that smeared it across the turf. Early in the fourth quarter, the scoreboard told an amazing story in bold block numbers: Brown 31, Holy Cross 10. The coach decided at that point to get his starters out and let the substitutes finish the mopping-up job.

As the regulars came out to the thunderous roar of the partisan crowd, everyone was high-fiving one another and bouncing around hugging each other. Everyone on the Brown sideline felt joy, happiness, and gladness. Everyone except Ron Brown.

He sat there on the brink of tears. He couldn't understand his own emotions. He had played one of the best, if not the very best game, of his career. He was to receive the game ball for his efforts. Yet, all he could think about was the terrible pressure he was under at that particular moment. Pressure he was putting on himself because of the television coverage and the many pro scouts in the stands.

"How could I have missed that tackle in the first quarter?" he bemoaned to himself. "If it weren't for me they wouldn't have even gotten their one touchdown.

"What in the world are the scouts thinking now?

"I bet they all left in disgust that they wasted their time coming clear up here to watch a nobody."

He sighed in despair as he thought of the ribbing he was sure to face in the dormitory, in the dining hall, on the campus. "I wonder if my friends saw my colossal error on that last play of the third quarter? No one will forget that for a long, long time."

In his panic, Ron walked wearily to the end of the bench and sat down. Everybody else continued to celebrate as the game wound down.

Brad, one of his best friends on the team, came to where he sat and looked down at him in unbelief. "Hey, Brown! Man, you look like you just lost your dad or somethin'."

"I know," Ron replied sadly. "That's just the way I feel—and I don't understand it."

On the team bus for the ride back to the locker room, after the victory was secured, the celebration continued. Everybody was jostling around, shouting, and giving victory cheers. Ron just sat there in his own personal gloom, staring blankly out the window. He didn't dare look around at anyone. He didn't want to be seen. But he listened keenly, waiting for someone to declare, "Did you see that play Ron messed up back in the third quarter?"

He was paranoid, sitting there with rabbit ears, waiting for taunting that never came. He was tight in mind and body. He wondered what Harry Walls would've said about this game. He was certain that even the ever optimistic Harry could not think of a compliment now. Ron went back to his dormitory room alone. He laid down on his bed in mental anguish. To break the spell, he tried counting the ceiling tiles over and over again. It didn't work.

"There's something terribly wrong," he admitted to himself. "Something just isn't right inside."

Brown University proceeded to win its next five games, only to lose to the David Shula-led Dartmouth Big Green for the Ivy League Championship. Nonetheless, the experts were saying that Ron had an outstanding season. Though the NFL draft was months away, rumors and opinions were rampant. People who supposedly were in the know kept Ron in turmoil and under pressure with their unsolicited views.

First one would say, "You'll be drafted in the third round."

That would make the young man giddy with excitement as the visions of a signing bonus and a six-figure salary raced through his mind.

Another would express his opinion, "You're bound to make it in the sixth round, seventh for sure."

With such queer, erratic pressure, Ron's mood swings were just as unpredictable. Besides his own discipline of sticking to his studies, there were two other release valves for him, two outlets which were strangely, diametrically opposites: the steadying influence of Audrey Dixon and the occasional carefree partying with his friends.

One such late night of carousing followed the senior fling at one of the Greek houses. Though Ron had never pledged to a fraternity, his status as an athlete made him a sought after guest for many functions.

He awoke the next morning with a brain-breaking hangover. To boot, he was bummed out with himself, the football hassle, the study grind, and life in general. Though it was exam time, he decided to forget all responsibilities for the day and just slouch around. Somehow he hoped to recover from the anguish raging in his body, which fluctuated between his churning stomach and throbbing head.

Audrey happened to encounter him in the student lounge. His body was contorted sideways in an overstuffed chair with his head propped uncomfortably on the armrest. She took one look at his rumpled appearance and knew there was big trouble. "Ron," she said calmly, hiding her annoyance at his irresponsible behavior, "what are you doing here? Don't you have a sociology exam at eleven?"

"I'm not goin'," he responded unevenly as he sat up in agony to face her. "I don't feel so good."

"You're drunk!" she scolded.

"Was drunk," he corrected, with a limp smile. "At the moment, I'm merely miserable."

"Well, miserable or not," she demanded, "you've got to get to that class."

"But, I'm not prepared," he admitted.

"Then fake it!" she advised as she grabbed his right arm with both her hands to force him to his feet. "With your intelligence, you'll make something out of it."

As he sat through the exam, preserving his grade point average, he took agonizing stock of himself. He came to three conclusions. One, he was an utter fool, because he had no clue who he was as a man. Two, he was thankful for Audrey Dixon, for she was a true friend who cared for him as a person. Three, he was going to be a pro football player because...because success was the only way he could prove himself worthy of life. Otherwise he was a loser. He just had to be drafted.

His self involvement and preoccupation with his own concerns was total. However, his concentration on himself was jarred a few weeks later when he got a call late one afternoon from Audrey's roommate. "Ron, Audrey needs you at the campus infirmary right away. There was an accident at the softball field and the doctor's examining her right now."

"What happened?" he insisted anxiously.

"She was standing on the sideline at the softball game and was hit by a wild throw from second base. It really looks serious. She was hit right at the edge of her left eye. She could lose her vision."

"I'll be right there," Ron promised.

Ron, dodging others as if returning an interception for a touchdown, ran all the way to the clinic. The news of the accident spread rapidly across campus. By the time Ron arrived, breathless, a half-dozen other friends of the popular young lady from New York were already there. Uncertain as to what the prognosis would be, they had huddled together in a corner of the lobby, hands linked together in a circle of prayer. Ron stood to one side, a solitary figure. He was thankful on the one hand that Audrey had so many concerned friends, but disgruntled on the other hand that he felt ill at ease. He didn't know how to join them in prayer.

When the doctor came out of the examining room fifteen minutes later, his opinion was guarded, and definitely not optimistic. "The swelling makes it impossible to check her vision thoroughly. Her eye suffered a terrific impact. The effects of the concussion will keep her in bed for at least a week."

He paused, then continued with a sigh, "There's a good chance she'll lose her vision."

Ron was devastated. "Why should anything so terrible happen to a person as kind and wonderful as Audrey?" he complained to himself.

"May we see her now?" her roommate asked.

"Yes, but just for a few minutes–and only two of you at a time."

Ron stood to one side. Partly he wanted to be a gentleman and let others go first. More importantly, he wanted to gather his thoughts so as to have something soothing to say when he saw her.

The room was quiet when he entered. All the others had gone. The sound of her breathing was exaggerated. With her nasal passages clogged, she sucked air in through her mouth. Ron was not prepared for the gruesome sight as he stepped to the edge of her bed. The smooth lines of her angular face were grotesquely distorted by swelling; black and blue blotches cast an eerie glow to her bronzed skin.

"Hey, Audrey, how you doin'?" Ron asked. He was at a loss for words as he took her right hand in his.

"Fine," she lied bravely.

"I wish like anything that this had happened to me instead of you," Ron declared as tears formed in his eyes.

"Well, if it had, you wouldn't be lying here," she replied. "You've been hit harder than this twenty times in a game—and you just bounce back."

"Yeah, but I have enough sense to wear a helmet," he joked.

She laughed lightly and began to cough.

"I'm sorry," he apologized. "I shouldn't be a clown at a time like this."

"No, no, that's all right," she assured him. "You're my favorite clown of all."

"Listen," he said, "I'd better get out of here so you can rest, but I'll be back tomorrow."

"Yes, I'm very tired," she agreed.

"Is there anything I can do for you?" he asked.

"Just pray for me," she advised.

"I sure will," he promised solemnly.

Throughout the night, Ron fretted about his vow. He knew he loved her. How then could he have committed himself to an empty promise? He didn't know anything about praying. Nevertheless, he gave it his best shot. "God," he said unfamiliarly, "Audrey is one of yours. I'm not. So I just ask you to take care of her. Take away her pain. Save her eyesight."

Next afternoon when he arrived at her room, Ron wasn't prepared for the commotion he encountered. Walking up to the door, he was certain he heard clapping and singing, as if it were a jam session. Sure enough! When he walked into her room, he was engulfed in praise music.

To God be the glory,
Great things He has done,
So loved He the world
That He gave us His son

Who yielded His life
An atonement for sin,
And opened the lifegate
That all may go in.

Praise the Lord, Praise the Lord,
Let the earth hear His voice!
Praise the Lord, Praise the Lord,
Let the people rejoice!

O come to the Father, through Jesus the Son,
And give Him the glory, great things He has done.

Obviously, he thought, as evidenced by all the excitement, the doctor had changed his opinion. Ron pushed around the worshipers with the hallelujahs on their lips and stepped to the edge of the bed.

His expression sagged. He was shocked. Instead of her big brown eyes looking up at him, huge gauze pads were taped over both sockets. She couldn't see a thing.

Audrey's roommate leaned over to speak into her ear to be heard above the praises, "Ron's here."

"Ron!" Audrey said adoringly as she lifted her right hand toward space to hopefully touch him.

He took her hand in his and crouched down low to speak, but as he did, the singing stopped and his first words were thunderous, "I don't understand . . .

"I don't understand," he repeated in normal voice. "When I heard all the praising I figured you must already be well, but . . . ."

She squeezed his hand firmly, understanding his dilemma as a nonbeliever. "The doctor wasn't very hopeful when he came in early this morning. The swelling is just too severe for him to check my vision. So he put these bandages on both eyes to protect them from any possible further strain. He should have a clear prognosis by the end of the week." She smiled in affirmation. "But I already know. I believe God will restore my vision."

"Amen! Amen! Praise the Lord!" her roomful of friends chorused variously.

Ron was speechless. He could not agree with such a radical, non-scientific view. Nor, at the same time, could he discredit or belittle their faith.

Day after day, he made his pilgrimage to the infirmary and the scene never varied. Christian friends attended her constantly with singing and clapping and faith-building praise. The attitude of the believers, rather than diminishing, reached out in ever growing assurance that a miracle of healing already had taken place.

Such faith in visible action is contagious. It got to Ron. Walking back to his dormitory that second day, his mind could not escape the contrast between the praises for God in Audrey's room and his own language habits. He made a decision. On the spot, he vowed, "No more profanity."

The next day, he encountered two of his football buddies on the steps of the John Carter Brown Library. "Hey, how's Audrey doin'?" one asked him.

"Praise God, she's feeling better today," he declared. The two looked at him suspiciously and responded, "Fine! Fine!" Then they beat a hurried retreat in the direction of the athletic field.

Ron walked slowly up the steps, glancing back over his shoulder at his friends, trying to figure out their weird reaction to him. Suddenly his face broke into a beaming, natural smile. He could hardly believe it himself. For the first time in his life, he had publicly honored God.

Gradually God Himself took a direct hand in discipling the young athlete. The changes weren't dramatic or earth shattering. No one else took much notice. But Ron knew he had turned a definite corner.

The doctor took the bandages off at the end of the week and made a complete examination. He was amazed. He then knew what several dozen Christians had known for days: there was no significant, permanent damage to her eyes. Her vision was 20/15. Two tiny scars were the only lasting evidence that anything traumatic had happened.

"They're sorta like beauty marks," Ron assured her.

"Oh! I'm so thankful that they're there," Audrey said firmly. "I don't ever want to forget this lesson. I really believe God allowed this to happen in order to correct me. I was becoming too lax in my walk with Him. This has jarred me back to a determination never to fail Him again."

Her words, "in order to correct me," seared themselves into Ron's spirit. As a nonbeliever, looking in from the outside, he couldn't see any room in her for improvement. But he could see plenty need of change in himself. If God had indeed corrected this precious young woman so sternly, what horror must be in store for a wretch like him.

Ron quit hanging out with the guys so much. In the midst of a party, he would look around and realize that something vitally important to him was missing. "I wish Audrey were here," he would complain quietly to no one and chastise himself for choosing to be there rather than with her and the God squad.

Increasingly he was aware of the gentle tug of God on his life.

However, he did not know how to respond. Or even if he should. His thoughts were consumed with the prospects of the NFL draft. That was of greatest importance to him. God would just have to wait.

CHAPTER 9

FIRST
THINGS FIRST

Gaining even a reserve position with a professional football team is accomplished by only a few hopefuls. It's not quite as easy as applying for a job at a nearby Wendy's. It is likewise even tougher than seeking a hard-to-find residency position at a major hospital after completing a grueling program of medical studies. It is highly sacrificial in nature.

It's a hard-nosed business in which men in management smile at young athletes who anxiously await a chance to grab the brass ring–and do so quickly if it is offered. No personal consideration is allowed to interfere or get in the way. The human elements, based on emotions, are cast aside and ignored. This is the real world. A twenty-two-year-old should be man enough to face up to a competitive and disgustingly impersonal bidding war for his physical talents and the stamina of his character. He is tested, timed, and examined as a hunk of flesh, then put on the auction block, much as if he were being judged for a Kentucky yearling sale.

From early in his junior season, for more than a year, Ron had been contacted by pro scouts from most of the twenty-eight NFL teams. At times they sought his favor. In other instances, they brushed past him to someone else as if he didn't even exist. The inconsistency of their attitude toward him kept him on edge–sometimes up, sometimes down. One particularly hopeful instance was right after the season finale against Columbia, his last game as a college athlete. A scout for Cincinnati said he would surely be drafted and that the Bengals were interested in him. It was the closest thing to an absolute offer he'd heard, though not an outright confirmation that he was pro material. There were other scouts who spoke in general terms about free agency.

With the end of the season, there was also an end to the almost steady, regular praise he had received from his coaches, the fans, and the press. All the glory quickly faded into a dim history. He was no longer a college athlete. That was over. A new phase of life was about to begin. The big question now—was he pro material or not?

Would any team want him? He hoped so. How he wished it! But because of the stress of the mind games the scouts played with him for months, he just didn't know.

Ron was so uncertain of what might come to pass that he intelligently kept one eye on graduate school. Come what may, he intended to pursue a master's degree in hospital administration. As a hedge against the future, in case he didn't make it as a pro, he applied to Columbia University.

Ron, always anxious to please, never wanting to offend, was a hapless target for a rare breed of opportunity seekers who year in and year out stalk the locker rooms of college campuses: professional agents. Like most other seniors eligible for the NFL draft that year, Ron very much wanted to make a team but was flush with a hundred questions as to how it happens. And just as surely as salmon go up river to spawn, every year would-be agents descend on college athletes to offer their services as a buffer between the athlete and the "big bad owners" of teams. Some are knowledgeable, honest, and sincere. Others, however, are pure and simple fortune hunters—seeking only to grab a quick buck and run.

Enter the agent.

"Hello, Ron, my name is Gus Dowling. I'd like to take you out to dinner tonight to talk about being your personal agent for your professional football career."

Gus was the first agent to approach him. And being interested in getting some answers to his many questions, Ron readily agreed. Dowling selected the finest of the many fine seafood restaurants in the city. During the meal, Ron was impressed with the man's mild manner; it fit his own style nicely. He enjoyed the small talk as they got acquainted.

Then Dowling got down to business. "I've been watching

your career closely for quite some time, Ron. Now that the draft is only a few months away, I'd like to team up with you as your agent.

"I already represent a number of players on several different teams. So team owners and scouts recognize me as a tough negotiator."

Though he was talking about himself, Dowling's words didn't sound like bragging. He was a man of the world. He spoke fast. Confident.

Ron was overwhelmed. He was also flattered that someone who was already in the big time as an agent for NFL players, wanted to represent him as well. "I'm pleased that you want to represent me, Mr. Dowling…"

"Gus!" he interrupted with emphasis.

"All right, Gus," Ron continued agreeably. "But, tell me, what can you do for me as an agent that I can't do for myself?"

"That's a good, intelligent question," Gus replied. "It's not so much what I can do for you, but what more can we accomplish working together as a team–after all, any final decision is always yours. My responsibility is to bargain in good faith on your behalf."

"Well, I certainly could use some help in knowing what to do," Ron admitted. "But," he continued awkwardly, not wanting to sound too mercenary, "how much is it going to cost to have you represent me? I know you guys don't work for free."

Gus laughed good naturedly. "You're right that I don't work for free. But my pay actually comes out of the owner's back pocket.

"You see," he continued in confidential tone, "since I've been through the procedure time and time again, I know what to ask for and how to get it. I'll be able to get you a higher signing bonus and, through negotiations, a better first-year salary. I may be able even to get you selected in a higher round.

"Now, my fee is just three percent of whatever you get. That's why I say that since I can get you more, you actually don't pay me anything–it's almost like an added fringe benefit. And I'll get more of those for you, too!"

Ron studied carefully the contract Gus Dowling laid out on the table in front of him. It was spelled out clearly that if Gus failed to negotiate a satisfactory contract for him, he owed the man nothing. That provision, more than anything else, lured him into believing everything else the man had claimed about himself. Ron's palms sweated. He was ripe with excitement as he pondered what to do.

He signed.

After he returned to his room, Ron read through the details of the contract again and again. At last it struck him clearly that it was for real. Finally! He knew he was on his way. From that point forward, his confidence level jumped noticeably. He had nothing to fear. His agent, who should know better than anyone else, assured him, without qualification, that he would be drafted somewhere between the fourth and tenth rounds.

"In fact," Dowling had concluded, "I wouldn't be surprised if you went in the third."

For the moment, Ron was elated. The fact of having a contract with an agent, however, left him with only momentary satisfaction. As the days of waiting for the draft turned into weeks, he became more and more sullen.

"What've I gotten myself into?" he mused. "Yes, I have a valid contract with an agent–whom I've never heard of before.

"But a man doesn't play in the National Football League for an agent! It takes a team contract!"

Would he rather have a team or an agent?

His emotions churned in turmoil throughout the long days leading up to the draft.

He prayed. But that was of no discernible help. He didn't believe in supernatural intervention anyway, although he was still bewildered by Audrey's "unexplainable" recovery. He was sinking in his spirit, tossed back and forth by every changing wave of the moment. He went to church twice. Yet he found no relief there. It was a profitless exercise. He heard nothing that was said or sung because he spent every minute recalling the names of every draftable player he could bring to mind.

Meticulously, he matched each of those mighty men, one round after another, with various NFL teams. Then, equally as methodically, he redrafted everyone again. Over and over, he continued the ridiculous numbers process endlessly.

As draft day approached, Ron had lots of well wishers, both by telephone and in person. But their words of encouragement were of only passing value, empty of substance. Daily, all they said disappeared from his mind as quickly as the sun hid from the earth. It was the long intervening hours that gave him the greatest stress. The intense internal insecurity which he kept hidden from the view of others haunted him throughout the night hours.

Audrey was his only anchor as he was tossed back and forth on the ebb and tide of his emotions. Her consistency of faith and cool demeanor helped him to hold somewhat steady. "Ron, I know how important being a pro football player is to you," she affirmed, as they arrived back at her dormitory after dinner one evening. "But, I also know something even more important! You must believe me that when the time for decision comes, God is going to be right there to help you.

"Listen to what it says here in Proverbs 3:5-6," she said as she reached for her ever present Bible.

> "Trust in the Lord with all your heart and lean not on your own understanding; in all your ways acknowledge him, and he will direct your paths.

"That's the key, Ron; you have to trust in Jesus!"

He listened carefully to her words, but they seemed not to penetrate. Nothing brought relief. He wanted only to be wanted by some professional football team. He didn't care who–just so he was drafted.

It seemed to Ron that the momentous draft day would never come. Then when it did arrive, he wanted to crawl deep under the covers and hide. Some college athletes, so sure of themselves and ready to celebrate, ganged up with others around America to listen to every detail of the draft broadcast. Not Ron Brown. He wanted to be alone.

As the drama of the draft unfolded, there were no early surprises. As widely expected, Tom Cousineau, a linebacker from Ohio State, was taken number one by the Buffalo Bills. Then, on and on it went. Painfully slow. When the third round ended without the mention of his name and selections moved into the fourth round, Ron began to pace the room. He hadn't listened to any of the introductory proceedings. Not expecting his name to come up in the early going, he had gone out to shoot baskets to ease the tension. Yet, that brought no relief. He was nervous inside and out. With each succeeding opportunity, he was baited with excitement to hear his name. But, alas, his name was ignored through the fourth round, the fifth, and the sixth as well.

The first day of the draft was over.

His stomach churned in anguish. He sat down to listen intently to the conclusion of the broadcast. But he couldn't relax. He stood.

Impossible, horrendous thoughts bombarded his brain. "What if I'm not drafted at all? What if nobody picks me?" He paused and caught a glimpse of himself in the mirror. He turned, leaned heavily with his outstretched hands on the dresser top, and looked at himself blankly. Unappreciatively, he considered the youthful face, topped with close cropped hair. He tried to look inside himself. He could see nothing. Nothing!

Ron slept poorly that night. His name had not been even hinted at. The final six rounds of the draft loomed ahead.

Next morning he lay in bed as long as he could to put off the day's proceedings. After a long shower, he flipped on the radio for the start of the broadcast. In his ears the din of the draft dragged on— and on. Words seemed to mingle meaninglessly with others. Names of players he never heard of were coughed up from colleges he'd never heard of. It appeared to him that scouts must have gone all the way to Mars to find someone to be inserted into a draft slot which should have been his. He wanted to hear every name, yet he wanted to hear none of them. Most of all, he wanted to hear his own name. When were they going to get around to Ron Brown of Brown?

Each selection created excitement. Everyone on radio was

expressing congratulations to others. They were happy. But there had to be some mistake, Ron kept insisting to himself. Still, they had missed the All-Conference defensive back from Brown University.

Ron felt empty. Yet, at the same time, as his emotions churned he felt nauseous.

He laid down on his bed. He stared at the ceiling. He wanted to block out the draft from his mind. Yet he did instant replays in his mind. Surely he had missed something. He lay quietly for a long time.

"No! I haven't missed anything!" he whispered to himself. "I just won't be chosen!"

His spirit sagged with the thought of giving up his dream.

He wanted to cry, but was ashamed to do so even in private.

"What can I ever do?" he asked the ceiling. "All I have dreamed of and worked for these last five or six years has been to play pro football."

But the ceiling ignored him as surely as the draft was doing. It stared blankly back at him.

Far from his mind were any positives of life. He was totally oblivious to the fact that he had accomplished a quality education and that he would be graduating in a couple of weeks. Such thoughts were far from him.

He wanted only to belong to a professional football team. There was no one present to give any promise or answer to his inward yearning. He was struck by the overwhelming silence of the room. For that matter, the entire building, the university, the world seemed to be in a trance with him.

A sudden jarring ring of the telephone snapped him back to reality. His first thought was to ignore it. He wanted to speak to no one.

It rang again. "Maybe it's my worthless agent! Where was he when twenty-eight teams spent two whole days selecting every athlete in the country except me?"

He let it ring.

Persistently, the phone demanded an answer a third and fourth time. "Hey, maybe they're calling with my draft notice," he declared aloud as he swung his feet over the side of the bed and reached for the receiver.

Suddenly, Ron thought he saw light at the end of the tunnel.

"Hello," he said hesitantly.

"Hello, Ron. This is Joe Roush of the Dallas Cowboys."

Ron's eyes lit up. Thankfully, he hadn't been forgotten. He'd been drafted after all. "Hey, Mr. Roush, are you drafting me?" Ron asked bluntly, brightly.

"Well, Ron, as you know the draft is about over–and it doesn't seem like anyone is going to select you. But we'd like to sign you to a free agent contract."

The bottom fell out of Ron's life a second time. He was sorry that he had blurted out something so sophomorish and stupid over the telephone. He was thankful at least that no one could see him squirming like a worm within himself. "Well, I don't know. To tell you the truth, I feel a bit down right now," Ron responded honestly.

"You wouldn't be human if you didn't feel low," Roush observed. "But come on down to my hotel and let's have lunch and talk it over."

Pride wanted to hide. Ego wanted to say no. But the desire to play pro football said, "I guess so. Where are you staying?"

"I'm at the Marriott. Tell you what. How about if I pick you up in front of your dorm in, say, an hour?"

"Sure. OK. I'll be ready," Ron agreed.

With that he flipped off the radio. He had no desire to hear the conclusion.

As he walked down the stairs and waited on the steps for the rendezvous, Ron was glad the place was rather deserted. He didn't want to see anyone he knew. He didn't want to have to explain why he wasn't drafted. Nor did he fancy listening to someone fumble for words to try to console him.

"Being a free agent isn't so bad," Ron reasoned to himself. "I'll get a chance to go to the training camp and earn a spot on the team. Several free agents make it in the NFL every year.

"And the Cowboys are 'America's Team.' More free agents make their team than any other squad in the NFL."

Ron was feeling much better about the whole affair when Roush picked him up shortly before one o'clock.

The noon crowd at the Marriott restaurant had thinned out considerably when they arrived. Throughout the meal, Roush talked glowingly about his view of free agency and what advantage the Cowboys had gained by their selections. "Ron, we're going to be choosy. We'll only sign contracts with twenty-three free agents. From those–along with our twelve draft picks, last year's veterans, and the off-season trades–will come next fall's squad.

"Ron, I realize how you and other athletes agonize through the drafting process–and not to be selected is tough. But being a free agent is actually better than being a late-round pick. This way you can select any team of your choice. Which gives you better negotiating power.

"And your chances of making the team aren't much diminished."

Ron gained a perspective on the draft proceedings from management's viewpoint that he hadn't considered before. He relaxed as they talked, and ate heartily to make up for the near fast he had endured during the draft.

As he enjoyed the last bit of dessert, Roush pushed the pie plate to the edge of the table and produced a contract. "Now it's time to get down to business, Ron. The Cowboys think you have talent and we'd like to give you a chance. This is our standard free agent agreement. We pay your expenses while in camp. If you earn a spot on the team, we guarantee a three-year contract with performance incentives and built-in cost of living increases.

"All you have to do is sign here on page three."

"Well, I'd like a day or two to think about it–and talk it over with my agent."

"Ron, I doubt that you'll ever hear from that man again. There was nothing in your contract with him that gave you any guarantees. Right now, I imagine he's out scraping the barrel, looking for someone who was drafted–and who needs an agent.

"Listen, I don't want to sound blunt, but there are a lot of good players around the country who weren't drafted. We can't afford to give you a lot of time to make up your mind while some competing team grabs up the others. So, here's the contract. Sign on the dotted line, or we'll go ahead and offer it to somebody else."

Roush might have disclaimed not wanting to sound blunt, but Ron reeled inside from the emotion of the blow.

"Will you excuse me for a moment?" Ron blurted out as he stood from the table. He was so disappointed he didn't know what to do. He left the man sitting there and pushed himself around tables and chairs and into the hall. "That's great!" he mumbled to himself. "Here I am! I've worked twenty-two years, all my life, to be the best athlete I could be. I wanted to be in a position where I could have a chance to maybe try professional sports. Now this guy, a total stranger no less, shoves a contract in front of my face and says sign on the dotted line–or else."

Once in the hallway, Ron had no direction as to where to go. So he just stood there. The lunch hour was over. He had the corridor pretty much to himself.

He searched for an intelligent thread of thought to cling to. His mind was blank. He felt purposeless, adrift on an uncrossable sea. He stood in silence for several moments, his back against the wall.

Suddenly a name flashed in his mind. A name he hardly knew. A fresh name. He thought of Jesus Christ.

Like a gentle flow of spring water over thirsty ground, that name brought refreshment to his troubled mind. Slowly he recalled from the preceding three years the bits and pieces of testimony he'd heard from a dozen different mouths. The words even of nameless God squadders melded into one intelligent message of love and hope and concern.

A relaxing smile creased his face as he thought again of Harry Walls and all that the man's life stood for. He wondered for a moment what Harry, always so positive in his outlook, would say at a time like this. Immediately a response filled his heart. He knew that the man would have words of praise and encouragement for him.

In the quietude of the hall, his thoughts focused on Audrey's last words to him. "Ron, you have to trust Jesus." He began to realize that was an affirmation to the often asked questions, "Do you love the Lord? Are you willing to follow the Lord?"

He sensed with stunning appreciation that he was not alone in the hallway. He was comforted. He began to speak earnestly, inwardly, with but a slight movement of his lips, to an Unseen Presence.

"Lord, you know my outward appearance looks good to a lot of people. I'm fooling a lot of folks. I'm fooling all the old people back home. They think I'm a fine, upstanding young man. I'm fooling all my friends back home because even though they think I'm a coach's pet and a teacher's pet, they have respect for me. I know that…"

Unconsciously tears welled up in his eyes.

"And I'm fooling all these people here in college. Yeah, I'm the class clown! And I look like I'm happy and having a good time. On the outside it looks like I'm doing well in school and sports! But on the inside my life is misery. It's a pressure cooker."

He gasped in anguish and wiped away a trickling tear.

"There are other people in the world who are going through a lot more hardship than Ron Brown is." He paused at the horror of the thought. "But at this moment, in this time, I feel worse than anybody in the world! I feel alone!

"Lord, I need you!"

At once, Ron knew that he had crossed a threshold. He entered into a sanctuary. That which he had rejected so forcefully for so long became his throbbing desire. With a seriousness of intent which he had never experienced before, he asked Jesus Christ to come into his heart.

Not with a flow of poetic words, but with sincerity he declared, "Jesus, I've heard a lot about you, but I don't know exactly what I'm doing. Up to now I haven't paid close attention. I don't know a lot about you. But I do know I need you in my life. And I'm going to follow you whatever it takes–and wherever you take me!"

That was a complete reversal of field for the "I Can Kid," the one who had professed to have all the answers. All at once, he knew that he didn't know anything. He had made a gigantic commitment. Not only had he climbed willingly into the wheelbarrow of the Master, he had done so as a blind man. He had no spiritual sight by which to judge.

All his life, he had believed in God. He had known that God was out there somewhere, controlling things. He realized he had been protected at birth, and as a kid from spending life on the streets. He knew that it was God who had brought him to a good home, a disciplined home where he was fed and brought up well. God had given him a chance to go to college and play football, something he loved to do. God had given him a good life. He believed all that.

But when the great crunch of life came, intellectual assent of God's existence was not enough. He needed something more on which to bank his life. He made his first deposit in trust to God. He reached out in faith with a decision for a working relationship with the Almighty.

Committing his life to Jesus Christ in that hallway was an intimate, personal experience. The most satisfying moment of his life. Far greater than any sporting thrill. In the twinkling of an eye, he stepped from darkness into light. And he knew it!

Having taken care of the most important matter of life, he was ready to go back and face Joe Roush and the matter of pro football.

As he returned to the restaurant, he wondered if one of those miracles that Audrey and others talked about would now unfold for him. Those fifteen or twenty minutes of time had changed the whole direction of his life. In the meantime, had God changed the mind of Roush and the Dallas Cowboys? Was an honest-to-goodness monied contract waiting for him?

He sat down across the table from the middle-aged scout. He looked at the free agent contract. Nothing had changed. "I think it would be wise for me to talk to my agent," Ron said with a newfound confidence.

"Fine. I'll be glad to talk to him as well," the scout said. "Let's go up to my room to finalize this."

From there Ron called his agent to explain the offer.

"Let me handle this," Dowling advised.

Ron handed the receiver to the scout who was lounged in a chair. Amazed at the rancor between the scout and his agent, Ron listened to one end of the conversation. It quickly degenerated into a heated argument about dollars. The scout was insistent, "We can give Ron no guarantees! How long have you been in this business, Dowling? Don't you understand that there are no assurances attached to free agency? If he makes it, then we negotiate."

There was silence in the room as the agent responded. Harsh murmuring was all Ron could overhear from the receiver.

"Dowling!" Roush spoke evenly into the telephone, with emotion. "I've been with the Dallas organization for ten years. In that time I've seen your kind come and go. The dollar sign is all you think about. You make big boasts to impressionable kids. But you're not interested in the game or the players. I wish we were rid of the likes of you." The two hung up in anger.

Understanding the uncertainty through which Ron was going, the scout called Dallas to explain the stalemate to his boss, John Wooten. Then he handed the telephone to Ron.

Wooten in turn repeated the previous ultimatum to Ron, "We have to have your decision now! If you don't sign, we have to look elsewhere quick. I know this is not the easiest decision you'll ever make, but it's not the hardest, either. Go ahead and sign the contract Roush has for you."

Ron stared at the papers in front of him for several minutes, trying to study them, but not really able to concentrate. To make matters worse, the scout kept applying pressure.

"Listen, Ron," Roush finally declared. "We need to wrap this up. I'm going to call the home office again to see if they think I should hang on any longer."

Roush talked for a couple of minutes, explaining the situation. Then he held the receiver out to Ron, "Gil Brandt, the general manager of the Cowboys, wants to talk with you."

Somewhat surprised by the opportunity to talk with the great Gil Brandt, Ron said, "Hello."

"Ron, this is Gil Brandt. I understand you have some uncertainty about our free agency offer. Your agent called me after he talked to you. He's very upset. I told him that at this point, the decision is up to you. I want you to know, Ron, that you were in our draft plans, but you were just down the list too far. But we have great confidence in your ability and would like to give you a chance to make the team.

"I hope you'll decide to give us a try. But take a few hours to think it over."

As he recradled the telephone, Ron was relieved and impressed. The man understood!

Later that evening, he signed.

He returned to the seclusion of his dormitory room to think through the day's events.

He'd just begun to relax when a scout for the New England Patriots called. "Ron," he said anxiously, "where have you been? We've tried to reach you all afternoon."

"I just got back from signing a free agency contract with the Dallas Cowboys."

"That's too bad," the man admitted woefully. "You were in our plans as well. But the best of luck to you, Ron."

Ron learned shortly that negotiating in the National Football League is a hard fought business. Joe Roush had performed his task for the Dallas Cowboys in perfect style. Even before the draft was concluded, he threw out his bait to his target, and then got him away from his own telephone in order to control the situation.

Not only had the Patriots tried in vain to reach him, but other teams had sought him out as well.

Yet Ron had no regrets. He had a free agent contract in his pocket, primarily due to the gentle persuasion of the renowned Gil Brandt.

But far surpassing that, or any other prize, he had a new covenant with God in his heart. That was not due to any act of man. It was a result solely of the remarkable, gentle, persistent wooing of the Holy Spirit. That contract, inscribed in his heart, was not provisional. He did not have to prove himself. God and he were bound in an eternal plan. Heaven or hell was at stake. Ron Brown was heaven-bound.

CHAPTER 10

DREAMS ARE HARD TO COME BY

J ust the privilege of finally signing a professional football contract, even as a free agent, proved to be a satisfying experience. As Ron laid in bed on that final night of the NFL draft, he was so excited that sleep was beyond his grasp. It had been an unbelievable day. He had made two awesome, gigantic decisions in tandem with one another! As his mind flowed like the constant slapping of ocean waves, it was impossible not to tie the two together. Had God planned a spectacular, successful professional career for him as a testimony to thousands?

Visions of bone-crushing tackles and high-leaping interceptions churned through his whole being in those early morning hours. This went on in spite of the fact that Audrey had cautioned otherwise. After signing the Dallas contract, he had made a beeline for Audrey's dorm to tell her every detail about the proposal from the Cowboys. More importantly, sitting on the couch in the lobby, he shared the joy of his commitment to Jesus Christ.

As he repeated the words of his simple prayer, tears coursed down her cheeks. She put her arms around him in a gentle embrace. A long minute passed. No words were exchanged. The moment was so special neither of them wanted to intrude upon it.

At length, Audrey spoke softly, her chin tucked over his shoulder, "Ron, I have prayed for your salvation so specifically for so long. Now I find it hard to believe that it has finally happened. I am so very happy."

Taking her by the arms, he pushed her back slightly to look directly into her eyes. "Audrey, I can never thank you enough for all your prayers and encouragement. I owe you a lot. I will never forget the thrill I had in the Marriott hallway when I realized that Jesus was real–just like you and others have been trying to tell me. But now I have experienced it for myself! Jesus Christ is truer than true. I've had hundreds of great highs in sports, but nothing can compare to that first moment of knowing Him."

They eyed one another closely–communicating in spirit. Then Ron continued, "You know, then, signing that contract seemed just the right thing to do."

"I agree," Audrey affirmed. "I believe that's God's plan for you."

"Man!" Ron declared. "I feel just great. You know, this morning as the draft was coming to a close, I felt lower than a worm under a rock. I felt that life was over. I just wanted to hide.

"When that scout called, I didn't even want to meet him. I felt even worse when he pressured me to sign that contract quick before he gave it to someone else. I was angry. I thought, 'Why has life fallen down on top of me?' I felt crushed. I just wanted to get out of there and avoid life.

"I only got as far as the hallway when I said to myself, 'OK, Brown! Where are you going to run to?'

"I was stumped. Cornered."

He paused in happy reflection.

"Then! There He was. Jesus Christ. As if He had been waiting in that hallway all eternity for Ron Brown to come to an end of himself! Jesus was there. And I knew it. And we made a deal. Praise God! We made a deal."

"I'm so happy for you," Audrey interjected. "But this is probably a good time to remind you of what the pastor said in church last Sunday."

"What was that?" Ron questioned.

"Remember, he said, 'Becoming a Christian is one of the easiest things in the world to do, but living the Christian life is one of the hardest things.' Ron," she continued, "it's not going to be easy for you in Dallas."

"Are you kiddin'?" he asked with a chuckle. "I know I have to keep making the right kind of choices, but it's so obvious that God is in this whole thing. Surely He's going to use my talent on the football field to bring honor to Himself."

The next week Ron was off to Dallas for the Cowboys' tryout camp. Much to his chagrin, as he got acquainted with others, he found out that he was surrounded by not just 22 other free agents as Joe Roush had promised. There were more than a hundred who had signed on the same dotted line. The Cowboys' obvious intention was to have a first look at them. Effectively, all that potential talent was safely tucked away from other teams.

Ron tried to act nonchalant, to take all the excitement in stride. But being in the same locker room with such stars as Tony Dorsett, Roger Staubach, Cliff Harris, and Charlie Waters was a heady experience. Here were men who had more than mere raw talent. Here were men who had achieved success in a grueling arena. Rather than being overwhelmed and intimidated by such giants of the game, however, Ron was determined to emulate them. He, too, would set high goals and attain them. He would look good, be a good player, and set a good image.

After just a couple of days, Coach Tom Landry sent word for Ron to meet him in his office. Ron was ecstatic. He knew he hadn't displayed anything special on the practice field yet, but evidently Landry had been looking over the scouting reports or had viewed highlights of some of his college games. "Oh, this is great!" he thought to himself as he headed to meet with the big man. "Landry wants me in his office. This can only mean that we are going to talk some serious contract negotiations."

He paused in his reveling to whisper a prayer, "Thank you, Lord, for giving me this opportunity."

Ron rolled into the office of the man who is a legend in his own time. Landry looked up from across his wide desk. His expression was calm as ever, giving no clue as to what was on his mind. But being a man of few words, he came immediately to the point. "Ron, we're sending you home. I'm sorry to tell you that you flunked the physical."

The words hit him like a splash of cold water, quenching the fire of his spirit. Stunned, he asked, "Flunked the physical? How?"

"It's your right shoulder, Ron. It just doesn't stand up well under the stress tests," Landry advised matter-of-factly.

Determined to reverse a horrible decision, Ron responded, "Coach, I've never missed a game in all my life. Yeah, I hurt this shoulder a couple of years ago. I missed a couple of practices, but I never missed a game. You know, Coach, it just doesn't bother me that much."

Landry looked at him sympathetically. Being the bearer of bad news to athletes was one detail of his work that he detested. Nonetheless, it was part of the job. He said, "Ron, I appreciate that. But we have a policy that we just don't take guys we think are injured. We just can't afford to put you on injured reserve all season long—and pay you all season long for not playing all season long. So, we have to go ahead and cut you right now. That's just team policy."

So in a matter of hours, Ron was "flying the friendly skies" back to Rhode Island.

Those were disquieting moments for the young athlete. His sports world, to which he had devoted himself so diligently, unsympathetically caved in upon him. For the second time in less than a month, he had been rejected by the very thing that had given him meaning in life: first he had not been drafted, now even free agency abandoned him. Athletics had been his ticket to recognition, respect, and a college education. He had counted heavily on the prestige of at least six or seven years in the NFL.

"How can it be," he moaned to himself as he stared out the tiny window at the star-studded sky, "that I flunked the physical? I've been in great shape all my life. I spent twenty-two years working out—to be at my best—and I go down there and fail a simple stress test."

He reasoned that he had given it his best shot. He was not at fault. But how could he explain this failure to his friends and family? Everyone had such high expectations for him. They had never seen him fail in anything he ever set out to do. Now he had to swallow hard, gulp down his pride, and face them.

"Why would God let this happen to me?" the newborn Christian asked himself in self pity. "What'll this look like to those who've heard about my commitment to Jesus?

"Lord," he cried softly through the gloom, "you know I only want to be a success to bring more glory to you."

No sooner were the words beyond his lips than he smiled to himself. He was new at the task of being a Christian, but he could almost hear God chuckling in response, "I have glory enough and enough to spare."

Because of the despair with which his trip began, it was a long flight to Providence. But by the time the plane touched down, God had spoken and given him a new definition of success. It was in stark contradiction to his former opinion of looking on the outside. "Son, what really counts with me is the inner man. I control the outer man. With or without an outstanding image on your part, I am in control. I have a different agenda than man. I'm more concerned with your inner being, your eternal soul. Let's work on shaping that up together!"

Though he was willing to learn from God, the first thing Ron wanted to do, back in Providence, was to hide. It was far easier to face God, whom he could not see, than old friends he could see. He had begun to sort things out with God, but he was ill prepared to face friends–even Audrey.

But news travels fast. Bad news even faster.

The semester had not yet ended, and the Christians at Brown University were waiting for him. The distinguishing trait of true friends is their sensitivity when one is hurting. Ron's heart skipped a beat at his first sight of six of them waiting to greet him on the main campus green, with Audrey at the front of the pack. His mood shifted dramatically. He was instantly encouraged in spirit.

Audrey rushed forward to give him a kiss on the cheek, but Alfred Cummings squeezed in quickly between them and was the first to speak. "Hey, Ron, flunking a physical is nothing to be ashamed of. Look at me."

Everyone, even Ron, burst into laughter at the comparison–fat, blimpy Alfred and trim, muscular Ron.

The group joyfully pulled him to a quiet side of the grass and agreed together, "Let's pray about this right now. Ron, if God wants you to play football, or whatever He wants you to do in life, He'll heal you. He'll strengthen you. He will give you victory so you can do that."

Ron knew full well the type of victory they were talking about. The girl next to him, whom he loved, had miraculously recovered from her accident just six weeks earlier. He'd seen it with his own eyes. "That sounds good to me," he agreed. "That's the best news I've heard all week."

The answer to their praying was instantaneous. Ron knew God had healed him. Immediately, he stopped doing special exercises for the shoulder and returned to a regular weight lifting routine as if he had a truly strong right shoulder.

The next week the semester ended. Audrey went home to New York City and Ron returned to the familiar surroundings of Martha's Vineyard.

In regard to old friends, his natural man wanted to hide from them, to avoid the shame of having failed, but they seemed not to blame him.

Within a matter of days, he began to relax from the strain he'd been under. Consistently, he expressed his faith to the Lord that he was accepting God's healing touch. Amazingly, against all opinion of the Dallas doctor, his shoulder became steadily stronger.

A month later, in mid-June, he received a call from the New England Patriots. "Ron, we read the details about you being released from the Cowboys, but we would still like to take a look at you. As you know, we tried to get you as a free agent on draft day.

"Why don't you come up and let our team doctor test you. If he gives you a clean bill of health, we'd like to have you."

Ron packed his bags at once and headed for Foxboro.

At Schaefer Stadium, the Patriots' doctor put Ron through the exact same shoulder tests the Cowboys' physician had given him in Dallas. The man came out of the x-ray room shaking his head. "I don't know what the Cowboys' doctor saw," he declared, "but there's nothing wrong with your shoulder."

Ron signed a contract on the spot, in front of the Patriots' popular talent expert, Bucko Kilroy. Whatever the problem might have been, it never bothered him again.

News of his second chance in the pros spread like wildfire across his island home. Once again, he was a local hero. Just like a light switch: then off, now on. Friends, even strangers, sought him out for an autograph–just in case he made it this time. One man, Kent Newsome, whom Ron knew slightly, came to him with a special request. "Ron, I have a sixteen-year-old son who doesn't have any goals in life. Would you please take him out for a Coke and just talk to him? He respects you and will listen to you."

Ron smiled sadly within himself, realizing the fickleness of sports fans. Just a few days earlier, before he had signed a new pro football contract, he hadn't been considered smart enough to tell anyone about the facts of life. Nevertheless, he gladly seized the opportunity and spent several hours talking with the kid.

Doubtless that encounter was good for the teenager, but it was equally important to the pro prospect. The counseling that afternoon set a life-changing pattern for Ron Brown. He loved the challenge of combining his Christian witness with athletics.

A few days later, as he drove to the Patriots training camp, the miles melted away. He was full in spirit. "You know," he said to himself, "this Christian life is wonderful. When you first accept the Lord, there is an instantaneous love relationship, a true love bond. You're really emotionally involved. It's marvelous.

"I know now what God is doing. He's been putting me through a little trial, but I'm going to make this team. Just like I've planned, I'm going to serve God while I play professional football."

He arrived at the Patriots camp in great physical condition. He proceeded to work hard under the direction of the coaching staff.

Off the field, however, he was a different man. His roommate observed, "Man, all you ever do is read that Bible. Don't you think you oughta be looking at the playbook some?"

But Ron found great comfort and security in God's Word. The playbook caused him nervousness and fear. He was no longer trying to put up a false front of self-confidence. He was beginning to face his own weaknesses.

He was studiously learning the Word of the Lord, on the one

hand, but on the practice field he didn't know any of the Patriots' defensive strategies. He was out of balance.

Therefore, in spite of observing righteous practices, he fell into a devilish trap of being overly self-involved. On the playing field, he was ill at ease, felt out of place, and found it difficult to keep his attention on anything, God or football. Consequently, he began looking around at his competition in the Patriot backfield. Standout stars like Mike Haynes, Raymond Claiborne, Tim Fox, Ricky Sanford–all former number one draft picks–playing the same position as he. He began to worry, wondering how in the world he would make the team. His normal determination to succeed was swallowed by insecurity. His attitude to do well suffered and sank.

Naturally, his performance dipped markedly. Instead of concentrating on what God could do with his life and talents, he thought continually about the obvious ability of others. Comparing himself to them, he began to fail miserably.

Others noticed as well. The defensive backfield coach was constantly on his case. In desperation one day, he screamed out, "Ron, you frustrate me! Here I am a Christian man and you're making me swear at you! You're just not concentrating and applying your talents!"

For the first time in his life, he looked for an easy way out. "I can't handle this anymore," he confessed to himself. "Football's a crazy sport anyway. I was accepted at Columbia. I might as well go on, quit wasting my time, and become a hospital administrator."

After harboring that thought for several days, Ron decided to test the waters. He would offer to pack it in. He was unsure of himself. Even so, there was a hope within him that the coach would beg him to stay. Maybe Coach would say, "Ron, you know, you're a pretty good player. I think you oughta stick with it. You have great potential. Don't worry yet; it's still early."

Fresh from the showers that afternoon, Ron went up to the Patriots head coach, Ron Earhardt, and said, "Coach, I'm done. I'd like for you to put me on waivers and let me go."

Without a hint of remorse, Earhardt responded, "Fine. Go."

So he quit that Friday afternoon.

The next morning, as he was packing his bags, the scout who had signed him walked by wordlessly.

A few minutes later, however, Raymond Berry, one of the Patriots assistants who had coached Ron on punt returns, came and sat down on the office couch next to Ron. Berry, in his playing career, had distinguished himself in the NFL as a Hall of Fame wide receiver, and also projected a solid Christian image.

"You're from Martha's Vineyard, aren't you?" the coach asked casually.

"Yeah," Ron answered singularly.

"I hear the fishin' down there is pretty good."

"Yeah," Ron agreed, "though I'm not much of a fisherman."

"Well, I'm sure it's a great place to live," Berry affirmed understandingly. "I wish you the best. Take care of yourself."

"Thanks."

Ron sighed deeply as he watched Berry walk away. The man had gone out of his way to uplift the fallen. And he had left behind a real Christian witness without having used any religious words.

Ron called his folks to explain what he was doing, and headed for New York City, graduate school, and Audrey. She, of course, was returning to Brown University, but they had several days to talk and pray together before the start of the fall semester.

"I've got a new life now," Ron explained to her. "No more wastin' time on a football dream. I'm going to serve the Lord as a hospital administrator."

Audrey was disquieted in spirit, but expressed only mild reservations. She remembered so clearly the prayers of May, asking God to mend Ron's shoulder, then the subsequent healing. She remembered his craving to be a pro football player. Then his elation at being invited to join the Patriots, his homestate team. But she wisely listened, giving no advice.

Ron also was ready for a commitment to the young woman. She, however, was not totally sure about that. She wanted to wait on God's definite guidance.

As Audrey left for Providence, Ron turned his attention to the demands of graduate studies. At the same time, he became involved in working with young, underprivileged kids. One of the kids, a four-year-old named Nathan, became like a little brother to him. Nathan lived with his grandmother in a troubled section of Queens. His mom was in prison. His dad was on tough times. He was growing up like a wild weed between the cracks in the sidewalk. He often spent time in a dingy park across the street from his building, just walking around. He was emotionally disturbed and getting to the point, even at his tender age, where he'd be beyond help.

Ron spent a lot of his spare moments with the little boy with the big brown eyes. "Now, don't you let life get you down," Ron encouraged him as they sat on the curb one afternoon. "Remember, God is a big God and He can take you to great places. I know He can! Now, don't you ever give up on life."

Nathan looked up at the man who was the nearest thing to a father he'd known. His hero. Adoringly, he said, "Someday I want to see you play football."

The words, though loving and well intentioned, shattered the man. Ron made no response. He reached out his big hand and tousled the boy's hair and laughed awkwardly. But he could not so easily brush away that simple sentence.

To himself, he yelled out a challenge. "Brown, you ought to be ashamed of yourself. Does it take a four-year-old to jar you into looking at the facts? You're a coward! You gave up on football on your own. Not because the Lord told you to. You gave up football because you doubted yourself. Now, how do you have the gall to tell this kid to never give up? You quit football because you were constantly comparing yourself to others and didn't like what you saw.

"You've been rationalizing around life. You've been hiding. You've been trying so hard to fool people again. You're just pretending to be happy with the idea of being a hospital administrator.

"You know that's a lie. Every time it comes to mind you turn it off because you can't stand the thought. Hey! When're you going to face the truth?"

After that flash of thoughts, Ron stood to his feet and said, "Good night, Nathan, I'll see you tomorrow."

As he traveled to the Medical Center campus, Ron became increasingly convinced that God had a message for him in the simple wish of the child. "I've been telling this kid that with God you continue, no matter what. You just don't give up on things. You have to keep on pushing. When the Lord tells you it's time to go somewhere else, He'll make a way. But right now, on my own accord, I've gone out on my own and strayed from God's best plan.

"No more! I'm getting back on track!"

And he did! Ron started a daily pounding of the streets of New York City. He began a steady program of weight lifting, joined the track club, doing everything to get back in shape, all while taking seven classes in graduate school. He signed on with the New Jersey Rams, a semi-pro team, to play in their regional games. It was a crazy schedule. Sometimes he thought he was out of his mind. Yet he knew he was doing it for the Lord. And at the same time, he was growing in his faith with God and in relationship with others. He studied the Bible faithfully, claiming along the way the promise of Jesus in Mark 10:27: "All things are possible with God."

He was strengthened in both body and spirit as that new attitude took hold and developed. He was doing it all. Rather, he was learning that God and he were accomplishing something special together.

Next on God's agenda for the former Brown University star athlete was a humility lesson. He started writing to NFL teams, "asking" for a chance to prove himself. Rejection letters piled on top of one another. The standard response was thanks, but no thanks. Often not even a whole paragraph.

But Ron was persistent, pushing past his previous problem of pride; he would post yet another proposal.

The odds against a positive reply, of course, were astronomical. With colleges and universities grinding out a fresh batch of potential candidates each and every year, the pro teams could be selective.

Then in March, ahead of the drafting frenzy, a letter arrived from the New York Jets. Ron walked slowly up the steps to his dormitory room, reading and re-reading the return address. His adrenaline was pumping as he sat down on the couch and tore open the envelope. The message was plain and simple: "Ron, we remember you as a player back at Brown University and we would like to sign you to a contract. Please give us a call as soon as possible."

Instinctively Ron's lips uttered, "Praise the Lord! It's true, 'with God all things are possible."

He realized that such an opportunity just doesn't happen. It was a blessing from God and he intended to make the most of it. He worked harder on his conditioning and got in perfect shape.

Again, his parents and friends back home, Audrey and the believers at Brown, and his newly acquired Christian friends in New York were enthused about his third chance in professional football. As he prayed about it, he was certain that God had prepared a way for him to be a success at last.

When he arrived at the Jets training camp, he was lean and hungry and ready to go. He knew he had an excellent shot at making the team. His position was wide open. The Jets had just traded their starting free safety, Burgess Owens, to the Oakland Raiders.

Gone were his inhibitions. He was not comparing or contrasting himself with anyone. He was determined that he could beat out anyone for a position. Correspondingly, the practices went perfectly for him.

Right at the close of the third day, however, he heard something pop. He grabbed his right thigh as if such a quick reflex could revert the blowout of his quad muscle. But, to no avail. He winced in pain and started hobbling around. He tried to do some extra running, but the defensive backfield coach came over to him and advised, "Ron, you'd better stay off that for the rest of the day."

His thigh swelled considerably. For four days, he was not able to practice, and had to content himself with riding the stationary bicycle.

He refused to let the injury get him down. He was going to make a success of pro football. He did a lot of praying, too.

Miraculously, the leg healed itself. Four days later he was back into the practice rhythm and playing well.

Everything was on track for his first season in the NFL.

Or so it seemed.

At six o'clock in the morning, the day before the first preseason game against the Giants, there was a knock at Ron's door. "Come on in," he moaned sleepily.

"Ron, Coach Michaels wants to see you in his office—and bring your playbook," the messenger declared.

Ron thought it was a little early to be going over plays, so he asked, "Can I eat breakfast first?"

"Yeah," was the soulful reply as the young man ducked his head back out the door.

As he walked into the coach's office, Ron, now wide awake, was instantly reminded of the Tom Landry scene just fourteen months earlier. An anxious gnawing bit into the pit of his stomach. His brain did a quick re-interpretation of the words, "Bring your playbook." That really meant, "Pack your bags."

Just as Landry had, Michaels remained seated for his unsavory task. Unlike Landry, though, his eyes were down, maybe to avoid the pain of seeing disappointment in the face of the likable young athlete. He said clearly, "Ron, we're sending you home."

"Coach," Ron asked with an unmistakable plea in his voice, "why're you cutting me a day before the first game?"

"Ron," he said, still without looking up, "we just don't think you're going to make the team. We'll put you on waivers. Maybe someone else will pick you up."

As he packed, Ron realized that the early morning call was a bit of a nicety—a guy could get all his gear out of the way before others arrived and wouldn't have to go through the humiliation of facing the successful ones.

Shame was the only word Ron had to describe it as he headed home for Martha's Vineyard. Actually, he would have preferred to have gone the other way—like to California. He was so down emotionally he wanted to roll way out of town, where nobody he knew would ever see him again.

That, though, was not possible. He was a man and had to face life. Not only that, but he was also maturing as a Christian and was certain that God had a plan. True, he was faced with a dark cloud of doubt, almost burdensomely. But he was at the same time sure that God wanted him to hold his head high as he walked patiently through to the answer on the other side, somewhere.

God was dealing with Ron Brown's inner man, fashioning a victor to His pattern. The outer man, unfortunately, was still cluttered with visions of success, fame, and glory.

To Ron, the trip home seemed endless. Once he was on his way, he just wanted to get there. He sighed heavily for the security he had always known in his parents' home.

Ron was puzzled. What was he supposed to do with his life now? He certainly needed more time at Columbia to finish his master's degree. But more than that he wanted to be a pro football player.

He turned to the One who had become his primary resource. "God!" he prayed. "What do you want me to do? Still inside I have a desire to play football. Is that crazy? Most people think I'm nuts. I've had three chances at making it big–and nobody gets a fourth chance.

"What am I to do? Please give me a sign."

The next day Ron went out for a walk. He was conscious of being peered at by strangers. Word had spread fast across the tiny town. Every sports page in America prints a daily list of those who are cut from pro football teams. On that day, that little blurb in the morning paper was Ron Brown's only claim to national fame. The last time he'd walked down that street, he was a success in everyone's eyes. He had just signed another pro contract. He was somebody to know. Somebody to take pride in. Everyone had wanted to talk to him. Now, no one stopped to speak.

At last, though, from down the street Ron was relieved to see a familiar face. Kent Newsome, who had asked him to talk to his son, was headed his way. The man looked up when he was about twenty feet away. Ron started to wave.

Newsome looked at him, turned his head, and walked across the street. The man, who a short time before had valued him as one to inspire his son, now viewed him as too much of a failure to even speak.

In the first rush of the rebuff, Ron was tempted to pity himself, but instead grabbed hold of another invaluable bit of instruction. "Father," he prayed within himself, "thank you for this lesson not to rely on the praise of men, but rather on your presence."

A few days later, another incident sealed the lesson in place. Ron was eating in a restaurant with a workout partner. An intoxicated man he didn't even know came up to his table and said, "You're Ron Brown, aren't you?"

"Yes, I am," Ron responded.

"You stink!" the man declared as he staggered away.

Ron was glad for the end of summer and its woeful disap-pointments. He returned to the discipline of his studies in New York and the pleasures of rich fellowship within the Christian group at Columbia Medical Center. He also had one full day with Audrey before she left for Brown.

Football still was not a thing of the past for Ron. In spite of the repetitious failures, he was holding on to hope to make a success of it in professional football. He was down but not out. There could yet be a miracle come his way. He joined the New Jersey Rams for a second season in 1980, anything to keep close to the real thing. He had an outstanding year, played well, was selected for All Conference honorable mention, and started a team Bible study.

Ron's best game of the season was at Bridgeport, Connecticut. He'd been struggling with a heel injury, but could still run. He decided to dedicate the game personally to Jesus Christ, to play for His glory. It was the first time he'd done such a thing. The only goal being to conform closer to Christ's image. To play the game the way Jesus would play. He forgot all about the painful heel, his prior "failures," his loneliness. It went well. He had two interceptions and ten tackles.

In May of 1981, Ron was contacted by yet another agent, from Buffalo, wanting to represent him. Why not, he thought. The agent arranged for Ron and several others to go to a Kansas City Chiefs tryout camp near Philadelphia at Cherry Hill, New Jersey.

On the way, the car broke down. There was Ron and the other athletes packing along Interstate 95 to get to a telephone. Naturally, they arrived late. To boot, it was a rainy day. He had little time to prepare for the first test in the tryout, running the forty. He wasn't loose. Instead of his normal speed of 4.5 or 4.6, he ran a 4.8. Way too slow for the pros. He lost his chance.

After he returned to New York, he lost his new agent as well. The man screamed through the telephone, "You didn't follow through. You just jerked it off." And that was it.

Bob Engle, the offensive coordinator for the Rams, however, was far more interested in seeing Ron make the grade. Engle, who in real life was the cover editor for *Newsweek*, was a closet football enthusiast. He had a genuine enjoyment in seeing others make it to the top. In mid-May, he arranged another tryout for Ron with the Patriots.

It was a humbling experience for Ron to return to Schaefer Stadium, where a year before he had walked away from a free agency contract. This time, however, he had a renewed confidence and determination. Six hundred athletes showed up, nearly a hundred of them defensive backs, vying for the two defensive back positions the Patriots needed to fill.

The first elimination step was the forty-yard dash. Ron was pleased to see that the timer was Raymond Berry, the Patriots coach who had spoken to him with such understanding the day he'd been cut. Ron ran the 40 in 4.65. He went on to the bench press and passed. In the standing broad jump, he covered thirty feet in three leaps. He was excellent in coverage of receivers; not one of his men caught a ball. He wound up as one of six final competitors, but was not one of the two signed.

Back in New York, on the surface, Ron had a lot for which to be thankful: exposure to a high grade of football, a wealth of excellent Christian friends, a satisfying ministry with needy kids, and a graduate degree almost in his pocket.

Underneath, however, he had two bothersome concerns: athletics and Audrey. She was constantly on his mind. Though he dated around, no one could match up to her, to their freedom of communication. He missed her. Unfortunately though, he knew she didn't miss him nearly as much.

But equally burdensome to him were the recurring doubts he had about his true motive for desiring to make it big in pro football.

In his third year with the Rams, their schedule became national rather than merely regional. It proved to be his best. He was chosen as captain, had four interceptions in one game and a total of seven by mid-season.

Then, in a game at Newark, he suffered a cartilage tear in his right knee. The doctor declared he'd never play again. However, Bob Engle got him in to see the New York Giants team doctor, Kim Sloan. After orthoscopic surgery by Sloan, Ron was back playing in three weeks. He went on to be named to the semi-pro All American team.

Meanwhile, he was finishing up his master's degree. A short time before graduation, Ron decided to take a one-day retreat–just him and God, alone for a time of reflection and meditation. He knew a spot high above the Harlem River. There, on a rock overlooking the valley below, he read his Bible and searched his heart.

He reasoned, "What's it going to take for me to admit defeat? I've failed three times in trying to make a pro football team. But does that make me a failure? What does the Lord really want from my life? Why am I in this world?"

He prayed, "God, I've searched the Scriptures and my own heart for purpose. I need to know what your definition of success is. I seem to be missing it. I have this yearning to play professional football. But can that be from you? I've been so close three times, and each time I thought you would bless me in it. Surely such an opportunity won't come around again.

"But, Lord, I have such a yearning to make it!"

He opened his Bible and read. He studied the account of Abraham and his faith that God would bless him with a son–even when the wait seemed humanly impossible and endless.

As he continued in his private study, the message of Isaiah 26:3 seemed to come alive: "You will keep in perfect peace him whose mind is steadfast, because he trusts in you."

"Lord, you know I trust you," he concluded. "So I will continue this course you have set for me."

He graduated shortly afterward, in May of 1982, with his master's degree from Columbia. The day was made special by the attendance of Irene Chase, then in her eighties. The woman who had worked so diligently in arranging his adoption twenty-four years earlier had watched his progress across the years with admiration. She took pride in his accomplishments in high school, at Brown University, and finally at Columbia, pleased to have lived to see yet another step in the life she had helped to save.

Unfortunately, Audrey was not there. She was struggling with her own career plans and simultaneously grappling with some difficult relationships. This had triggered a lot of unresolved conflicts from her childhood. She had finished at Brown and was home in New York City, awaiting her entrance into graduate school. But to Ron's telephone call she insisted, "I don't want you to come by."

He tried to get a valid reason from her, but the best she could offer was, "Ron, it's not you, it's me. I just have a lot of things to sort through."

From that point on, they were no longer "buddies." The one whom God had used greatly to bring him to Christ began to move away from Ron emotionally. For Ron, it was a rejection which stung more than the three pro football cuts put together. It could never again be quite the same.

Ron, however, didn't have time to go into a tailspin. A few days after graduation he received a telephone call from Chicago that stirred the slumbering chords of his athletic soul. Miraculously, the Bears invited him to come to their mini-camp for a tryout. "We need a defensive back," they explained. "We have a prepaid plane ticket waiting for you at LaGuardia. A cab is on its way to pick you up. You have just an hour to make the flight."

A tear trickled down the cheek of the macho athlete as he

recradled the telephone. "How can this be? I know I just talked to the man and this is no joke. What a great opportunity. God is blessing me beyond reason. Now! This must be the time for the success I've been seeking–God has been testing and teaching me through these other trials."

This was a case of Bob Engle's influence once again. He had contacted the Bears when he heard they were looking for a man with Ron's particular talents.

"Can he run 4.6 and is he physical?" were the only two questions they asked.

Engle assured them of Ron's abilities and sent them a game film to prove it. The film he selected was the 1980 Bridgeport game, which Ron had dedicated to Jesus Christ. The Bears coaching staff viewed the film and agreed that Ron was capable of playing their type of physical game.

He arrived at the Bears camp with high expectations. The unsolicited invitation to even be there was interesting in itself. No, more than that, it was unbelievable. Such a call just does not go out to a man who's been out of college for three years and who's not played a minute in a pro game.

On the first day of practice, Ron was pleased with himself. They were doing some defensive back drills and he was in top form. But after practice, he didn't know what to think when he saw the coach, Mike Ditka, headed his way. Three previous personal encounters with head coaches had been disastrous–and this time it was only day one of the camp.

Ditka, who was in his first year as coach of the Bears, came up to Ron and put his arm around his shoulder. "Ron," he said, "you don't look like a rookie. You look like a pretty good player. We watched some film on you before. You've got a chance. You've really got a chance."

"Thanks, Coach," he responded as Ditka walked away. Ron was flabbergasted. Such a compliment is almost never heard by a free agent. But of course, in a sense, he wasn't a rookie anymore. He'd been to lots of camps and had gotten better.

He was on top of the world.

On the second day of practice, they ran more defensive drills. The kind Ron had been through a thousand times before. Expertly he went up to grab a pass in mid-air. But he came down with a crunch. His right knee blew out. He lay on the ground writhing in misery, looking up to a gathering circle of concerned individuals. Ditka, Buddy Ryan, and a crowd of Bears looked down at him. Their faces told a singular story: "Too bad, but that's it for him."

Ron looked beyond them to the blue sky above and asked, "Lord, why're you dangling the carrot stick? Why? Why're you doing this to me? You know I've been seeking you and I've been praying and I've been working awfully hard at it. I have a good attitude and I've turned my life around in your name. Why're you doing this? Why do you keep giving me a desire to keep on? Why don't you just give me a desire for something else?"

As they laid him on the stretcher and wheeled him off the field, a heavy gray cloud drifted across the sky.

CHAPTER 11

GOD'S BEST

O nce again, Ron dreaded going back to his family and friends. A failure. A loser. He could imagine varied whispered conversations behind his back:

"Why's he continuing with this?"

"He's a nut!"

"Why doesn't he go on, be a hospital administrator? At least that would be steady. He should make some money, and get on with his life."

"Why does he insist on pursuing these childish games?"

"He'll never be a success!"

Though he received consistent support and understanding from his parents, Ron knew there was no way he could follow through with achieving his dream on the island. There were too many prying minds in the tiny community. He decided to return to the safety of anonymity in New York City.

Yet, he didn't have to go alone. Inside his soul he felt that still, small voice of the Lord saying, "Stay with it. Stay with it. There's a plan for you."

Ron secured a fundraising position at Columbia to help pay expenses while he concentrated on rehabilitating his knee; the Bears had promised to bring him back if his knee was restored fully. Or perhaps a fifth chance from elsewhere would come his way. If it did, he wanted to be ready.

A professional spot in football was his primary purpose. But he also blossomed in the task at hand, becoming a top fund raiser. He was promoted to assistant director of the office with responsibility for training and overseeing new employees. In terms of career, those under him were like Ron in many ways: aspiring actors, actresses, musicians, writers, and dancers—all waiting for their "big break." Without his realizing it at the time, that became his first coaching opportunity. God's plan was at work.

In addition, the Columbia School of Public Health helped open another door. He was hired by Blue Cross-Blue Shield as a corporate fitness consultant. In front of their offices at 34th and Park Avenue in downtown Manhattan, he gave noon hour seminars right out on the street with a microphone. While jumping rope, he talked about fitness, diets, footwear, and heart rate. The company promotion heralded him as a defensive back with the Chicago Bears. Blue Cross was excited with the response and intended to use him again the following summer. But when the time came, since they could no longer tout him as a pro football player, the company reneged on the promise.

Meanwhile, he was in no condition to play the 1982 fall season with the New Jersey Rams. Instead they asked him to be defensive coordinator and defensive backfield coach. He had no desire to be on the sideline. He wanted to play. Nonetheless, in order to stay involved, he accepted the challenge. It also kept him in touch with the Rams Bible study which he'd helped get started back in 1980.

He gained respect at both work and play. But only in his relationship with God did Ron feel true satisfaction with life. That, along with the bonding and support from the other believers, kept him from sinking into despair. True, he was maturing as a Christian. God mattered most to him. But in what was next in order of importance to him, he was a failure. He doubted that he would ever succeed in athletics. Yet, he could not turn his back on the dream of his youth. In spite of setbacks, football was still real to him.

Ron continued to work hard on bringing strength back to his knee. As part of his training program for another try at pro football, he began running with an AAU track team in Harlem called the Pioneers. It was an active and aggressive program, highly competitive. It had to be. In New York City there are lots of fast guys, on the outside looking in, wanting a chance. So, in order to encourage as many kids as possible to get off the streets and into action, membership in the AAU was not required to be able to compete in meets.

Because of his fascination with speed, Ron took keen interest in the hundred-meter dash at one particular meet held on Randalls Island. Four guys lined up for the race. Two had paid their registration fee and belonged to the Pioneers. The other two were cold, right off the street.

The four took the mark. The team members looked sharp in their uniforms and regulation shoes. They totally outclassed the other two in swimming trunks, running in ragged tennis shoes. The gun sounded. Like a shot, the two ragamuffins were off. The team members saw only the backsides of the street kids who finished first and second. The two Pioneers clocked in third and fourth.

Ron scanned the sports section of the newspaper the next morning for the meet results. To his amazement, the guys who finished third and fourth were listed as finishing first and second. The other two runners weren't even mentioned. At lunch he saw one of the other Pioneers and asked, "How did the results of yesterday's 100-meter dash get misprinted in the paper? I saw what happened and those two street kids beat our boys by a full second."

"Well, you see," his friend explained, "we let anyone run in the races who wants to, but it only counts if they're on the team."

That afternoon, on his way to the Rams Bible study, Ron thought through that contrast and the importance of being on God's team. As he did so, the Lord brought a clear understanding into his heart as to how it applied to him. "You see, son," that now familiar inner voice explained, "there are a lot of people in life who are running good races, fast races. There are a lot of people in life who look like they're winning. Their business is an outstanding achievement. They are renowned world success stories. They have a nice home in the suburbs, wonderful kids, a beautiful wife or handsome husband, a great job, and they make a lot of money. They seem to be rolling along just fine in life. They may play in the NFL or NBA, or sing and dance on the stage or TV or movies.

"But, son, I have something better for you than that. I want you to get beyond that idea of success.

"More than being successful, I want you to be faithful!"

For the first time in his life, Ron truly understood the difference. His heart had been searching for God's plan for two years, but his mind had been stuck in a worldly frame of what it means to be a successful person.

At the Bible study, he recounted to the Rams what he had learned from the experience. "You see," he explained, "God has His own newspaper sports page. It's called the Book of Life. If you have not joined His team, then your race doesn't count. It's just like Jesus says in Matthew 7:21-23:

> "'Not everyone who says to me, "Lord, Lord," will enter the kingdom of heaven, but only he who does the will of my Father who is in heaven. Many will say to me on that day, "Lord, Lord, did we not prophesy in your name, and in your name drive out demons and perform many miracles." Then I will tell them plainly, "I never knew you. Away from me, you evildoers!"'

"If we haven't made Jesus Christ our Lord and Savior, then we're not on the team. We could be running apparently faster than anyone else, doing things better than everybody else, but in the end it won't count. Our names won't show up in God's publication of the Book of Life. That means eternity in hell."

In his earnestness, Ron had spoken just as significantly to himself as he had to the others. The analogy opened up a new freedom of choice for him in his own life. The pressure from the driving desire to succeed in the eyes of the world began at last to ease.

In another area of importance, Ron also settled into a trust with God concerning the woman for his life. The right lady would come along at the right time. He dated freely. Audrey faded from the picture. He thought of her often because she had made an invaluable contribution to his life, but the passion was gone.

Memories rushed to the forefront momentarily, however, when she called in early January 1983. The sound of her voice was familiar, yet there was a faraway tone in her greeting.

"Audrey, it's great to hear from you," he responded. "How're you doin'?"

"Ronny, I'm OK except for one problem—and I called because I need your advice." Her speech was strained.

"Sure!" he pledged. "What is it?"

"Well, there's this guy I've been dating—his name is Ralph. We get along great most of the time. However, I just don't know what to do. He's not interested in spiritual matters at all."

Ron listened patiently through her problem. It was evident to him that she needed to forget Ralph and move on with her life. "Listen, Audrey, I think you need to take time out from whatever you're doing to get back your focus on the Lord. You need to get your priorities in order. Then what you do with Ralph or grad school or anything else will fit in its proper place."

She thanked him politely, but he could tell she was disappointed that he'd not given the advice she wanted to hear. She had wanted license to do as she pleased, not to change direction.

He was sorry she was going through such a struggle, yet as he cradled the phone back on its holder, a wave of peace washed his heart. He had faithfully repaid the debt to the one God had used so specifically in his life. He was set free from that tie.

Ron continued to train to get himself physically fit. As he did so, he also strained to find a fifth opportunity in pro football. But he struck out on both counts. The knee never came around, and consequently the search was in vain. No football team looks for a hobbled defensive back.

The door was shut.

At least the door he wanted was barred. The door he had pounded on so relentlessly would not budge. It was locked.

Ron was confused and felt unsure of his purpose. Most of all, though, he had no desire to make a career step outside of football. However, because so many things were up in the air, he searched anxiously for different career options.

But without his designing it, another door into the fabulous football world opened.

Wondering as to where his future was going, Ron talked to Andy Talley, who formerly was running back coach at Brown and then head coach at Villanova. Talley suggested that Ron give coaching serious consideration. "Ron, you would be good at it. Listen, I know that John Anderson is looking for someone at Brown. You ought to give him a call."

Ron followed the advice. The coach wasn't in when Ron called, so he left a message. Shortly the call was returned.

"Ron, this is John Anderson," the man on the telephone identified himself. "I'm glad you called. I'd like you to interview for a position on our staff here at Brown. I heard about your dilemma and wondered if you were interested in staying in football via coaching? I need a freshman coach. However, we need to talk about it and see how the interview goes first. You see, I have over four hundred applications for the position from experienced college coaches out of work and former pro athletes wanting to get into coaching.

"Could you come up next week so we can discuss it?"

Ron was shocked by the suddenness of the invitation and responded with some hesitation. "Well, as you know, this call is unexpected. And I don't know what I want to do. But," he affirmed with a quick decision, "I'll be glad to meet with you to talk about it."

The intervening week was hectic. With all his other responsibilities, Ron had little chance to think through the prospect of being a full-time coach. From his earliest days as an athlete, he'd had no such desire. He wanted to be a player. That's where the glory is.

The evening before he was to meet with Coach Anderson, he was studying the basketball scores on the sports page when a short article at the side caught his attention. It was set off in a bold bordered box and titled with a question:

Is Fleeting Fame Too High A Price?

In America today macho image is one of the most compelling forces of our society. And of all such image makers, none is greater than that of men who make up the National Football League. These stalwart figures of weekend glory in the gridiron battles are held in highest esteem, not only by the youth, but by a broad section of the adult population as well. They are honored in their communities, sought after by the mighty and the lowly, and hounded by the press for morsels of comment to foment ever more suspense for impending games.

From August, through a seemingly endless season, and on through a sometimes tiring series of championships, professional football players hold status against rumors of wars, a rising or falling economy, crime in the streets, and fights in the family.

America has a love affair with its football players and pay a handsome price to watch their mastery of talent. But what price do these faithful gladiators pay? The cost to them is high, sad to say. The average NFL player is dead at 55, twenty years ahead of his non-athletic peers.

About 80% who go into the NFL married come out divorced.

About 50%, in spite of the incredible salaries earned, come out bankrupt.

The question perhaps is unanswerable, but needs to be asked nevertheless: is such a cost to family and self too great a price to pay for fleeting fame?

On the long train ride to Providence the next morning, the article was very much on Ron's mind. It was the focus of attention as he and God had plenty of undisturbed time to reason together.

"God, what is it you really want for my life?" he prayed as he rode along. "Is this potential offer from Coach Anderson something you have for me, or is it a detour? I know that article in yesterday's paper was true: there are some crazy things that go on in pro football. But there are some legitimate, good people in pro football."

"Absolutely!" came a resounding response to his spirit. "I have key people in all kinds of highly placed positions. And they are an honor to me. And they will continue to gain the praises of men because they have learned that those honors mean little. They have attained a success that lasts. They're not flattered by men. They have my peace and satisfaction within."

"Lord?" Ron asked his co-passenger. "Do you mean that I've been on this wild four-year rollercoaster just to learn a simple lesson that outward image is not important? But, Lord, I've known that. At least, I've been trying to pattern my life that way."

"Yes, son," the reassuring voice spoke softly, "you've been learning well. However, success or prestige or honor in the eyes of men must be worn like a loose garment. You put it on. You take it off. Then you go on to the next thing.

"But you've allowed the whole desire for image in life to cling to you like a fine fitted suit. But, Ronny, status, in and of itself, is neither of importance nor of lasting significance."

The words had breathed softly on his spirit in love, but they cut him to the quick like a sharp knife. Like a double edged sword.

He was humbled.

More significantly, he was also set free, for the first time in his life, from the fear of failing.

"Lord," he repented, "I'm so sorry. Pro football is something I thought I had to have. I've not possessed it. It has possessed me. Thank you for being so patient with me. I now gladly release it all to you."

With that issue resolved, he concentrated on the opportunity at Brown. After interviewing for the job, he called his closest Christian friends and asked for counsel. One such friend whose opinion he valued greatly was one of his high school football coaches, Bob Tankard.

The response he received from all sources was firm and enthusiastic that he should go into coaching. He sensed from this that God indeed had been gently nudging him to enter football professionally. But as a coach, not as a player.

He was offered the job and accepted.

It was not his selected course, but it would keep him on the inside of the sport he loved, serving the Lord he had learned to love even more.

From his first day on the job at Brown, Ron realized that having knocked around four NFL training camps had not been a total washout. It had been good instruction. When he sat down with the rest of the staff for a planning session, he was not a novice. He had rubbed elbows with some of the truly outstanding strategists of the game, men like Tom Landry, Mike Ditka, Raymond Berry, and other great coaches. He had run in competition with guys like Walter Payton and Wesley Walker. He had been a good student of the game. Perhaps he could become a good teacher.

A few weeks before the start of practice that August, Ron took advantage of a lull in his schedule for a vacation back in New York City. He wanted to have some parting hours with those who'd been such a support to him during his search for direction in life.

But again, God had an unexpected blessing in store for him. Ron had first met Molvina Carter in January at a dinner party. He was instantly interested, for she was a very impressive woman. She had studied at Stanford, Oxford, and Columbia. Yet she was at the same time an extremely compassionate Christian. She had an unabashed love for those who are socially disadvantaged.

Until he met Molvina, relationships with women had been very discouraging. He had dated a few nice Christian gals, but he was impatient and restless; none lasted. He therefore had hesitated to try courting Molvina.

However, on his return to the city, the fascination of her inspired him to plunge ahead. He aggressively sought her company, and she complied. They discovered countless ways to share time together at church and with groups, but their favorite style of outing was for a quiet picnic in Central Park with lots of time to talk.

This woman was strong. She had a keen mind and insight for truth. There was a refreshing boldness and intensity for accuracy and attention to detail in her every endeavor. Yet it was accomplished with a powerful gift of compassion and loyalty, seasoned with a dash of shyness.

Ron saw Molvina's humility as her greatest quality. In the public, ego-boosting profession of athletics on which he was about to embark, Molvina had a much-needed and balancing devotion to privacy and excellence when no one else was looking. She desired neither praise nor recognition from the world. Just love and support from her Lord, family, and close friends.

Molvina Carter was a barrier to hypocrisy. No macho stuff or popularity seeking with this young lady. Ron Brown welcomed this special person in his heart. She was to become God's gift of balance in his life.

When summer ended and Ron returned to Rhode Island, he missed her and longed for her company. They maintained an intimate communication. No doubt about it, Ron Brown was falling in love. He had no intentions of ever losing her.

Romantically, they agreed that July 29, 1984, one year from the time of their first date, they would be joined by the Lord in marriage.

Having not met Molvina's family, Ron decided to introduce himself to her parents by letter.

April 26, 1984

Dear Mr. and Mrs. Carter,

Let me start by saying that this is somewhat of a difficult letter to write because of the unique circumstances involved, yet a very pleasurable one as well, because of the great joy in my heart.

Molvina speaks fondly of you. From listening to her and examining her life, I visualize you as strong Christians and consequently love-oriented. That's basically what I wanted to share with you in this letter: what God has done with love in my life.

As you've heard, I'm very much in love with your daughter. I know that the word gets tossed around often, but here God has intervened, tremendously. I met Molvina at a dinner party in January of 1983 in New York. Yes, I must admit I was instantly attracted to her—not love at first sight, but certainly "lots of like." The dinner party contained "Stanfords" and "Princetons" and lots of "Ivy League" talk. I, myself, was trying very hard to concentrate on television.

It just so happened that on this particular evening, the Super Bowl game was a little more interesting to me than Wall Street.

However, I couldn't help overhearing Molvina's comments. I was extremely impressed that she was more people-oriented than money-oriented. Her stand inspired me to turn my attention away from the Super Bowl and to join forces with her in the discussion. When I left the apartment that night, I was impressed with her. I bragged about her to my roommate for three days.

Relationships in my life had left a lot to be desired, and I felt I could never love again. However, God wouldn't let me give up. One day I was inspired to call Molvina. It seemed like a risk, but that risk turned out to be a gold mine for me. Little did we know that in less than a year we'd be talking about marrying each other.

I'm traditional–and I'm asking for your blessing to marry your daughter, Molvina. I want you to approve of me.

I plan to love Molvina by giving my all to her–relinquishing my silly pride and ego–and rather cooperating and inspiring her to the fulfillment of her God-given talents. I know she'll do the same for me.

We believe God approves of our union. I hope you concur. My family certainly approves of Molvina. She is so special. I'm amazed at how much I love her.

Thank you so much for enduring this letter. It was emotional for me to write. I hope you've gotten a little better idea of who I am and what I'm all about.

I really am looking forward to meeting you and the family. May the LORD bless you. You have my love.

Sincerely,

Ronald A. Brown

Meanwhile, Ron had directed the Brown frosh to a 1 and 5 season. Not an outstanding beginning to a coaching career. But freshman play is regarded as an important proving ground; winning is not all-important as it is with the varsity. Young guys, fresh out of high school, have an opportunity to mature in competition with a select group of their peers. Neither the press nor the electronic media give much concern to that level of play, but it is just as significant to collegiate football as farm teams are to professional baseball.

In addition to the satisfaction of being intimately involved with some dedicated young athletes and the camaraderie of the coaching staff, Ron loved the challenge of academics at that great institution. Being an alumnus also afforded him ready recognition on campus. He was remembered not only for his football and academic achievements, but he was well remembered for the clean image he had left behind. He was respected. Notably so.

Though coaching, training, and recruiting players was the profession which began to unfold before him, his primary purpose was to be God's man, a witness. Whether one-on-one with a troubled student or in group Bible studies, he began to carve a niche for himself in the spiritual fiber of the campus.

Although 1983 could be qualified as a good testing time for the freshman team, the season was a disaster for the varsity Brown Bruins. Even for a school which prides itself principally on being an academic institution, a 4 and 5 record was unthinkable. Consequently, with pressure from alumni, fans, and disgruntled students, the entire football coaching staff was fired. The sacking included the freshman staff as well, which spelled an apparent early doom to Ron's newfound career.

A few days after the house cleaning, Ron was home on the island with his parents.

"Son, what are you going to do now?" his father asked with concern. "Everything seemed to be going so well for you."

"I don't know, Dad," Ron answered. "This decision was sudden, but not really unexpected. I mean, coaching is a tough profession. Coaches have to produce. The staff just didn't put up the right won-loss record.

"At this point I have no idea what to do next. I was really beginning to enjoy the job. I thought this was God's plan for me! And then boom!"

"But why did they fire you? I can see why they got rid of the head coach. But why you?" his dad questioned.

"That's the way it works, Dad," Ron explained flatly. "You see, he had the say as to whom he wanted on his staff. So when he goes, we all go. That way when a new coach is hired he's free to choose a staff to his liking. This way there was a total clean sweep."

Though he tried to act low key about it with his folks, Ron was in turmoil about the sudden shift in job security for a reason other than what it meant to him. His relationship with Molvina had progressed steadily. They were together at every opportunity and planned to make it permanent. The date was firm for a wedding at her home in San Diego. How could he go through with the responsibilities of marriage and be on the streets looking for work at the same time?

Ron returned to campus the next day just as the news broke publicly. The trustees had wasted no time in selecting a new head coach. John Rosenberg, former defensive backfield coach at Penn State and the USFL's Philadelphia Stars, was hired and hit town in full stride. Though Brown University has no spring football program, Rosenberg had a lot of work to do in order to build a staff and get them involved in his new system. One of his first orders of business was to contact Ron and ask him to come to his office. After a brief greeting and introduction, he got right to the matter at hand.

He put Ron to an on-the-spot test of his knowledge of football. He was aware that in addition to being head freshman coach, Ron had assisted the varsity defensive back coach. "Ron, step up to the chalkboard and diagram a few defensive back techniques and coverages for me."

Without questioning why, Ron took chalk in hand and explained in detail five or six defensive coverages and the individual techniques associated with them.

Rosenberg listened attentively. After Ron had run through schemes for fifteen minutes, the coach interrupted him. "Thanks, Ron. Sit down over here and let's talk.

"Ron, I've heard a lot about you for years. You had quite an impact on the Ivy League as a player. But more importantly, now, you did a great job with the freshmen players this last year, in spite of the 1 and 5 record. However, I think Anderson made a mistake in putting you in that spot."

Ron gulped. The ax was about to fall.

"You have a great potential in coaching," Rosenberg continued. "I'd like for you to consider moving up to the varsity as defensive back coach. How about it?"

Ron was shocked by the offer. He wasn't being fired. He was being promoted. And into an area of specific expertise. He was amazed at the sudden turn of events, yet he smiled inwardly as he realized who had opened up this expanded opportunity for him. God was in charge. This was the Lord's stamp of approval on coaching as a career for him.

It seemed that a whole lifetime flashed before his eyes as he saw God leading him into the future, but his instant response to the offer was, "Yes, sir! I can handle that."

And handle it he did. Within two years, the media dubbed the defensive backfield for the Bruins as "The Wreckin' Crew." This was accomplished in spite of an off-and-on conflict within the coaching staff against the head coach. Even Ron was frequently at odds with Rosenberg over strategy and principles, though they maintained a good working relationship.

Meanwhile, Ron gained the stabilizing support of a strong Christian wife. He and Molvina tied the knot just as they had planned. No longer did he have to look around for a confirming opinion (or contrary advice) on key issues. Molvina was always there, although low key, with encouragement or challenge.

Ron's fourth year at Brown was a difficult one. Recurring problems with the head coach were too much for both players and assistant coaches. Some left. Ron had a job offer from Hank Small at Lehigh. Yet he held steady.

The coaching staff that remained was in continuing turmoil over a key decision by Rosenberg to not give John Townsend the assignment as defensive coordinator. JT had been in college football for many years at several major Division I schools. He and Ron not only shared coaching similarities, but because both were black, they were united in some common life issues as well. Rosenberg devised a unique plan to rotate his defensive assistants to coordinate the defense on a game-by-game basis. The decision was an obvious hindrance to continuity. It strained many relationships, even between Ron and JT. Eventually, though, they were able to reaffirm their friendship stronger than ever.

God also gave Ron a new ally in the Christian outreach on campus. Biff Poggi came on board as an assistant coach. In short order the two men became great friends. Together they organized a Bible study for all coaches at the university. Later, after Poggi had moved on to a coaching job in Baltimore, they shared their individual dreams with each other for helping underprivileged kids. They realized that they had one and the same vision. So they teamed up to start an I CAN camp, first in South Carolina, and later in Nebraska.

In all the busy involvement as a coach, with its heavy schedule of travel for recruiting and being constantly on call for every need of athletes, Ron maintained one thing as more important: his relationship with God came first.

He abandoned forever the ego need of building an image for himself. He knew that God's main purpose for him was to use athletics as a platform from which to share the truth of Christ.

CHAPTER 12

REALITY
BEYOND THE DREAM

Ron Brown had dreamed big from the first time he donned a pair of sneakers and got into athletics. He wanted more than anything to be right smack dab in the middle of professional sports. It was the apparent, right thing for him to do. He wasn't kidding himself. He had some basic talent. He could go far.

It was not just a case of youthful ego on his part. He received continuous reinforcing encouragement along the way from a host of people. His coaches goaded him toward perfect performance. His parents watched adoringly from the sideline. Whatever it was he secretly lacked in inner confidence, others made up for with unbridled support. For instance, when he was only beginning to develop his physical skills and was an unproven quantity, his basketball coach at Martha's Vineyard helped him gain a vision of the future. Jay Schofield drilled him consistently not only in fundamentals of basketball but in the basics of life also, hitting hard on academic and social development. Schofield kept feeding the youngster with enthusiasm for stretching beyond, to dream. And then to dream again.

Yet, for balance there was Gerry Gerolamo, the high school's head football coach. He wisely added the challenge for Ron to remain humble in the light of what Gerolamo was certain would be success.

Years later when Ron returned home after being cut by the Dallas Cowboys, another former coach, a strong born again Christian, Bob Tankard, came right over to see him. "Now, Ronny," he said firmly, somewhat fatherly, "I know you're feeling down. Who wouldn't? You had a great chance and it was just snatched away from you!

"But, Ronny, that's not the end. Sure, Dallas is big time. But so are the 49ers, the Bears, the Broncos, and the Patriots."

"Sure, there are other teams in the NFL," Ron moaned, "but who's going to give a second chance to a reject?"

"You're not a reject, man!" Tankard affirmed. "Let's get that shoulder back in shape and try again. You can do it!"

With such affirmation continually coming his way, Ron pressed persistently on with his dream. Certainly if it had not been for Christ's transforming influence, he would've fallen by the wayside. Jesus was the one who made the significant difference. He put others in Ron's life to further strengthen him in his pursuit as they often supplied the confidence when he had little or none.

Naturally, Ron met other disappointed dreamers along the way. Unfulfilled in their hopes, they all seemed to have two basic things in common: at least a bit of talent and a driving desire to be famous. Some wanted the glory of limelight success in sports so badly that they lost view of anything and everything else. There was no balance in their lives.

One such man left a lasting, tragic impression on Ron. He first met Jim Tressler on the coaching staff at Brown. When the whole staff was fired the following year, Tressler's bubble burst. He had dreamed, but it was greatly exaggerated, and he had no follow through of his own. He slid from the pinnacle and faded away. With no further goal or plan, Jim drifted back to his old hometown in Ohio to sell cars. Disillusioned. Purposeless. Frustrated.

He was only in his mid-forties, with a wonderful wife and two daughters in college. One day, while all alone and depressed, convinced that no one cared, he shot himself. The newspaper account was a shock. Ron wept as he read the news aloud to Molvina at the breakfast table. He laid the newspaper aside silently, and thought deeply as he slowly regained his composure. How gracious God had been in giving him a purpose far beyond this world's fame for which to live.

Unfortunately, the death of this one fine man was not an isolated incident.

Tragedy struck again. Later at the University of Nebraska, another coaching acquaintance also committed suicide. Ron sorrowed because of the loss of such energetic men at the prime of life. "But," he observed to Molvina after the second coach's funeral, "don't we also have a bit of these men in us? If it weren't for God being in control of our lives, we'd be just as prone to disaster. The way these guys died was tragic. But the reason they died is worse. They died for want of a reputation in the eyes of the world, feeling they had fallen short of success. I remember the feeling," he admitted quietly.

"But how thankful I am that God kept the dream alive in me until I was able to get beyond it to the reality He has for me–us."

Molvina did not reply. The truth was too solemn.

"You know," Ron continued momentarily, "a Christian friend came up to me my first year back at Brown as a coach and said, 'This isn't so bad, Ron. At least you got God's second best.'"

"A friend, you say," Molvina responded.

Ron smiled at her unguarded support. "At least God was able to use his comment to my benefit. I gave a lot of thought to what he said. Had I been forced to settle for God's second best? The more I thought about it, the more I knew he was wrong, the more satisfied I became of what God was doing in my life. The Lord showed me that the whole definition of success that I'd been geared to, even after I became a Christian, was still flawed with outward emphasis. Looking always for image.

"I found that the real answer is only in the Word of God. This is our playbook," Ron continued as he reached for his Bible on a nearby stand, "showing us through obedience His formula for lasting satisfaction. The Lord explained it perfectly to the children of Israel in Joshua 1:8-9." He turned the pages to the passage and read aloud:

"'Do not let this Book of the Law depart from your mouth; meditate on it day and night, so that you may be careful to do everything written in it. Then you will be prosperous and successful. Have I not commanded you? Be strong and courageous. Do not be terrified; do not be discouraged, for the Lord your God will be with you wherever you go.'

"Now, I've gained a different dream, a higher goal. I just want to please Jesus Christ."

"I agree," Molvina affirmed. "It seems to me that God designed all along for you to be a coach. He simply used the so-called failures in pro football as your training ground. Like young David, running from Saul for years before God raised him to be king as he had promised. Or like Paul, spending three years in the desert before exploding on the scene for a worldwide ministry."

A short time after that, Ron sat in his car one day, praying before going to work at Brown University. He began to talk to God about his future in coaching. He was feeling apprehensive. "I'm at a small Ivy League school–the least experienced coach on the staff. Is there a future for a black coach? Will people ever feel comfortable about hiring black head football coaches? Is it always going to be such a struggle?"

He prayed for wisdom.

God responded quietly with assurance to Ron's heart, "Don't seek anything first–except conforming to Christ. Don't wait to become a head coach before you start having an impact on people spiritually. Start now. Go hard. Use my gifts now–even as an assistant coach to bring glory to me.

"I'll handle the promotions. Trust in Matthew 6:33 and Psalm 75. Just be faithful."

Ron and Molvina enjoyed the four seasons at his alma mater. It was an important proving ground for Ron in his God-ordained profession. But it was time, he considered, to move on.

He began testing the waters. He interviewed first at Baylor with head football coach Grant Taeff, who also had a powerful Christian witness. Taeff eventually decided to hire someone else. But he appreciated Ron's talent so much that he promised to recommend him for another position elsewhere.

That vow was shortly fulfilled.

Tom Osborne, head football coach at the University of Nebraska, heard about Ron from Mike Church, defensive coordinator at the University of Texas-El Paso, who had coached with Ron at Brown University. Osborne called Ron to get acquainted.

Ron promptly called Taeff and asked him to speak to Osborne on his behalf. Taeff did so.

Osborne invited Ron to Lincoln for an interview, after which he narrowed the field down to Brown and one other. Ron and Molvina prayed about the opportunity and were in agreement to accept the job of receivers coach for the Cornhuskers if it was offered.

Osborne decided on Brown.

With a Big Eight, Division I school like Nebraska, spring football is an invaluable training time. So Ron and Molvina made a quick transfer from Providence to Lincoln in order to be on the job for the April sessions.

As the Huskers' receivers coach, Ron knew from the first day of practice at Nebraska that he was into a much higher caliber of college football. The media attention directed toward him as an assistant coach for the Big Red was more intense than anything Ron had experienced at Brown. The press back in Rhode Island had never cared so much. Ron realized right off that "fish bowl" living would be at its highest in the football-crazed state of Nebraska.

Ron dove into the challenge of working under the direction of Tom Osborne with excitement. It was an outstanding opportunity to learn through the tutelage of one of the most respected college football coaches of the last quarter century.

He envisioned also that he could make an impact in the realm of race relations. After a decline in the 1970s, racial incidents on college campuses had begun to increase dramatically during the 1980s. The often quoted words of Edmund Burke, "All it takes for evil to prevail is for good men to do nothing," were etched deep into his character. Ron was committed to making a difference.

"I'd like to raise the level of consciousness of whites, blacks, everyone, and remove the ignorance," he told an Omaha sports reporter. "Racism, subtle or overt, hurts not only minority-race people. It diminishes us all.

"God created men and women of all colors equal. They ought to be looked at for the content of their character, not the color of their skin. We have to defeat the stereotypes."

Another dream Ron had nurtured for years and which he took along to Nebraska was his desire to continue to minister meaningfully to underprivileged kids. He had been involved in such outreach from his early days as a Christian while in New York City. This vision to do something lasting wouldn't go away.

In New York City, Ron had prayed about what had become a burning passion. "Father, I really want to be able to do something to help underprivileged kids. I don't know exactly what you have for me next, but I do know it's not to be a hospital administrator. Oh! I'm going to finish this master's degree. But that's not for me. I just ask that whatever else you have for me, please use me for the sake of kids.

"And," he concluded with a dream from his youth, "I want to be a positive role model. There are so many injustices in society. I promise you that every chance you give me to be heard, I will give Jesus Christ all the credit for any success I have."

There had been countless opportunities to help individual kids, yet Ron was restless for something more. He devised a plan to search out possibilities in the south. While coaching at Brown, he realized that schools of the Ivy League didn't frequent the south to recruit. Ron convinced Coach Rosenberg that there was a gold mine of potential talent down there for Brown University.

On a ten-day swing through the southeastern states, Ron searched out athletes and also gained invaluable coaching clues by observing spring practices at major universities. But his side agenda was to see firsthand the poverty and inequalities of life in remote rural areas. In one town after another, he walked through the streets and visited with young and old alike.

As he headed back to Providence, a vision began to form, a plan to bring disadvantaged kids together for a few hours each day for a week. Sports would be a main feature, but a challenge to excellence in all areas of endeavor would be the focus.

That vision became reality as well when he and Biff Poggi got their first I CAN summer camp underway in 1987 in Beaufort, South Carolina. With the help of the local chapter of the Boy's Club, children between the ages of ten and fifteen were carefully selected from neighborhoods throughout the area to ensure a broad mix of racial and social backgrounds, the idea being to break down the insidious barriers that even divide kids.

Ron and Biff wanted a way of combining the best in athletics and academics, while at the same time transforming attitudes. Since most underprivileged kids have experienced a negative view of life, living under a dark shadow of doubt both about themselves and their opportunities, an understandable response to challenge often is, "I Can't!"

Ron and Biff came up with the positive strategy of I CAN, an acronym for Ideal of Christian Athademitudes in the Neighborhood.

"There is no such word as 'athademitudes,'" Biff challenged when Ron first coined the word.

"There is now," Ron laughed. "Look! It puts into one expression everything we want to accomplish with the kids: athletics, academics, and attitudes. And we want them to understand that with the right attitude, they can accomplish anything."

So, in addition to his optimism for a meaningful career of coaching at a football powerhouse like Nebraska, Ron knew that God had other purposes for him. Surely, an ever expanding I CAN also was transplanted with him to the lands along the Platte.

CHAPTER 13

THE SURPRISE DECISION

Working throughout the off-season as a recruiter for the Nebraska football program is equivalent to a full-time job in itself. Yet Ron savored every bit of it. He loved the challenge of building rapport one-on-one. Compared to the laid back style of the Ivy League from which he came, the Big Eight search for talent is intense and aggressive. Days on the road and in the air were long, exhausting, and extensive. But such effort brought Ron face to face with some of the finest high school and junior college athletes in the nation. It had been in his first such recruiting year at Nebraska that Ron came into contact with Victor Stachmus, built a friendship, and won the struggle for the gifted young man's commitment to play football for the Big Red, and was there to help him into Christ's wheelbarrow of faith.

In addition to Victor, 1987 produced a bumper crop of young men for Nebraska as other future standout players signed on the dotted line. There were guys like Lance Lewis, Mike Grant, Bruce Pickens, William Washington, Tyrone Hughes, and Jon Bostick. The Cornhusker staff had done a great job.

Ron, however, had little time to rejoice with the rest of the coaching staff as that signing season ended. He was organizing his plans for spring practice when word came of his father's unexpected death on April 9, 1988. Ironically, Victor Stachmus was diagnosed with leukemia just one week later. It proved to be a tough spring.

Ron and his father had quietly enjoyed a very close, meaningful relationship between themselves. That was quite an accomplishment for two men who for years found difficulty in expressing themselves emotionally. Though the bond between them was basically unspoken, it was at the same time unbreakable. The son always knew that his dad was there for him, and the father had impeccable trust in the boy. They liked each other and enjoyed being together. They just didn't find words to talk much about it.

During Ron's last year on the staff at Brown University, his dad asked if they could make a trip together in the summer of '86. "Ronny, let's go south–to see the new south. I haven't been down there since I was in the army during World War II. Even though I had a uniform on, I had to go to the back of the bus–in America, no less. I would love to see how much things have changed–maybe even ride in the front of a bus–just for the fun of it."

"Sure, Dad! That would be great. I can take a couple weeks off this summer. You and I can have a great trip." They made plans. Ron eagerly anticipated the time alone with his dad. But when the time came for them to leave, the southern tier of states was gripped in a terrific heat wave. His long years of hard work had taken their toll on Arthur Brown–he couldn't stand hot weather. They had to cancel the trip. Instead, they sensibly stayed home in the relatively cool comfort of Martha's Vineyard.

It was a preordained time. Ron had yearned for years to have an uninterrupted time to talk to his dad about Jesus, just as he had with hundreds of others. In contrast, his mom was easy to talk to about spiritual matters; she had been converted in her own living room one night after watching Billy Graham on television. But his dad had maintained a respectable distance in spiritual matters. He always had been a devout, religious man. He'd gone to church all his life and saw to it that his kids did too. But he kept talk about God to a minimum.

One evening as the two of them sat on the front porch, the conversation flowed naturally into the subject which was of greatest importance to Ron: Jesus Christ and what God had accomplished in him and for him personally.

"Ronny," his dad confessed openly, "I've been around this earth for 68 years and I've never had that kind of satisfaction you talk about. I've worked hard and no one has ever given me anything.

"Now, I'm not complainin' about the work. I think that's how it's supposed to be. But I've been put down and closed out of opportunities that white folk take for granted, and just because I'm black. I think that's mighty unfair.

"I think your mom and you and your sister woulda had it a whole lot easier if we'd not been born black."

Ron looked at his dad in amazement. The man had stood as a sentinel of cool understanding throughout the years of unfair racism and had kept his counsel to himself. Never had he insinuated any bitterness in his soul. Bitterness, not that he was black–he was proud of that–but anger because society made that into a critical barrier.

"Dad," Ron said with spiritual insight, "you know, no one who comes into this world can determine how they're going to be born. But God does give us the option to be born again–to start a new life in Jesus Christ."

His dad looked at him intently. Listening.

Ron continued, "Dad, it really begins at the point of our recognizing our need for something more. We look at our mistakes, our sins, our anger, then we turn to God for an answer.

"First John 1:9 says, 'If we confess our sins, he is faithful and just and will forgive us our sins and purify us from all unrighteousness.' And we all need forgiveness–you, me, mom, everyone who ever lived–except Jesus.

"That's what Paul meant when he wrote in Romans 3:23, 'For all have sinned and fall short of the glory of God.' But then he adds the promise in Romans 6:23: 'The wages of sin is death, but the gift of God is eternal life through Jesus Christ our Lord.'

"Dad, Jesus Christ accomplished all that for us when He died on the cross. He died that we might be forgiven and begin to live for Him."

"Ronny," his dad interrupted, "I believe this and would love to. I'm just not sure that I can."

"Dad, you can!" Ron insisted, and without pausing for breath plunged ahead boldly. "Would you like to pray right now and ask Jesus to come into your life as your Lord and Savior?"

His father looked at him admiringly, knowing that his son had given him the words that he himself should have taught his son many years before. His voice, however, did not quaver as he replied, "Yes, son, I would."

As the two of them sat praying in the cool of the evening, Ron was overwhelmed with gratitude to God for this rare opportunity with his dad.

With firm voice, Arthur Brown poured out the burden of his heart to God in repentance and acceptance. Silence punctuated his conclusion. Tears welled up in his eyes as he declared in simple appreciation, "Thank you, Ronny. Thank you, Ronny."

Less than two years later, as he took that forced break in spring training to be with his mother and sister, Ron wrote in epitaph of his father:

My Dad had a great ability to see potential in someone—and make that person feel good about himself.

Here's a man who by the world's standards was not highly educated, nor influential in the public forum. Yet he was wiser than many because he knew how to communicate easily with people from ages two to ninety-two. I never saw him uncomfortable around people. He could make you laugh or he could be stern and command attention, whatever it took to get his wisdom across.

His most admirable qualities were his loyalty, love, and commitment to his wife, my mom. He treated her with such great respect. All the little things. He was home every night, and even though he worked during the day, his heart was always home. His relationship with my mom was extremely inspirational to me and my wife.

Back in 1957, he and my mom decided to adopt a child from a foundling home in New York City. That was me, and two years later my parents went back to the same place to adopt my sister Theresa. It was so natural for that man and his wife to love, no matter if you were miles away. They knew love and commitment, and exemplified it. I am so blessed because I still am a recipient of that love even after his death.

The greatest memory I have of my dad came just two years ago, in the summer of 1986. We were sitting on the porch and began to talk about life in a very serious way. He shared with me his 68 years of ups and downs. He realized that life was more than paying bills, going to work, and wishing the best for his wife and children. We talked about God, and although he spent most of his life going to church on a regular basis, he realized that he had never personally made Jesus Christ the center of his life. The next thing we knew, for the first time ever, we were actually praying together. And he asked Christ to be the center of his life. I treasure that day with all my heart.

His favorite jazz musician was Jimmy Smith. He often played a song from one of Smith's albums called "I'll Close My Eyes." On April 9, 1988, Arthur Brown closed his eyes for the last time here on earth. However, at the instant of death, he opened his eyes to a new life—eternity with the Lord. I love my dad. I miss him. Yet he's preserved for a future date when we will reunite.

With the death of the man who meant more to him than any other, and then on the heels of that the death of the recruit who was so close to his heart, Ron was all the more determined to share the message of Jesus Christ with all who would listen—especially his players. He wanted them to know success. The kind of achievement that you don't have to be a winner to obtain. The style of status that keeps you feelin' good even when the going is rough.

Being introduced as the receivers coach for the University of Nebraska sounds impressive in itself, but loyal fans of the team sometimes chuckle. Head coach Tom Osborne believes in running the ball, running the ball, running the ball. Even if it doesn't work for the first three quarters, he sticks to his game plan. The Cornhusker pass receivers and their coach often are like the proverbial Maytag repairman, the loneliest man in town.

Yet Ron Brown is one who, from his first day, never laughed at the task. He knew that receivers have another significant function.

They don't just stand around on the gridiron waiting for a pass to come their way once in a lifetime. Receivers must also block well if a running game is to work at all. Much to the credit of the blocking prowess of the receivers, the Nebraska Cornhuskers lead the nation in rushing yardage.

Ron also determined from the beginning of his tenure in Lincoln that if Coach Osborne called for only one pass in a game, he intended for his man to catch the ball. He drilled his tight ends, wing backs, and split ends to high proficiency. They responded to the challenge, and in 1989 Nebraska finished in the top ten in the United States in touchdown passes caught and tied the Big Eight record for most touchdown passes thrown in a season. Not only so, but the Husker receivers also had one of the highest yards per catch averages (18.8 yards) in the nation.

The walls of Ron Brown's South Stadium office in Lincoln are covered with charts, all the information any young man needs to know in learning to catch a football. Yet, failure can be summed up easily. In it all, there are basically three reasons why a person drops a ball that's within reach.

Number one. The receiver goes out on his pass pattern, turns around, and sees the ball coming just six inches away. All he has to do is take it. Suddenly, however, a thought runs through his mind: "Humh, when I catch this ball I'm goin' to make a move on this defender like he's never seen before. I'm goin' to spin away from him. I'm goin' to start wrigglin' and streakin' down the sideline, avoid some other tacklers, score a touchdown, the fans are goin' to go crazy, my name's in the newspaper, my face on television. It's goin' to be great!"

All of that thought process takes just a split second while the ball is still approaching those yearning hands; he takes his eyes off the ball to head downfield, and it drops to the ground.

Never take your eyes off the ball. It's the first lesson!

But, that in itself doesn't necessarily spell success for a receiver. On the Cornhusker practice field it sometimes sounds like an incantation as Coach Brown reminds his charges over and over, "Watch the ball in! Look the ball in. All the way in."

Dutifully, ironically, young men stare at the pigskin as it hits them in the helmet or flops off their fingertips. That underscores the second reason for failure to catch a well-thrown pass: lack of concentration. A man may be looking at the ball but his mind is not on the ball. He's thinking about a bad grade he got from a tough professor, or a misunderstanding with a girl that made him mad, or the "silly" passing drill itself.

All kinds of things can race through a person's mind if his real intent is not on the matter at hand: catching the ball.

The third reason why some players drop the ball was evident in the Cornhuskers' 1988 game at UCLA. Dana Brinson, all 160 spry pounds of him, leaped up and stretched out to grab a pass. Just as the ball hit his fingertips, he was smashed hard by a UCLA linebacker. Dana was knocked out cold. He caught the ball, but he lay on the ground for a long time.

Fans cheered as he eventually got to his feet, but the unexpressed question was, "After a hit like that, will that boy ever overcome fear when another pass comes his way?" For a lot of players, when they come racing across the field, even though there is no one else around, there is fear because they've been through the frightening experience of being flattened by a bruising tackle and those hands don't go up with the same authority. And the ball slides off the fingers.

In sharing Christ with one of his players one morning, Ron reminded him of the three reasons why passes fall incomplete. "That's why, for the first twenty-two years of my life, I couldn't catch on to God's plan," he admitted.

"God is like the quarterback, getting ready to throw the ball. The ball is in the form of His Son, Jesus Christ. I didn't have my eyes on Jesus. I had my eyes on the world. I wanted popularity. I wanted to please people. I couldn't accept Christ. I wasn't looking His way.

"In college, I began to understand something about Jesus Christ because people were talking about Him, but my mind wasn't on Him. My mind was on the success of fulfilling other's expectations. My priorities were different. Jesus was way down the list. Even though I believed in Him, I wasn't making Him number one in my life. I was dropping the ball because my full concentration wasn't on Him.

"Also, there was the fear. The fear of failure. The fear of wondering if my life was such a miserable mess, how could I honor God. The fear of what my buddies would think if I became a God Squad member.

"But God is very merciful. God sent me two receivers coaches, a guy named Harry and a gal named Audrey. They weren't the answer in my life. God is the answer. But He used them to help me see Him. To help me, by the example of their lives, to have courage to reach out and make the most important catch of my life–Jesus Christ.

"I want to encourage you too. God is throwing you a pass. If you haven't made Jesus Christ your Lord and Savior, if you haven't made that great catch, I encourage you to do that. Reach out of your heart and make the greatest catch of your life. There is no greater joy than that. I have no regrets. I would never turn back."

"Thanks, Coach," the young player nodded in agreement. He too wanted to get on God's team–as a starter.

In his first three seasons on the coaching staff at Nebraska, Ron assisted in helping the Cornhuskers roll up an impressive record of 31 wins against only six losses. And, as had been the pattern for years, the Big Red went on to three consecutive postseason bowl appearances.

Early in the 1989 campaign, several of the recurring powerhouses in college football had disappointing losses. The national press was looking for someone to tag number one in the country. Nebraska, though a young team, had surprised everyone with early, lopsided victories. In contrast to other perennial favorites which stumbled coming out of the starting gate, the Cornhuskers performed well under the field leadership of senior first-year-starting quarterback Gerry Godowski.

Then came the Colorado game. Hype was high. Sportsmen used that often overused phrase "game of the decade." It was plain to see that the winner would be heralded as number one.

Unbelievably, on the first play from scrimmage, Tom Osborne–the run, run, run coach–called for a pass. Within seconds, the deft hands of Bryan Carpenter reached out for the ball, pulled it to his chest, and raced into the end zone. Flash: Nebraska 7, Colorado 0.

The fans who had traveled to Boulder, joined by thousands in front of their television screens, rocked with enthusiasm.

However, college football is composed of four equal quarters. The team ahead at the end wins. Final score: Colorado 27, Nebraska 21.

For some die hard Nebraska fans, it was the end of the season. For them, a loss to Colorado or Oklahoma is a wipeout.

Fortunately, college coaches and athletes cannot key in on just one game. Those who are at the task full time know that one game does not make a season. Their eyes are just as much on continuity and progress as on the win or loss column. They don't have the luxury of brooding over defeats or gloating over victories.

At three o'clock sharp the next afternoon, the Cornhusker coaches were back at work, preparing themselves for the next battle. Though another trip to the Orange Bowl undoubtedly was lost along with the Colorado game, it was not the end of the season. There were skills to be refined.

But besides heading back constantly to the drawing board, well disciplined coaches also build variety into their lives. Ron Brown is in demand continually as a speaker. Immediately after the Kansas State game in 1989, for instance, as soon as he completed his responsibilities with the team and homecoming alumni, he rushed out to the nearby Lincoln Correctional Center to share the message of Christ in his life with a fellowship of inmates. All as a part of his promise to God to honor Him in everything.

At about that same time, Ron had an unexpected challenge cross his path. Along with many others in the coaching fraternity, he had been aware for months that there were problems within the football program back at Brown University. But he had no idea that he would be singled out as a leading prospect for the head job.

At first, he kept the news to himself. He and Molvina talked it through. There were many uncertainties about making a move. They were well settled in their home and happily had established a broad base of relationships. Equally important, the opportunities for ministry in the name of Jesus, within the state and beyond, had given Ron a high profile. He was well known in his stance of openly proclaiming the truth of Christ, insisting on an end to racial bigotry, and seeking assistance for orphans and the underprivileged. Also, the I CAN program was going well with a third camp on line to begin in northern Nebraska among Native American children.

Though all of those circumstances were important considerations, he nevertheless was a football coach, and going to Brown could be a significant career move. He talked to many football people for their general opinions. But he strongly considered the advice of a few trusted friends and sought their prayer support.

Ron swallowed hard one morning as he stepped out of his office in the South Stadium. It was time to talk to the one man in Lincoln he respected most in regard to football and whom he also held in high admiration as a Christian. Tom Osborne had brought him to Lincoln and introduced him to the power football of the Big Eight. They had become good friends. Nonetheless, Ron was nervous. He didn't want to appear to be an opportunist.

"Coach," he began after they had settled down in high-backed chairs in Osborne's office, "I think you should be one of the first to know that I've been approached by Brown University in regard to the head coach's job there. At this point, they have several people they're considering. Certainly the job isn't mine for the asking. But I didn't want you to hear a rumor about it from someone else."

"I appreciate that, Ron," Coach Osborne replied in his own inimitable, unruffled way. "But, I must say I'm not surprised."

An expression of shock registered on Ron's face.

"Oh, certainly I didn't know about Brown University's approach," Tom continued. "I just mean I believe that a man of your ability is always going to be sought after as a coach."

"I just don't want you to think that I'm using you and the University of Nebraska as a stepping stone—especially since I just came here from Brown three years ago," Ron explained.

"No, don't worry about that," Osborne assured him. "I know you better than that. I'd certainly hate to lose your talents, but this could be a great opportunity for you. Do they want to interview you?"

"I told them I couldn't come for an interview until after Thanksgiving–after the season's over but before we begin practice for the Fiesta Bowl," Ron explained.

"You have my support, Ron, whether you stay or go. Be sure to keep me posted, though," Osborne advised.

The unhurried meditation and search for an answer then came to an abrupt halt. Before Ron and Molvina could thoroughly sort through their own thoughts on the matter, the news broke across the campus and in the press. Immediately, they were inundated with perhaps well-meaning, but unsolicited, advice from every corner. Being the football mecca that it is, Nebraska is not short of "experts" on every facet of the game. Many offered an opinion.

Ron, however, had acquired one immeasurable asset in decision making. Prayer had become for him not an empty ritual performance but a time of personal communion with God. Through patient reflection and waiting, he had learned to lay matters before his Heavenly Father, and then trust in the resulting leadership.

This dependence upon God was truly important in the face of conflicting conclusions from two individuals whose opinion he valued greatly: his mother and one high school coach.

When Coach Tankard learned that Ron was in consideration for the top job at Brown, he was elated and enthused. He had no doubts on the matter. He told Pearl Brown, "Absolutely, Ron, should take the job! Why, here he's only thirty-three years old and can step into leadership at one of the most respected institutions in the Ivy League.

"Not only that, he would also be the first black head football coach in the history of the league–as well as one of just a few in America today. It would be a great step for advancing not only himself but society too.

"And this is a rebuilding time at Brown. He can put his own individual stamp on the program.

"With God's help, and a few successful years at his alma mater, Division I schools will be beating a path to his door."

Ron, of course, was flattered, though not surprised, by Tankard's endorsement. From their first association in high school days, the coach always had given him solid support without laying a heavy drag on him.

On the other hand, Ron was totally astonished by the response of his mother. He had assumed that she would be excited about him being back so near to home–especially because of the recent loss of her husband and her own advancing years. However, there was no selfishness in her opinion. She, too, was adamant. "Ronny, why would you even think of leaving Nebraska? God has been so good to you there. You have everything a young man could want: a great wife, a fine home, a job you like, respect in the community.

"No, son! I don't think you should go back to Brown!"

When the possibility of being head coach for the Bruins first presented itself, Ron was one of many applicants. He flew east to interview for the position in November. By early December, the list had been pared to four. Ron was a leading candidate. But he was also informed that a "small number of alumni" were not in favor of being the first in the league to hire a black head coach. They didn't want to set a precedent.

Nonetheless, the university officials were made of sterner stuff. On Christmas Eve, Ron was told that the job was his if he wanted it. He sought to postpone a final decision until after the Cornhuskers' Fiesta Bowl contest, but the officials at Brown under-standably wanted to put an end to speculations. They set December 30 as a deadline for his answer.

Not only did Brown University demand an answer, but it seemed that everyone in Nebraska wanted the inside scoop as well. Big Red fans take their football seriously. Consequently, while trying to concentrate on his responsibilities to the team, Ron was beset on every hand. The telephone in his room at the Fiesta Bowl site was constantly ringing–inquiring minds wanting to know. His players were nagged continually by reporters trying to get an inside exclusive as to what Ron was going to do. Coming out of practice sessions he was besieged by media people. Television cameras and tape recorders were stuck in his face. The hounding seemed endless.

Molvina gave quiet assurance that she would stand by whatever Ron determined was best. Biff Poggi telephoned to give his support. Ron set aside two hours to be alone to sort through his desires and emotions in order to determine God's will and plan.

First off, he looked at it logically from the viewpoint of his career. Certainly, as the world judges success, the idea in the coaching profession is to be at the top of the heap. Some would do anything, short of murder, to grasp what he was being offered. "Could it be a stepping stone to something even greater, as Bob Tankard and others think?" he pondered.

"But how could I ever get greater national exposure than being at Nebraska–a team always ranked at the top? At Brown I'd be a bigger duck–but in a much smaller pond."

How to judge the difference in that scale was impossible for him.

Ron was also faced with considerable pressure from 220 members of the Black Coaches Association, of which he was an officer. Many saw this as a chance to break new ground. His steady response was, "I've been brought up to believe that being black doesn't mean being desperate. I need to make a prayerful decision based on wisdom, knowledge, and insight.

"The need now is for black coaches to have head positions where they can have sustained opportunities and the resources to win consistently."

Ron, from his earliest days, had an unyielding desire to help bridge the gap in race relations. But, he determined, he was already involved in that task as an assistant coach at Nebraska. He didn't have to go to the east coast to find racial tensions. Ron decided that this was not solely a racial choice.

During the early afternoon before the Cornhuskers' Fiesta Bowl practice, Ron threshed through his mind all the possibilities between going and staying. As he did so, one word kept surfacing. That word was not success, of which he had been so enthralled as a young black boy from a modest home. Nor was it fame, of which he had dreamed as an aspiring athlete. No, the word was not of what he could gain but of what he could give. That word was ministry. During three short years in Lincoln, God had confirmed to Ron that his high profile position was given to him as a trust. He was to be a witness, to give expression to his faith in Jesus Christ. And to prove it, God had opened up amazing opportunities all over America.

Ron chuckled to himself as he compared the extreme satisfaction of speaking in the name of Jesus to the dream of empty success which had haunted him just a few years earlier. He realized that he had not yearned to be a pro footballer just for the honors and opportunity; the quest for fame had been in neon as well.

Now he was confronted with another opportunity which would afford him high prominence in his profession. The sports media was abuzz daily in anticipation of his decision. Most people were certain of what he would decide. Who wouldn't take hold of a head coaching position?

Ron Brown wouldn't!

In his search for peace in the matter, he focused first on professional fact. He was a coach whether he stayed at Nebraska or returned to Providence. So what was the issue? To the mind of most people in the world, one must grab every chance to climb the ladder to success and recognition. Not to do so is folly.

However, Ron had an allegiance to a higher goal. His perspective for gauging life was centered in his personal responsibility as a child of God. He was to bear witness to the truth in Jesus Christ.

One significant opinion came from his friend Ron Dickerson, another strong Christian, who at the time was defensive back coach at Penn State. His advice centered on a verse of Scripture, James 1:5:

> "If any of you lacks wisdom, he should ask God, who gives generously to all without finding fault, and it will be given to him."

"Listen, Ron," Dickerson declared, "close out everyone else's opinion and get God's wisdom–and stick to your guns." Ron and Molvina proceeded to stay awake all night on December 29, meditating on that verse and praying.

The next day he had his answer.

When he called John Parry, athletic director at Brown, with his decision, Parry was perplexed by the refusal, but he didn't pry for an explanation. As Ron made his surprise statement to the press that he was staying at Nebraska, those normally bursting with commentary were without words.

It was left to Ron to explain simply, "God has given me a real peace about staying as an assistant under Coach Osborne." Newsmen didn't want to get into a "Jesus" story, so they let the interview hang at that point.

Ron didn't expect people to necessarily understand his decision. In the final analysis, it was too simple. A complex society wants mystery and intrigue. There was neither in Ron's story. He had found peace not in success but in service.

A couple of days later, Ron received a letter from the father of David Seizys, a Nebraska player. Tony Seizys and Ron had grown to admire one another. In the letter, Tony explained that he had not wanted to influence Ron's thinking, so he had waited until the decision was made before sending the letter, which clearly was written prior to the decision. Tony shared a Bible verse which was to help Ron immensely in the following months of second guessing. It was John 6:27:

> "Do not work for food that spoils, but for food that endures to eternal life, which the Son of Man will give you. On him God the Father has placed his seal of approval."

Ron was questioned daily by Nebraska fans, as well as college, pro, and high school coaches around the country about his decision to turn the Brown job down. Many just could not grasp it. Their barrage of inquiries caused him to wonder to himself, "Who, in a world bent on getting, can understand giving?"

He smiled as he thought back through his own pilgrimage. "For years, like others, I couldn't have fathomed God's plan," he admitted. "But now I can!"

Subsequent events proved to confirm Ron's decision to stay at Nebraska. The opportunities to speak out on three matters of great concern to him multiplied: adoption, race relations, and the plight of underprivileged kids.

From what started as the first I CAN camp at a rustic farm in South Carolina, his desire to help poor kids has attracted support from many sources. Most striking of all was when the mayor of a nearby town drove out to a camp to see what was going on. He parked his car across the field and watched from a distance. He couldn't hear what was being said, but he saw what was being done with the kids. He then drove back into town and wrote out a check for $15,000 of his own money.

Requests come in for information on how to expand the camps to other areas. That poses one question for Ron and Biff Poggi as they see their vision expand: should they give into the pressure to tone down the Gospel message in order to have even more camps?

Never!

"I'll never forget the first camp," Ron said with excitement to a reporter. "We had no idea what to expect. We didn't even know much about how to organize it. But the last night, as I shared my testimony as to how Christ transformed my life, every kid but one gave his life to Jesus.

"It was one of the most incredible experiences of my life. That's the real purpose of the camps. Sure, we want kids to get a good grasp on life and a right attitude. But without Jesus Christ, that's impossible."

Another pleasing opportunity for Ron was when he and his mother were able to do a television commercial together on the topic of adoption. It became even more important to him when he sat next to her hospital bed as she was waiting for bypass surgery.

They had plenty of time to reflect on their life together. His mother had often assured him and his sister that their birth mothers had loved them very much because they decided to give them life instead of death. That had to have been a difficult decision, but what an impact it had on so many lives!

Would Arthur and Pearl Brown have come to know Christ if they had not brought a club-footed child into their home? If he had been cut out of his mother's womb and thrown away like a piece of trash, would Victor Stachmus have had someone at his bedside to lead him into peace with God when he was so fearful of what lay beyond death?

But as Ron held his mother's hand that day, he thought more of what was facing her at that moment. She asked him to read to her from the Psalms. When the orderly came to wheel her away to surgery, she assured her son, "I'm in the Lord's hands."

Her words were prophetic. The last he ever heard her utter. Pearl Brown never awoke from the surgery.

So is the life of Ron Brown. Basically a story about an insecure, weak person, who failed so often in his personal life, who had to say at one time, "I CAN'T" in order to achieve real success in life. Yet, one day he allowed the blood of a Man named Jesus to erase that apostrophe T forever:

I CAN'T̶ do all things through Christ who gives me strength.
Philippians 4:13

CHAPTER 14

ONWARD TO THE 1994 NATIONAL CHAMPIONSHIP

During his first six seasons at Nebraska, Ron had helped coach the Cornhuskers in consecutive bowl appearances, only to come up short each time. The 1993 season appeared to be different. The team had relatively easy wins in the first two games against North Texas and Texas Tech, but then had a struggle against a powerful UCLA squad in Pasadena before coming out on top, 14-13. The remainder of the campaign required some come-from-behind victories en route to an unblemished record. The Big Red was ranked No. 1 in the nation, slated to go up against No. 2 Florida State in the Orange Bowl.

In that tightly fought national championship game, Byron Bennett kicked a field goal with 1:16 left in the game, putting Nebraska ahead, 16-15. Excitement ripped along the sideline with the players and exploded in the stands amid the fans. Cornhusker players screamed and hugged one another, tasting victory, a long-awaited first national title for Coach Tom Osborne.

Seconds later, however, on the ensuing kickoff, the ball went out of bounds, giving Florida State good field position on its own 35-yard line. Behind the quarterback leadership of Charlie Ward, the Seminoles marched deep inside Nebraska territory and kicked a go-ahead field goal of their own. With the score 18-16, and with precious seconds left on the clock, it was evident that Bobby Bowden was about to win his first national championship as coach for Florida State.

But the Cornhuskers were not ready to throw in the towel. The offense rallied behind quarterback Tommie Frazier, who hit Trumane Bell with a pass into Florida State territory. With time for just one more play, Nebraska set up for a game-winning, 48-yard field goal attempt. Tension mounted throughout the Orange Bowl. The snap came from the center to David Seizys, who deftly placed the ball for Bennett's kick attempt. The football sailed unerring toward the goal posts, only to hook wide to the left. Nebraska had come within inches, but would have to build for another year to gain a national title.

Within weeks of that loss, Ron Brown was approached by Bobby Bowden to move to Florida State as coach for the wide receivers. Though he was very content with his position at Nebraska under Coach Tom Osborne, he considered the offer seriously. From a professional viewpoint, a move to FSU could enhance his professional status. At Nebraska, he had been a coach in a power option-run, play-action passing system. Florida State, on the other hand, would provide a more wide open drop-back passing attack. Such a move would help round out his experience and improve his opportunities to move up the ladder professionally.

In the final analysis, however, Ron had to consider something far superior to the world's concept of success. He had to determine what God wanted him to do. During seven years with the Cornhuskers, God had leveraged Ron from the Nebraska football platform with Christian camps for underprivileged children, a Christian radio ministry, and extensive writing and speaking opportunities. Searching the will of God in prayer, he and his wife determined that the time was not right for him to leave the ministries to which God had entrusted him.

Many could not understand his turning down such an attractive offer. It would have been a feather in his cap to have worked under two of the premier coaches in America–Tom Osborne and Bobby Bowden. But, for Ron, such decision-making had become perennial. In 1992, the issue arose nationwide that there were no black head football coaches at any major university. Consequently, he was considered a candidate when his close friend Ron Dickerson became head coach at Temple University. This set a new precedent and attracted considerable media attention. Dickerson asked Ron to join his staff as offensive coordinator, which, after prayerful consideration with his family's input, he declined.

In the course of life, everyone–whether a Christian or not–is encouraged to "move up the ladder." It is the thing to do, to get ahead. Success is normally attributed to the one who gets the most promotions, the largest salary, the biggest house, the most prestigious title. There is nothing intrinsically wrong with any of that, but the most important thing that a child of God must know is the certainty that he or she is in conformity with the will of the Heavenly Father. That concept is powerfully stated in Ephesians 1:11: "In him we were also chosen, having been predestined according to the plan of him who works out everything in conformity with the purpose of his will."

Anyone who is ever tempted to "grab the brass ring, which only comes around once," needs to take a long hard look at the temptation of Jesus in Luke chapter 4. Making a wrong career choice can lead a person far afield of what God intended, what God designed for that life. No one else in all the history of the world has been offered so much as Satan suggested to Jesus. The devil said, "I can give you all of this!" Jesus turned him down. He said no–and firmly so. He knew of an eternal plan, confirmed before the creation of the world. He set His face as a flint to accomplish a higher purpose than anything this world could ever come close to offering–even though He saw the cross looming ahead in His immediate future. It is essential for the child of God to be able always to discern between a divine appointment and the mount of temptation.

Every man, woman, and child who ever lived has had to contend with the powers, authorities, and attractions of this world. Nonetheless, the admonition of Romans 12:2 must be the defining distinction for every believer: "Do not conform to the pattern of this world, but be transformed by the renewing of your mind. Then you will be able to test and approve what God's will is –his good, pleasing and perfect will." Each person needs to understand this command before he or she can begin to minister.

However, the struggle with this biblical concept would continually be a "thorn in the flesh" to Ron. With the determination to stay in Lincoln, Ron, along with the rest of the coaching staff, set his focus on preparation for the 1994 season. In the ensuing months, emotions ran especially strong in Nebraska in anticipation of the fall campaign. Practically anyone who knew anything about football was certain that the Cornhuskers would return to Miami the next December at the head of the pack. This was not mindless, wishful thinking. The Big Red would be able to field a talented defense, a powerful offensive line, and quarterback Tommie Frazier was expected to be awesome with two years of experience under his jersey.

As the season progressed, however, the distinction of the 1994 Cornhuskers was power through weakness. The team was invited to play a preseason game in the Kickoff Classic against West Virginia, a team which had been powerful the year before and was in the hunt for the national crown. The Big Red won that game handily, then rolled over Texas Tech and UCLA. Next in line was Pacific, and though the coaches and players took no team for granted, fans saw an easy win. Tommie Frazier had injured a calf muscle in the UCLA game and the coaches considered holding him out of the Pacific contest to give it a rest. Hoping that the injury wasn't serious, Frazier started the game. After taking just nine snaps from center, however, he experienced debilitating tightness in his calf muscle and wasn't able to continue.

Brook Berringer, on the other hand, was in excellent health. He had been bothered somewhat in the previous two seasons with persistent bursitis in his right elbow, but that was behind him. His throwing arm was stronger than ever and his timing was excellent on pass patterns with Coach Brown's receivers. Though unexpectedly thrown into the contest to take control, he performed admirably. Fans were elated that he was able to secure the win against a relatively weak Pacific team, but Wyoming was coming to town the next week. Everyone hoped that Frazier, doubtlessly the best option quarterback in the country, would be back in charge.

There was a statewide sigh of despair the following Monday when it was announced that Tommie's injury was serious–even life threatening. He was diagnosed with blood clot problems, and on doctor's orders he was sidelined. In a state where Big Red football is a major topic of discussion "thirteen months out of the year," men, women, and children were in shock. Nonetheless, focusing optimistically on the hopes for a national championship, they rallied around the relatively unknown substitute.

Concern, but not yet despair, gripped the fans in Memorial Stadium at halftime. Wyoming had jumped out to a 14-point lead, then traded touchdowns with the Cornhuskers and led 21-7. But with just twelve seconds left in the second quarter, Berringer plowed into the end zone, sandwiched between two defenders. The helmet of the second player crushed into Brook's chest, partially collapsing his left lung. During the intermission, with his team down 14-21, he gave little thought to the ache in his side. His concentration was on accomplishing the task at hand. The game was at stake.

Neither the Wyoming opposition nor the Nebraska faithful would have guessed that there was anything wrong with the big kid from Kansas by the way he performed at the start of the third quarter. He ran for two of Nebraska's three touchdowns in an eight-minute burst, keeping an unbeaten season alive.

Again, jittery Cornhusker fans were not able to savor victory for long. Doubts crept into every conversation when they learned that the new starting quarterback had been sent to the hospital with chest pains. X-rays and tests showed his left lung was forty percent collapsed. Doctors made an incision in his side to insert a tube to re-inflate the lung. After an uncomfortable night in the hospital for observation, Brook was sent home Sunday and was back throwing the ball on the practice field on Tuesday. Certainly he still had some pain. "There's a difference between being hurt and being injured," he said. "Everybody plays hurt sometime. It's hard to tell the difference because everybody plays through some pain."

Team trainers devised a special flack jacket to protect him against further injury. He had little opportunity to get used to it before trotting out onto the field to start the next game against Oklahoma State. It was sluggish going against a tough Cowboy team, however, and Nebraska eked out a 9-3 lead after two quarters.

Husker hearts skipped a beat when the teams returned to the field for the start of the second half. Tommie Frazier was walking the sideline in street clothes, Brook Berringer was nowhere to be seen, and walk-on quarterback Matt Turman was called upon to lead the team. It had been determined ahead of time that physicians would X-ray Berringer during the break in action. The exam showed that he had re-injured himself. Once again the lung had partially collapsed.

Turman, untried as a third-stringer, rose to the occasion. He was instantaneously heralded as "The Turmanator," leading the determined Cornhuskers to their sixth straight win of the season.

A nationally-ranked and vastly improved Kansas State team, winless against Nebraska in two decades, was elated to host the Big Red the following week. Perhaps against a team so depleted at the quarterback position they could finally put together a victory. Still nursing sore ribs, Berringer watched from the sideline as Turman had the first start of his career. With the Nebraska offense somewhat limited, the Huskers were ahead 7-6 when Berringer was inserted for the last series of the second quarter and then started the second half.

Two things worked well for the visiting team. Dominance by the Blackshirts made it a miserable day for the highly touted Kansas quarterback Chad May. They sacked the NFL prospect six times for a total loss of 53 yards. On the offensive side of the ball, Nebraska proved that it didn't need to depend on its usual pattern of options and quarterback keepers. Avoiding the possibility of a direct hit to his lungs, Brook marshaled his squad to a 17-6 victory.

In time for the Missouri game, showing no signs of his injury, Berringer was back to full speed. Again the defense was stingy and succumbed only to a 34-yard touchdown pass with about seven minutes to play. Berringer completed 9 of 13 passes for 152 yards and 3 touchdowns, and Nebraska breezed to a 42-7 win.

Still there were skeptics across the nation. Colorado was ranked number one and the Cornhuskers second as the Buffaloes came to Lincoln the following Saturday for a nationally televised matchup of unbeaten powerhouses. The Huskers jumped to a 24-0 lead in the game, helped greatly by their kicking game, which repeatedly pinned Colorado deep in its own territory. The Buffaloes began nine of their 13 possessions from no better than the 20-yard line. With a final score of 24-7, Nebraska jumped to No. 1 in the national ratings.

In the following two weeks, the Big Red machine rolled over Kansas and Iowa State in relatively easy fashion. A bit of a quarterback controversy showed on the horizon as the team prepared for its season finale against Oklahoma. Tommie Frazier had been working hard to get himself back in shape. He made the trip to Norman, and for the first time in more than two months, he was suited up and on the sideline. If needed, he was available against the Sooners. Brook Berringer's seventh start of the year proved to be the toughest test of all. In a hard-fought defensive game, Brook capped a 10-play, 82-yard drive in the third quarter for the game's only touchdown.

In spite of being hampered at quarterback for most of the season, the Nebraska Cornhuskers were again going to Miami undefeated to play for the national championship. Three different men had started games and even a team manager had suited up to give some depth at the position. But the entire team had awakened to the need for teamwork. Players accepted the challenge to focus on what they considered unfinished business from the year before. They still had the bitter taste in their memory of the near miss in the previous Orange Bowl. They had something to prove.

In their unity of purpose, the Big Red squad had earned national respect. The defense had played superbly in the eight games when Frazier was sidelined with his blood clot problems, holding the opposition to a mere 87 points. Meanwhile, the aggressive offense had tripled that figure with a total score racked up of 243.

With Frazier cleared by his doctors for full-contact practice, a "quarterback controversy" emerged in the press, yet the Huskers as a team did not lose their concentration. As quickly as they returned from the win over Oklahoma, they began preparations in earnest for their trip to Miami. It helped that in his return to uniform, Frazier kept a low profile, declining all requests for interviews.

Coach Osborne and quarterback coach Turner Gill had a difficult decision facing them as to who would start at quarterback against Miami. On the street and even in the media, many thought it was a choice between two effective players with contrasting styles–Berringer the passer and Frazier the runner. But the overriding policy for the coaches was that a starter can't lose his position due to injury. Brook had started seven games and had helped to win an eighth, but Tommie was back and was healthy. He was given the starting role.

The Big Red offense was unimpressive in the first quarter and fell behind 10-0 as Miami hit a field goal and then marched 97 yards down the field for the first touchdown of the game. Just as Osborne had assured everyone for weeks that he intended to use both quarterbacks, Berringer was inserted at that point. After two series of downs, Nebraska had to punt. Then Miami punted back. A persistent Husker offense ended with a 19-yard touchdown pass from Berringer to Mark Gilman on a play-action fake. The extra point was good. Nebraska was back in the game at 10-7.

Although the Cornhuskers moved the ball better than their opponent, both teams had to punt on their next two possessions, and the half ended with that narrow score. Miami returned to the field from the locker room with enthusiasm. The Hurricanes took the kickoff, swept down the field in less than two minutes, and scored on a touchdown pass from quarterback Frank Costa to take a stunning 17-7 lead.

Once again, Nebraska failed to move the ball–three and out. The ensuing punt pinned Miami deep, and an aggressive defense pushed the 'Canes even deeper, inside the 5-yard line. That powerful defense narrowed the margin to 17-9, scoring two points as Nebraska linebacker Dwayne Harris wrapped up Costa in the end zone for a safety.

Neither team could gain further offensive advantage as the third quarter came to a close with Miami in possession of the ball. As so often happens in football, Nebraska had a golden opportunity as the final quarter got underway. Miami couldn't move the ball and was forced to punt on fourth down. The snap was fumbled, however, and the Cornhuskers had the ball, first and goal, on the 4-yard line. The instant call by Osborne was for a pass play. Eric Alford was momentarily open in the end zone, but under pressure, rolling to his right, Berringer held onto the ball a second too long. Attempting to throw the ball out of the end zone, it was intercepted by inches.

Fortunately for the Huskers, Miami was unable to move the ball, and Nebraska took possession with 12:07 left in the game. Frazier resumed command at quarterback, but was unable to gain a first down. For a third straight time, with the Blackshirts playing outstanding defense, Miami was three and out.

Nebraska got the ball with great field position on the 40-yard line. Lawrence Phillips broke loose for a 30-yard burst to the 15, and Cory Schlesinger romped through a weary Hurricane defense into the end zone. Frazier connected on a two-point conversion pass to Eric Alford, and it was a brand new ball game, tied 17-17.

With barely six and a half minutes to play, the highly touted offense of the 'Canes once again sputtered–three and out. They had to punt.

Nebraska moved the ball, seemingly with ease, down the field. Once again, refusing to be stopped, Schlesinger plunged into the end zone for his second touchdown of the quarter. Nebraska, for the first time, was in charge of the score, 24-17.

The ensuing kickoff gave the ball to Miami at its own 17-yard line. Two ferocious sacks of the quarterback left them in an almost impossible hole. On fourth down, in desperation, Costa heaved the ball 50 yards in the air. Up for grabs, Nebraska intercepted the pass, and with that gained its first national championship under Coach Osborne. Celebration erupted instantaneously along the Nebraska sideline and into the stands with the Nebraska faithful. The sweet savor of success was wonderful. While enjoying that moment, Ron Brown couldn't help but notice the bent shoulders and saddened expressions of dozens of Miami players. In football, success is so one-sided.

The after-game rejoicing continued for a long time, but then reality set in. "We had achieved a mountaintop," Ron observed. "But what's next? It's a long way to the next mountaintop! I enjoyed that sweet taste of success like everyone else. But it was a lot like chewing gum–you put a stick in your mouth and enjoy all that flavor, but after a half-hour it becomes tasteless; you're ready for something fresh."

CHAPTER 15

FAITHFULLY ADHERING TO A HIGHER LAW

In the walk of life, men and women are often faced with doing what is most expedient, what is expected. Instead, the focus for the faithful in Christ must be on the big picture. Immediate self-gratification is the standard of the world. The goal of the believer is something far more gratifying, that which is expressed by the Lord Jesus in John 10:10: "I have come that they may have life, and have it to the full." But in order to attain to God's offering of life, a believer must give himself or herself faithfully to the higher law.

Doing nothing when faced with a decision is not an option for the child of God. For every individual believer, it is a matter of knowing what is worth fighting for. The words of "Such a Time as This" by the Maranatha Praise Band is a pointed inspiration in this regard, coming from the faithfulness of Ruth in the Old Testament:

> For such a time as this
> For such a time as this
> We've been summoned here by God
> For such a time as this.
> We will not be silent
> We will not hold back
> By His grace we will rise up
> For such a time as this.
>
> Through the moving
> Of His Spirit
> Through a mercy
> We do not deserve
> We've been rescued

From apathy
To live the legacy
of Christ in this world.

To make a difference
In our generation,
Advance His Kingdom
On every side
To write history
Throughout our intercession
And see thousands and thousands
Come to Christ.

David Seizys is an outstanding example of faithfulness from Nebraska football. From the standpoint of faithfulness and giving it his all, David is a prime example of what it is to be a team player. No task was insignificant to him if it was for the benefit of the team. Also, once he committed his life to Jesus Christ, he was totally abandoned to the best God had for him.

Ron Brown remembers a tough situation in which David, without hesitation, made his stand for Christ. "David was incredibly faithful to the Lord, an enthusiastic Christian dedicated to the highest cause, the highest law–the Lord God Almighty. He played that way, but he also conducted himself that way in meetings. On one occasion, we had a former great player in the NFL come and speak to our team on the woes of drugs and alcohol and other social abuses. In conclusion, the pro asked, 'What can we do? What has to take place for youngsters to get off of drugs and alcohol, to take the preventative measures?'

"A couple of players made comments which were general in nature. Then David Seizys raised his hand. When the NFL repre-sentative asked him what his opinion was, he responded simply, 'You need a spiritual life.' It got real quiet in the room. Then the pro said, 'All right. Now someone give me a real answer, where we can deal with reality.' This was an obvious put-down to what David was trying to say. But it didn't even faze him. I looked at him to see if there was any hint of embarrassment at all. There was none. He was loyal to the highest cause, the highest law, and of course, Almighty God."

Often when Ron has stood to speak in front of a secular audience, there has been that temptation to obey the false premonitions inside of him that tell him to water down the "Jesus" portion of the message. Ken Kaelin, former Husker fullback, once related that he often battled spiritual warfare regarding the numerous messages he delivered. When he first told of this struggle, Ron didn't understand it. Since then, Ron has begun to get a much clearer picture of this spiritual opposition–the flesh versus the spirit– which rages on in the inner man.

The Apostle Paul often admitted to a sense of fear and trepidation in his proclamation of the Gospel. Consider that Paul was a bold ambassador for Christ. This would lead one to believe that courage is not the absense of fear; rather, it is doing the right thing in the midst of fear.

CHAPTER 16

A VISION
BEYOND THE IMMEDIATE

There is no doubt that in the world in which we live we will face opposition, and that is good. Without it, life has no meaning; without it, there is no challenge, no opportunity; without it, there would be no football game. How we handle opposition, however, is one of the most crucial determining factors of life. This is especially true for a child of God. Too often we tend to give in to the forces of evil pushing unkindly against us. Resiliency must be the resolve by which we pursue God's will for our lives. This is why we have the challenge to perseverance in James 1:2-4:

> "Consider it pure joy, my brothers, whenever you face trials of many kinds because you know that the testing of your faith develops perseverance. Perseverance must finish its work so that you may be mature and complete, not lacking anything."

An illustration which Ron Brown often uses expresses clearly that how we handle the pressures of life is dependent upon our inner strength. With an open palm, he says, "Here is a piece of paper. If I squeeze it as hard as I can, it becomes all crumpled up, useless. And even when I release it, there is no response; it stays all messed up. Why? Because it has no resiliency. But if I take a rubber ball and squeeze it as hard as I can, when I release it, it pops back into shape. Is it because of the outward pressure? No! The pressure on the outside is the same for both. It's what's on the inside that makes the difference. The rubber ball has resiliency, the ability to pop back into shape once it's squeezed. If Christ is our inner power, we will be able to withstand any pressure."

It also helps to have an accurate perspective on a situation. God sees the big picture. He is able to look beyond the opposition and through the tribulation. Our limited scope of things on the sideline of life, with all of our stuff in the way and all the commotion going on at once, is very confusing to us. That is why we have to rely on the Holy Spirit, that voice from above Who sees it all, and speaks to us that all is well.

Possibly nothing describes Ron himself better than the words by which we are admonished from the tenth chapter of Daniel: "Do not be afraid." For, if nothing else, he is bold in speaking out about Christ. At the same time, Ron is an interesting contrast of temperaments within himself. If it were up to him, he would be the same reflective, reserved, and private person that he was in his youth. There is a deeper force at work within him, however, which compels him to have such enthusiasm. On one hand, he is known for his boldness in speaking out clearly on issues which are of significance to him. On the other hand, he is a shy and, at times, insecure, withdrawn person who will shrink into a corner of a crowded room.

Before coming to Christ at the end of his college experience at Brown University, his focus was rather narrow, mainly eyeing himself and sports. He wanted to be a success at both, but feared failure above all else. Though blessed with natural physical abilities, Ron drove himself constantly toward perfection, devoting himself to lifting weights while some of his peers caroused the town. At the same time, he pushed himself to put on a good front, an image he didn't feel he possessed. And he didn't.

Possibly the greatest challenge Ron had to face in regard to a coaching opportunity came in 1995 from Tony Dungy, coach of the Tampa Bay Buccaneers. Dungy offered Ron a "dream come true" job to coach Tampa Bay's wide receivers. That would have been a major career advancement with more money and a great pension plan. Besides that, Ron had high regard for Dungy, who also had a strong commitment to Jesus Christ. The two men had an opportunity previously to get well-acquainted in Black Mountain, North

Carolina, at a Fellowship of Christian Athletes camp. What nailed Ron, however, was a not-often-quoted verse from Colossians 4:17: "And say to Archippus, 'Take heed to the ministry which thou hast received in the Lord, that thou fulfill it'" (KJV). In other words, Ron sensed that in this case, God was saying that His ministry in Nebraska was not yet fulfilled.

In declining that offer, Ron also began to envision that there needed to be additional legs to what he had been doing in the name of Christ, a team working in follow up, a man to come alongside in ministering. The end result of praying about it was that God gave Ron a sensitivity to His desire that He wanted a "full court press" in the state of Nebraska with an urgency to reveal Christ. Ron knew this was God's call on his life to join Him in this cause across Nebraska for at least the present time.

To balance the demands of family, coaching, recruiting, and an expanding speaking schedule, Ron asked a local pastor, Tom Rempel, to suggest someone to handle the scheduling. Rempel thought a faithful member of his congregation, Penne Hanus, might be a good fit.

Penne and her husband, John, got together with Ron and Molvina for the first time in March 1995. "I've been around people who have had excellent knowledge of Scripture, people who really know the Bible," Penne said. "But Ron, in addition to knowing Scripture, allows God to transform him, mold him to be more like Christ. And he's never satisfied in his conforming; he believes he can always be more Christ-like."

In her hometown of Summerfield, Kansas, Penne had learned early in life about Jesus. Her mother was a leader in Child Evangelism Fellowship for years, and Penne made her first commitment to Christ at her mother's knee when she was only seven. She and John married when she was eighteen, and they have two children: a daughter, Jonica; and a son, Jeramy.

"In having a husband with the integrity that John has," she confided with assurance, "and to work for a man who lives out his faith as Ron does, I'm extremely blessed. By watching Ron up close, I've seen more clearly how to use God's Word in our lives."

She speaks enthusiastically of what she sees as a three-pronged responsibility: 1) prioritizing the flood of messages that come to Ron; 2) scheduling speaking engagements, arranging transportation, handling honorariums (a large portion of which has been used to fund the I CAN and Mission Nebraska ministries), and covering public relations details; and most significantly of all, 3) freeing up time for Ron to be with his family. "Penne and John were God-sends," Ron said. "I am sure their relationship to Molvina and me is a God thing. God knew that I could not and should not handle the increasing volume of requests and needs. Understanding John and Penne's background, God was matching our families from day one. God has blessed Penne with a real gift of helps and a big dose of patience as she spends literally hours per day on the phone preparing and nurturing my schedule. That combined with John's gift of helps and his love to pray has freed up much family time for me."

"Working with Ron has made me aware of the responsibility that faces Christians," Penne said. "Because people associated my name with his, I realized that we are linked in a ministry, and it's important for me to always present a positive attitude to everyone. Then it dawned on me—I should have been doing this to promote Christ all along! The moment I became a Christian, my attitude should have changed to one of loving and accepting all people.

"Ron often quotes Psalm 119:46, 'I will speak of your statutes before kings and will not be put to shame.' John and I both are a lot bolder in our faith now than when we first took part in this ministry. We really do find ways to verbalize what we believe."

Of great importance to Ron Brown is the concept of the I CAN camps, which he and his friend Biff Poggi conceived while he was still coaching at Brown University. Their desire in the late 1980s was to bind together the best in athletics and academics in order to transform attitudes. They saw that kids living in disadvantaged circumstances were insecure about both themselves and the opportunities afforded to others. Ron was convinced that with a few days under concerted Christian instruction, young lives could be lifted to a brighter outlook on life. With that transformation in perspective, they would begin to believe they could accomplish anything.

The goal of the I CAN camps—for children between 9 and 11 years of age—is to raise their aspirations of what they can become, to challenge them to something higher. But more significantly, through a relationship with Jesus Christ, to release God-given energy within them so they will have the necessary power to get there. These camps, in turn, have given an entry point into various communities. If there is to be a sweep across the state for Christ, His people must fully follow Him, which includes moving with compassion into areas of social decay.

Ron's relationship with the Young Men's Christian Association (YMCA) has been an interesting and spiritually rewarding collaboration. The YMCA's love for children prompted its sponsorship of some of the I CAN camps in Nebraska (Lincoln, Scottsbluff, Columbus, and Norfolk). Ron's desire to see the "C" in the YMCA promoted and exalted has helped to keep a "marriage" between the I CAN camps and the YMCA.

With his heavy schedule, Ron has needed lots of help in reaching as many young people as possible. Hundreds of people have served in various capacities over the years. Some have become so enthusiastic about what God accomplishes in the I CAN camps that they make serving in this ministry a priority in their lives.

Shelli Graves attended her first camps—at Lincoln and Macy, Nebraska—in 1994. She thought she was going to observe, to get an idea of what was going on, but she pitched in from the beginning and started to help. She was hooked from the start. She saw with great satisfaction the result of her and others' efforts, as campers made commitments to give their lives to Christ by the end of the week. This excitement has only grown since then.

Shelli met Ron Brown for the first time in 1989. She was impressed and challenged by what he was doing with kids when he spoke later at an FCA Adult Chapter luncheon in Lincoln. "There are a few people I know," she says with candor, "who are rock solid in their faith in Christ. Ron Brown is one of them."

In 1995, Shelli stepped into the task of being the I CAN admin-istrator for the Lincoln camp, but that expanded quickly into assisting in the work statewide. She oversees the whole range of details—teachers, supplies, transportation—for the camps in Lexington, Norfolk, Columbus, and Macy. Besides the brief camps during the summer, there are also follow-up activities throughout the year. Everyone involved in the ministry realizes how essential it is to keep the kids encouraged in Christ after they have come to Him in faith.

Through her work with the I CAN camps, Shelli has realized that God has blessed her with the gift of administration. In that regard, she looks for opportunities for further service. In addition to her work with Cedars Youth Services (foster care), she volunteers her organizational skills with the Fellowship of Christian Athletes and a Christian karate school in Lincoln.

God blessed Ron in ministry by leading him to a woman who had the same heart for kids and tolerance that Ron possessed. Ron had been hearing racist remarks about the Nebraska Indian population, and on more than one occasion, Ron responded with high intensity to both Christians and non-Christians who made such comments. He hated how Indians were talked about negatively, yet he himself didn't know them. Ron couldn't get his mind off of these honorable people who were being slandered, but felt a sense of inadequacy to do anything substantial for them. What was God saying to him about these people who, like Ron, lived in Nebraska, but were as foreign to him as one from another nation? God began to answer this question.

Ron heard about a white schoolteacher on the Omaha Nation Indian Reservation in Macy, Nebraska. Her name was Linda Ganzel. Linda was a Christian woman with a huge heart for the Native Americans in Macy. Ron invited her to check out the Lincoln I CAN camp to see what it was all about. Linda was not only impressed but began to wonder if the coach could do something similar on the reservation.

Shortly thereafter, a frustrating experience made God's direction clear just after the first Lincoln I CAN camp. Ron headed for South Carolina to help with an I CAN camp there. Because of air traffic congestion, Ron's plane arrived too late to meet its connecting flight in Chicago. Dejected, he went to a hotel for the night. Too mad at God to read his Bible, he turned the TV on to see what was playing. As he flipped through the channels, he stopped at a man who was reading a Bible. The man was speaking about Squanto, the great Indian leader who became a Christian and helped protect the early settlers and pilgrims back in the 1600s. Ron listened in awe of not only this great man's testimony, courage, and compassion, but recognized why God had him miss that connecting flight. God knew of a TV show in Chicago that Ron needed to see. It wasn't a coincidence; rather, a divine appointment. It was clear God wanted Ron to begin an I CAN camp on the Omaha Nation Indian Reservation in Macy, Nebraska, with the help of Linda Ganzel and many others. This I CAN camp has now been in existence for over a decade. Numbers of souls from the reservation have come to know Christ.

God continued to provide direction and guidance to Ron, often through new relationships with people. For years, Don French, a Lincoln businessman, suffered under a strong inner conflict in regard to religion. Every time he entertained any thoughts on the subject, his stomach would turn sick; he was scared about where he was going, where he was headed in life. On the one hand, deep down inside, he had a burning desire to help others. But on the other hand, he was little help to the person closest to him. He wasn't being the husband God would want him to be. He realized, especially with a baby on the way, it was time to be a better man.

But where could he begin? He did not feel comfortable talking to his wife, or with anyone else, for that matter, about Christ. "I could feel everything building up inside me," he said. "Though I was at a loss of what to do, I never felt like I could totally give up on God. I knew something had to give, but I had no one to guide me."

One evening while channel surfing, he saw Ron Brown on the public access television. Being a typical, avid Cornhusker fan, he stopped to listen, thinking Ron would be talking about Nebraska football. Instead, Ron was discussing his favorite subject: Jesus. Don listened briefly, but being in such inner turmoil, he turned the channel. Over a period of two weeks, however, he saw bits of the program a couple more times. The fourth time he decided to listen. What Coach Brown said made him really think about his life. Several times after that, he thought about calling Ron to see if he could help him. But the two had never met. He couldn't bring himself to talk about Christ with someone he had never met. "Certainly I wanted help," he confided, "but I couldn't imagine that a big-time college coach, after winning back-to-back national championships, would even take the time to help one person." So he didn't call.

Then April 22, 1996, became a significant turning point in his life. "The day of Brook Berringer's funeral, I was outside doing yard work, and I decided to listen to the funeral on my walkman. There were three speakers out of eight who made a deep impact on my life —Ron Brown, Art Lindsay, and Turner Gill. Listening to them brought up some emotions that made me cry about everything that was going on in my life. Again I had a deep urge to call Ron, but again, I was afraid to call."

About two weeks later, an older couple, Henry and Ruth Harms, friends of Ron and Molvina, stopped in Don's restaurant. Little did he realize that this retired minister and his wife, a former Christian education missionary, were to be a link to God's answer for his life. In their usual manner, they struck up a conversation with him. "Right off," he said, "they asked me where I went to church. And they asked me questions about my life. It was strange to me because I had never felt comfortable talking to anyone about myself. But for some reason they were so easy to talk to."

Eventually it came out that the Harmses knew Ron Brown. "Right there it hit!" Don declared. He knew that God had brought them together that day—the couple knew the man whom Don wanted to call for advice and guidance.

Don explained to the Harmses how Ron had influenced his life and how he had thought about calling him. Ruth asked him to write down his telephone number. She soon told Ron about the meeting in the restaurant and gave him Don's number. Two weeks later, Don received a call from the coach.

"We talked to each other for about an hour," Don reflected. "Then Ron told me that in July he had an I CAN camp in Columbus and asked me to ride along to get better acquainted. I was thankful for the chance to further our relationship. That night at the camp, when the invitation was given, I committed myself to Jesus Christ as my personal Savior.

"Since then I have traveled with Ron throughout the state to I CAN camps and his various speaking engagements. It's a small ministry on my part to do the driving, but it's a great help to Ron as he has time to reflect and write out notes on whatever God lays on him for that occasion.

"I praise God for using Ron to make me a stronger Christian. My whole life has changed for the better because of this relationship. If there is one thing that Ron said to me that is the most important thing in my life, it is this: 'Without God in my life, I wasn't prepared to die. And if you're not prepared to die, how can you live? How can you live life as a son or daughter, brother or sister, husband or wife, father or mother, or even just a friend?'

"I know what it's like to live now because I'm prepared to die. I ask anyone—are you prepared to die?"

CHAPTER 17

1995
NATIONAL CHAMPIONSHIP

The desire of God is that men and women get beyond debating His existence and simply start obeying His commandments. Jesus Christ said that only in this way may we know God fully. "Whoever has my commands and obeys them, he is the one who loves me. He who loves me will be loved by my Father, and I too will love him and show myself to him" (John 14:21). Knowledge of God and growth in Him begins with obedience. Without obedience to a higher authority, a person has no standard by which to gauge himself or herself. Can you imagine a football team without obedience? There would certainly be no national championship. As believers we need a coach. And even if the coach is our Father, we need to be obedient to Him in every aspect.

In simple terms, obedience on the football field is translated into being coachable. No matter how great a talent a player might have, if he can't bend to authority, he can never reach his full potential. Through endless hours of practice, Coach Brown repeats to his players constantly, "Keep moving to the ball. Never give up on a play; finish it–finish what you start." That determination ultimately results in victory, which in turn becomes an inspiration to others to never give up, never give up, never give up.

If any word of Scripture addresses this matter, it comes from the inspiration of Paul in 1 Corinthians 16:13. "Be on your guard; stand firm in the faith; be men of courage; be strong." This certainly is the attitude required of any child of God if he or she is going to be a positive influence in a difficult world. Though their goal was a worldly crown, such tenacity of will also expresses the essence of the 1995 Big Red football team. Wrapped in a season of great turmoil,

Nebraska swept to a second national championship in spite of a plethora of controversies and a storm of media scrutiny. More than anything else, those months revealed the strength and resiliency of Coach Tom Osborne, his staff, and individual team members.

Months before the season began, the press did its best to create a quarterback controversy. In the 1994 campaign, Tommie Frazier and Brook Berringer had each made significant contributions to gaining the national championship. Which of them should be the starter for the ensuing season was a question mark for the media, but not for Coach Osborne. His standard always had been that a starter could not lose his position because of injury. Nonetheless, radio, television, and press people, brushing aside that fact, tried to light wet kindling–it's the thing commercials depend on. Berringer pushed him, and that was good for the team. But through grading and performance during the fall camp, Frazier came out on top.

Indeed, it was especially fortunate for the Cornhuskers not to have a lingering question about the quarterback position. As the season progressed, the team had to stand strong against a barrage of unfortunate incidents. At least there was no doubt about Frazier's leadership. From his freshman year, he had been outstanding in running the option. Then, in the off season, he had worked hard on his passing ability. Every time the team huddled on the field, there was never any doubt as to who was in command. He exuded authority both in confidence and competency His season's performance would finally rank him as runner-up in the hunt for the Heisman. Without a doubt, he was the single most stabilizing factor on the team.

Lawrence Phillips, on the other hand, proved to be a major detraction. Undoubtedly, Phillips was one of the best running backs ever to play for the Cornhuskers. He had grit and determination, and often made something out of nothing, no matter what defense the opposition might design against him. It was only his junior year, but he was an early odds-on favorite to win the Heisman Trophy. Pro scouts watched his every move.

Then came the second game of the season. The Huskers

traveled to East Lansing, Michigan, to take on Michigan State. It was a bright, crisp afternoon, and Phillips played a brilliant game as the Big Red posted an impressive 50-10 victory. All he had to do was fly back to Lincoln with the team, get a good night's sleep, and wake up to glowing press reports in the Sunday newspapers. Instead, a confrontation with his former girlfriend ensued, and Tom Osborne had to discipline Phillips under great national scrutiny.

How suddenly a media darling can become a target of ridicule. Instantly the story was emblazoned across the nation. Instead of the focus being on a superb team of players possessing the dual punch of an outstanding offense and a crushing defense, sportswriters and sportscasters stumbled over one another to get to the "truth."

The national media challenged Osborne's decision not to remove Phillips from the team. Osborne decided to let the law of the land figure out the player's case. Yet, not ignoring Phillips' decision to wrecklessly hurt another individual, he suspended him for most of the regular season. He also insisted (and enforced) that Phillips attend school and counseling sessions.

More significantly, however, the team members met in their own quiet confabulation. They faced the crisis head-on, deciding as a unit not to be distracted from their goal of another national championship. Through years of experience, they knew that media scrutiny would be worse than ever. They agreed that no one would comment on the matter, pro or con. Instead, they would get ready for the next game.

If that had been the only shockwave to hit the Huskers during the season, their stalwart attitude would have been commendable, but not out of the ordinary. Unbelievably, however, other players tripped over the legal boundary and energized new bold headlines. The television show *48 Hours* focused its magnifying glass on Nebraska football. It was a rough condemnation, but the team refused to be sidetracked. The Huskers went on to win the final Big Eight Championship and set their sights on the Fiesta Bowl.

In reflecting on those events, Ron observed, "Tom Osborne is a good example of someone who has learned to see through the opposition. People are quick to remember his national titles. Yet, Tom was falsely accused of being a man of less integrity with the reckless criticism he endured during our second straight championship drive. The way he handled that opposition, in being submissive to God, was a great testimony to me. In a Bible study in which we were involved at the time, Tom shared how he came to an end of himself and had to just totally depend on God."

Not to worry, however. The Huskers were united in their mission. They were determined to repeat as national champions.

Of course, no one was taking the opposition for granted. The Florida Gators were ably coached by Steve Spurrier, and the quarterback, Danny Wuerffel, was one of the premier passers in the country.

No one went to the Sun Devil Stadium that night, though, expecting a blowout. In spite of fidgeting in the first quarter, the Cornhuskers rammed through a convincing 62-24 victory.

In his pregame comments to the team, Coach Tom Osborne keyed in on one very forceful verse of Scripture, 2 Timothy 1:7: "For God did not give us a spirit of timidity, but a spirit of power, of love, and of self-discipline." Besides running out onto the field well-prepared for the task at hand, the Big Red also played an inspired evening of football. Their reward was another Sears Trophy and national acclaim.

Just as significantly, perhaps more so, the conclusion of that game also resulted in one of the greatest picture portrayals of prayer and unity one could ever imagine. It also served as inspiration for the front cover of this book. Ron Brown recalled, "Right after the game ended, Danny Wuerffel walked up to me and said, 'Coach Brown, I know that you pray with your players after the game. Would you mind if I got in the huddle and prayed with you?' I was shocked because Danny had just played probably the worst game of his life, and they were embarrassed as a team nationally. That was not a very normal response from most people in his situation, but very reflective of his love for Christ.

"I assured him, 'Danny, you're welcome to do that. I usually open and you can close. How's that?' He said, 'That'd be great, Coach.' So we go over and kneel down, and there are Nebraska and Florida players together. I didn't realize that right next to me, kneeling on the other side, was Brook Berringer.

"When I saw that picture later, I realized that I was surrounded by the two most disappointed guys on the football field, one on the winning team, one on the losing team. The one on the losing team for obvious reasons. The one on the winning team hardly played at all; in fact, he had drifted into obscurity that whole season. But Brook fell to his knees and poured out his heart in praise to God anyhow. Little did any one of us know that just a few months later Brook would die, while Danny lives. Brook's death created huge ministry opportunities for God's glory as people came to Christ. In death, Brook Berringer glorified God.

"Danny Wuerffel lives and goes on the next year to get his national championship, win the coveted Heisman Trophy, and stand before America declaring that Jesus Christ is Lord and it was because of faith in Him that he was able to see the thing through.

"In reflecting on that scene, I just thought for a moment, 'Man, that's what it's all about.' As Paul says, 'For to me, to live is Christ and to die is gain' (Philippians 1:21). I have to say, that is the perfect picture because that's where we are. We're either living or dying. In both we're to glorify God.

"In the shame and frustration of those two players is the perfect picture of obedience. Whether we're on the losing team or the winning team, we all go through our personal struggles. In that moment they were two of the loneliest people in the world, surrounded by the hoopla of a national championship. Yet, these guys were honoring God. And God used these two to glorify Himself."

For the child of God, there may be no trophy to set on the mantle. There may be no praise from those who watch. But perhaps there is no other verse in the Bible which better spurs every believer in Jesus Christ to be a witness in his or her spheres of influence. Then 1 John 4:4: "Because the one who is in you is greater than the one who is in the world." Get rid of all hesitancy. Put the awesome power of the Almighty to work, focusing on Ephesians 1:18-20: "I pray also that the eyes of your heart may be enlightened in order that you may know the hope to which he has called you, the riches of his glorious inheritance in the saints, and his incomparably great power for us who believe. That power is like the working of his mighty strength which he exerted in Christ when he raised him from the dead and seated him at his right hand in the heavenly realms."

CHAPTER 18

BROOK BERRINGER

I t was not just his play, but the attitude by which he approached life which set Brook Berringer apart from others. Though he certainly had great ability, the greater attribute of his life was his availability. He was always ready to fill any gap, often unheralded. The true measure of who he was came into focus only later.

Carl Sandburg, the great American poet, one time wrote, "A tree is best measured when it has fallen." That has certainly proven true in the case of Brook Berringer, who was a primary catalyst in the 1994 national championship and a consistent enthusiast along the sideline toward the repeat title in 1995.

Ron Brown had a special interest in Brook because he had the privilege of recruiting the tall, talented athlete from Goodland, Kansas. In that process, he had built personal ties with both the quarterback and his family, which was especially close-knit due to the death of his father when he was only seven.

Besides wanting Brook to develop his football talents, he also had a prayerful interest in the young man's relationship with God. It was therefore with great pleasure that he interviewed Brook for his weekly radio show, just before the 1996 Fiesta Bowl (1995 National Championship Game) in Tempe, Arizona.

In the midst of that broadcast, Brook declared, "When I have something more specific to focus on, like eternal life and my faith in Christianity and my yearning just to grow in that faith, it brings everything, the whole scheme of things, into focus better. It's amazing the difference it has made in my life. I know where I'm headed. I know the ultimate goal, and it brings everything into perspective; it really prioritizes things in my life."

A year and a half after that interview, Ron Brown observed, "Those words were profound in the light of eternity. Little did any of us know that just three and a half months later Brook would enter into that eternity. On April 18, 1996, Brook Berringer died in a plane crash in a field near Raymond, Nebraska. You see, eight months prior to his death, Brook trusted the only One Who gives eternal life–Jesus Christ–as his Savior and Lord."

The night Brook died, Coach Tom Osborne, in addressing more than a thousand people at the annual Fellowship of Christian Athletes banquet, said, "Sometimes it's horrible, like the events of today. But God can use every situation. The question we have to ask is, how are we going to relate to that situation? How are we going to yield it up to Him and honor Him in the way we meet that situation? That's why I mention to you tonight that there was no question of what we needed to do tonight to honor God, because that's what Brook would want us to do. Absolutely no question as to what it would be! I know Brook would want this event to honor God. Brook honored God with his life."

Aaron Graham, former center for the Cornhuskers and now playing in the NFL, was a good friend of Brook. He felt a tremendous sense of urgency to share the Good News of the Gospel in spite of the emotional pain of losing such a close companion like Brook. "It's been rough," he said, "because he was such a good friend of mine; but on the other hand, the tears I've cried for him have not been tears of sadness. It's been more tears of joy. It has impacted me tremendously. I really feel that there is an urgency now because we're not guaranteed anything–we're not guaranteed tomorrow. God doesn't want us to sit back on our laurels and just watch time pass by. He wants us to be active in sharing. I think Brook's death has made me be a lot more bold in that sense."

Those were not just empty words on Aaron's part. Leaving the Devaney Center after the FCA event, his heart was heavy with grief. "But driving back to my apartment," he said, "I gained a real peace. I knew where Brook was and I was glad for him. My tears were gone when I arrived home where my girlfriend, Jill, and my roommate,

Phil, and his girlfriend were waiting. They were all still shaken up over the news of Brook's death and were amazed that I had gained such a calm.

"Phil and his girlfriend left shortly. I knew it was time for Jill and me to have a serious talk. I told her that if she and I were going to have a lasting relationship, she needed to know Jesus personally also. She was more than ready. I got my Bible and we went through John 3:16, Romans 3:23 and 6:23. Then we looked at John 14:6 and flipped back to Romans 10:9. I asked Jill if she wanted to pray and give her life to Christ, and she did." Jill later became Aaron's wife.

In light of the brevity of life which Brook's death demonstrated so clearly, many others have shared Aaron's sentiments on the necessity to share the Gospel. UNL graduate assistant coach Chad Stanley has a keen insight on Brook. He was Brook's freshman year roommate, Husker teammate, and fellow Kansan. Speaking of Brook's last day on earth, he remembers, "I got to eat lunch that day with Brook for the last time. In a way, it was like this was my last meal with him before God called him home. It really impacted my life. I know I couldn't have gotten through it (his death) without my spiritual life.

"The memories I hold of Brook are those of starting out in this football program as freshmen, a little tentative and scared at first. Being away from home for the first time and confined to a small dorm room, though, you really grow with a person. We found out a lot about each other during long talks into the night. He referred to his father a lot, especially the hunting and fishing trips they had together. Brook was very young when his father tragically got cancer and died. That had a great impact on him. He'd talk well into the night about all the little fishing holes his dad took him to. He'd often get choked up talking about it as it tore at him. Not a day went by without him thinking about his father, who had a great, great impact on his life at a young age.

"Brook was a man of character–the way he carried himself just walking down the street, the way he dealt with people. He was just as comfortable talking with a three-year-old as he was a ninety-year-old. He was just that type of guy. He had a lot of charisma and had all the right personality traits. In fact, I always said Brook could have run for governor in Nebraska or Kansas. He just carried himself with a lot of confidence no matter what he was doing, whether it was in the classroom or something simple like playing darts or throwing the football. A lot of that stems from the way his dad had an impact on him before his death. Also, his mother did a great job the way she raised him as a single parent. She was a woman of God, and that had an impact on him, too.

"Then, after Brook became saved and really dedicated his life to Christ, you really saw a Brook Berringer who picked up on such things as community speaking events. He was a guy that always had a lot of irons in the fire, but after that point, Brook really reached out and tried to help anyone he could. He might visit someone sick in the hospital, speak to a Ducks Unlimited group or Pheasants Forever. He was always going out, trying to reach out to people and help them and support them in any way he could. You really saw that part of Brook come out as his confidence grew and his spiritual role grew in Christ."

Not so much of who he was, but because of God's refinement within him, Brook Berringer is a prime example of character to us all. In Christ, God is able to take anyone–from the lowest to the highest–and to transform them beyond any human measure to life as it is really meant to be. "Do not conform any longer to the pattern of this world, but be transformed by the renewing of your mind. Then you will be able to test and approve what God's will is–his good, pleasing and perfect will" (Romans 12:2).

Brook's mother, Jan, a schoolteacher, has been an incredible inspiration to everyone due to her determination to push onward despite crushing circumstances. She lost two obviously important men in her life: her husband, Warren, who lost his fight with cancer when Brook was just seven years old; and Brook, her only son, at the tender age of twenty-two. "Of course," she said, "I want to be with my son again, and I want to be with my husband again. I never dreamed that we would have to go through this again. Losing

Warren was so hard. The day before Brook's accident, I was preparing for the draft party. I began to cry because it was the anniversary of Warren's funeral, and he wasn't going to be here to see his son get drafted. It just tore me up that this was going to be another special event that Warren was going to miss. Then the next day I got a phone call that Brook's not here, either.

"I want to be with them again. You don't know what life is going to deal you. It's just a reminder that our time on this earth is so short, and it is so important to use it as a time to get ready for our next life.

"There has been a big impact on my life since Brook's death in strengthening my faith. It has made me so much more aware of people who are strong in their faith. Going around on the book tour (*One Final Pass*), I have made a lot of contacts with incredible people who have such strong faith, and that really bolsters me. I'm very supported by a lot of people who cared a lot about Brook—the whole state of Nebraska has been like a big family to me and my daughters. It's been hard in some ways because I'm so vulnerable and exposed as I'm out speaking and doing book signings, trying to spread the message that's in the book. But it has been wonderful, too, that there are so many people who cared so much about Brook and that the message has impacted a lot of people. I figure that if one person is able to hear and respond to the Gospel because of that book, then the whole thing has been worth it.

"I think that as time goes on, instead of Brook being forgotten, we're actually going in the opposite direction. I think he's impacting more lives now than even at the beginning. I get letters from people who tell me what a difference Brook—or the book—has made in their lives. It amazes me that it's ongoing, that people haven't forgotten about him yet. And I'm happy about that.

"I have really appreciated Ron Brown and all of his uplifting comfort. That goes as well for Turner Gill and Tom Osborne and all the staff in the football department at Nebraska who care a lot about us—that has been incredible."

Ron Brown's admiration for Jan Berringer is unparalleled. Ron said, "I love Jan deeply from both afar and up close. I obviously admire how she has been able to keep on after the tragedies in her life. If I didn't know Jan personally, I would be one of the thousands that do admire her from a distance. But through the recruitment, playing career, and death of Brook, my wife Molvina and I have entered into a close friendship with her and both sides of her family. As far as we are concerned, she and her family are members of our family."

On the first anniversary of Brook's death, Ron Brown encouraged his radio audience, "Perhaps a number of you have experienced such a loss of a close family member similar to Jan Berringer. For you, I'd like to comfort you from God's Word, Matthew 11:28-30:

> 'Come to me, all you who are weary and burdened, and I will give you rest. Take my yoke upon you and learn from me, for I am gentle and humble in heart, and you will find rest for your souls. For my yoke is easy and my burden is light.'"

In further reflection of that fateful day of April 18, 1996, Ron observed, "It was no coincidence that the Fellowship of Christian Athletes Banquet in Lincoln occurred on the night of Brook's death. Several fellow athletes shared their Christian testimonies. Brook was scheduled to be one of those who shared. Instead, the man God used to lead Brook Berringer to faith in Jesus Christ, Arthur Lindsay, a Lincoln businessman, had the awesome responsibility of speaking on behalf of Brook." This is part of what he had to say.

"I remember so clearly the first time God told me to pray for Brook. It intensified across the years to the point where I was praying for him every day. When we finally got together, I just shared the Good News about Jesus Christ with him from the very start.

"Then last August 24, we sat down on the steps of his home and I said to him, 'Brook, we've talked about Christ a lot, and I've challenged you to give your life to Him. Have you given your life to Him yet?'

"He said, 'I have never really understood what that meant.'

"So I said, as I opened the Bible, 'Well, Brook, it begins right here, John 3:16,' and we read, 'For God so loved the world that he gave his one and only Son that whoever believes in him shall not perish, but shall have eternal life.' I said, 'That's the basis that God begins with.'

"I flipped over to the book of Romans, chapter 3, verse 23. I said, 'But, Brook, you have a problem: "For all have sinned and fall short of the glory of God." That's you. That's me.'

"We went on to Romans 6:23, '"For the wages of sin is death, but the gift of God is eternal life in Christ Jesus our Lord." Brook, you can't pay the penalty. Jesus paid the penalty. The only thing you and I deserve is eternity in hell! But the gift of God is offered to us freely in Christ.'

"We went on over to Romans 10:9, 'That if you confess with your mouth that Jesus is Lord, and believe in your heart that God raised him from the dead you will be saved.'

"Then we capped it off that evening with 1 John 1:9: 'If we confess our sins, He is faithful and just and will forgive us our sins and purify us from all unrighteousness.'

"I said, 'Brook, does that make sense?'

"He said, 'Yes.'

"I said, 'Would you like to pray about it?'

"He said, 'Yes.'

"We joined together in prayer for several minutes as he committed his life to Christ.

"The next week I brought him a Bible. When I gave it to him, I asked, 'Brook, when you came to the University of Nebraska, how many plays did you know?'

"He said, 'I didn't know any.'

"I said, 'Well, how many do you know now?"

"He said, 'I know them all!'

"I said, 'Oh, so Tom calls a play, you run down to the locker room, get out the playbook, look it up to see what the play is, you run back on the field and you run the play.'

"He said, 'No, Coach calls a play–we run it!'

"I said, 'Brook, this is your playbook. You have to know this Book just as well, and better than you know the University of Nebraska playbook.'

"So Brook started memorizing Scripture. Each week I'd give him one or two more verses. I'd like to share with you just a couple of his favorites. From Psalm 103, the first three verses:

'Praise the Lord, O my soul; all my inmost being, praise his holy name. Praise the Lord, O my soul, and forget not all his benefits, Who forgives all your sins and heals all your diseases.'

"Another one of Brook's favorite verses was 2 Corinthians 5:17: 'Therefore, if anyone is in Christ he is a new creation: the old has gone, the new has come.'

"Last fall, it seems like it was maybe October, Brook and I were sitting at the training table. We had shared some Scriptures together, and we were ready to have prayer. With the potential of his NFL career in mind, I asked him, 'Brook, what do you really want?'

"He said, 'What do you mean?'

"I said, 'You know, what do you want to see happen in the next four or five years?'

"His eyes sparkled intently as he answered, 'All I really want is to grow in my relationship with Jesus Christ. This is the greatest thing that ever happened to me!'

"Oh, the beauty of this young man's life! Isn't it marvelous that God can accomplish so much in one young life in just 22 years? What a tremendous, tremendous challenge He gives to us.

"If any of you, any of you who knew him, ever want to see him again, you have to go to heaven. If you ever want to see him again, that's where Brook is.

"I just praise God for the delight of this young man who knew what he wanted, and more than anything else, he wanted to glorify Christ in his life. And he does that."

In the months that followed what most people considered a tragic event, Brook's testimony of life and faith spread rapidly across the Midwest. Thousands attended his memorial service in Goodland, Kansas, while tens of thousands more watched on television and listened by radio. The earnestness by which his friends and family spoke of their hope and faith in an all-knowing God was a lasting inspiration to multitudes. Ron Brown summed it up about as well as anyone with his poignant challenge, "If you're not ready to die, you're not ready to live!" Brook Berringer was ready for both.

Through the publication of his life story, *One Final Pass*, five months later, countless lives have been transformed through its vital message that in the last nine months of his life, Brook's primary desire was "to grow in my relationship with Jesus Christ. This is the greatest thing that ever happened to me."

"And by faith he still speaks,
even though he is dead" (Hebrews 11:4).

CHAPTER 19

PRAYER— A FOUNDATION

W e live in the midst of a violent generation, spurred on by a media which seems to relish the reporting of what is most bizarre and ungodly. In such a topsy-turvy world, it is natural for so many to want to tune it all out and be left alone. But just the opposite should be the battle cry of every believer. Persistence, regardless of apparent circumstances, is so vital to the walk of every man and woman of God. Endurance under trial and perseverance against all obstacles is what every child of God should demand of himself or herself.

The most unusual coaching invitation Ron ever received came after the 1995 championship from the head coach of the New England Patriots, who asked him, "How would you feel about coming home?" Naturally, returning to the East was of interest, but nothing more. In another instance, it was reported on the news that Ron was going to the University of Pittsburgh. The truth of the matter is that he had never been contacted. Even so, unless one is careful, Satan will used such falsehoods to get one's eyes off the Lord and create desires that are not in God's will. We must be in constant communication with God to learn His plan for our lives.

Persistency of purpose in pressing on toward the goal is the key. In the game of football, it is self-evident. A player on one team sticks to his assignment like glue. An opposing player gives up before the whistle. That makes all the difference.

The need for persistence is the same in the spiritual realm. Jesus Christ taught that our first responsibility is to take care of the little matters first. In the parable of the talents in chapter 19 of Luke, He commended and rewarded the good servant, "because you have been trustworthy in a very small matter." Communicating with God in prayer will make us ready when unexpected opportunities present themselves. We can pray during seemingly inconsequential moments while waiting for an appointment, at the checkout counter, or in heavy traffic on a hot afternoon. Dr. Frank Laubauch, in his powerful little book, *Prayer–the Mightiest Force in the Universe*, challenged God's people to fill the innumerable chinks of time in their daily lives with prayer.

Throughout the Word of God, the primary spiritual injunction to men and women is that they should pray, that they should turn to the Lord God Creator first and foremost. This must seem like a small matter to most, since very few take it to heart. There is this emphasis for two reasons. First of all–and this is the underlying truth of all the Holy Scriptures–God deeply desires to be in intimate communion with men and women and boys and girls. Second, it is their ultimate source of strength. In his Gospel, Luke wrote, "Jesus told his disciples a parable to show them that they should always pray and not give up" (18:1).

This unique relationship, which a believer can have with the Almighty, was observed by Moses more than 3,400 years ago: "What other nation is so great as to have their gods near them the way the Lord our God is near us whenever we pray to him?" (Deuteronomy 4:7)

Who, then, is the primary beneficiary of prayer? Who needs it most, God or man? It has been said that prayer changes things. But that is not true. "Things" has little to do with it. What prayer does change–indeed, transforms–is the one involved in the praying, the persistent pursuer of God. Leo Tolstoy, Russian novelist and social critic at the turn of the century, wrote, "Everybody thinks of changing humanity, and nobody thinks of changing himself."

The one challenge that God gave the world–which is guaranteed to bring about change in those involved–is prayer. Loren Sanny, former president of the Navigators, taught that "prayer is not request time. It is reporting for duty time." It is an opportune time for the created to get directions directly from the Creator.

Elisha, in 2 Kings chapter 6, is a sterling example of a man who was not disheartened by any threat of the world because he was in intimate communion with God. Elisha talked with and knew and trusted the Lord. His servant, on the other hand, obviously was not a man of prayer; he was terrified because of the army of Arameans surrounding them, seeking to snare Elisha.

"'Oh, my lord, what shall we do?' the servant asked.
"'Don't be afraid,' the prophet answered. 'Those who are with us are more than those who are with them.'
"And Elisha prayed, 'O Lord, open his eyes so he may see.' Then the Lord opened the servant's eyes, and he looked and saw the hills full of horses and chariots of fire all around Elisha" (2 Kings 6:15-17).

Anyone who knows Ron Brown at all realizes very soon that he recognizes the invaluable contribution many people make to his life in prayer. "I have found that women, especially, have had an incredible impact on my ministry," he says with apparent appreciation. "Nancy Wach and Cindy McKillip are outstanding examples, among many, that God has raised up in intercessory ministry. They are ranchers' wives way out in western Nebraska who have developed an incredible outreach for God through their dedication as prayer warriors. And another woman who not only is a blessing to me, but to many others, is Grandma Cooley. The amazing vitality God gives this ninety-two-year-old saint has also made her a favorite among the kids as a regular inspirational speaker at the I CAN camps."

Ron, too, realizes his own personal need for prayer time. Certainly he is known for scouring the Scriptures, to which his well-worn and marked-up Bible is testimony. But he admits that God has been challenging him to develop a more advanced, more intimate prayer life based on his love for Scripture. There have been days when he has allowed his hectic schedule to negotiate the "non-negotiable" of quiet time, and Ron has paid for it dearly. He insists, though, that "public worship without one's own quiet time is like a dark cloud without rain." It is in spending time alone with God that a man or woman builds inspiration and determination to express that joy and peace outwardly.

Without that inner strength, Ron Brown and others like him would surely cave in to the pressures that mount against anyone who takes such a bold stand for God. Amazingly, Ron gets a share of hate mail. That might be understandable if he were advocating some devious plan to cause harm to others or to bring honor to himself. If he were speaking lies and ill will, condemnation might be deserved. But his message of challenge consistently has been to bring meaning to life through the Lordship of Jesus Christ and unity among all believers. The instruction of Ephesians 4:2-6 is clear and straightforward:

> "Be completely humble and gentle; be patient, bearing with one another in love. Make every effort to keep the unity of the Spirit through the bond of peace. There is one body and one Spirit–just as you were called to one hope when you were called–one Lord, one faith, one baptism; one God and Father of all, who is over all and through all and in all."

One shining example of unity for which he has been an instigator and motivator is a circle of prayer in the middle of the field after every Cornhusker football game, home or away. A few times in the decade, it has been a contingent of only Nebraska players and coaches, but more gratifyingly, almost always there is a mixture of team jerseys–winners and losers–bowing in honor and praise to the Lord God Almighty. Increasingly, across the years, more and more fans watch and wait as the prayer circle goes on beyond their hearing. Then, as they finally stand and begin moving toward locker rooms at either end of the field, appreciative, powerful applause arises from the thousands of people still watching from the stands.

Not everyone, unfortunately, approves. The American Civil Liberties Union protests strongly about the postgame prayer and other Christian activities, but no injunctions have been issued.

In our walk with Christ, however, we are not to be concerned with what others say about us or do to us. That is not our standard by which we march. We do not pray "on street corners to be seen of men" (Matthew 6:5). It is a matter of giving open praise and glory to God for His countless blessings. Knowing that they would face opposition, in some of His final words to His disciples, the Lord Jesus said:

> "'If the world hates you, keep in mind that it hated me first. If you belonged to the world, it would love you as its own. As it is, you do not belong to the world, but I have chosen you out of the world. That is why the world hates you'" (John 15:18-19).

It was with this understanding–and the assurance it gives in a hostile world–that Peter and John were able to withstand the threats of rulers.

> "Then they called them in again and commanded them not to speak or teach at all in the name of Jesus. But Peter and John replied, 'Judge for yourselves whether it is right in God's sight to obey you rather than God. For we cannot help speaking about what we have seen and heard'" (Acts 4:18-20).

It is time for the children of God to get serious about their individual responsibility of bearing witness to the truth that is in Jesus Christ. To stand against the forces of evil which are so prevalent and pervasive in this world, a man, a woman, a child must be bathed in prayer. The mighty strength of the Eternal Father is always available–only a prayer away.

CHAPTER 20

LESSONS IN LOSING

Not everything we experience in life is to our liking. Indeed, if we were able to design every circumstance, it would be far different from the harsh reality which often befalls us. It is so important, therefore, for a believer to be able to see what is happening and to know what is really going on—what God's plan is. Nowhere in Scripture does God promise to change our circumstances; instead, His encouragement is that He will enable us to live above them. That is why we need always to be alert to a higher goal—His goal. Our assurance, therefore, does not come from what happens, but from the One who has a plan. A verse which has been a powerful uplift for Ron Brown, and one he quotes often, is Psalm 84:11: "For the Lord God is a sun and shield; the Lord will give grace and glory; no good thing will he withhold from them who walk uprightly" (KJV).

Certainly this insight was sorely needed by the 1996 version of the Nebraska Cornhuskers. It would have been good to be able to see beyond their present circumstances to something greater that God had for them. Expected to be the first team ever to win three consecutive national championships in football, they started out in glorious fashion, whipping Michigan State convincingly, 55-14. The Big Red was way ahead in the polls, holding on to the #1 position, just as they had in the preseason voting. *Sports Illustrated* featured Nebraska as its cover story.

Things couldn't be better in Lincoln, Nebraska.

Indeed, everything might have been okay if they could just have stayed at home. But the Cornhuskers had a return trip to Sun Devil Stadium where at the first of the year they had overwhelmed Florida. Anticipation for a relatively easy win was rampant for the nationally televised evening performance. Thousands of ardent fans flew to Tempe for the contest. Tens of thousands of others set up TV parties in their homes and places of business. Some, looking ahead and not wanting to miss the big show, booked their New Year's flights and hotel accommodations in New Orleans for the national championship game.

Perhaps the team members were also looking ahead. Or perhaps they just lost their focus. At any rate, the defense stalled and the offense sputtered. Seemingly without warning, the wheels came off the Big Red machine, and it crashed to a 19-0 loss, falling to Arizona State. Incredibly, Nebraska gave up six points by suffering three safeties in the game.

As hard as it was to do, players and coaches had to "suck it up," put the game behind them, and start serious preparations for the next game the next week. They had no time to bemoan the loss.

Some irate fans replayed the game over and over. In doing so, many lost their perspective. It was such a difficult turn of events for some that a local television station announced an 800 number for people to call for free distress counseling.

With back-to-back national championships to their credit, the coaching staff was almost beyond reproach. Player for player, the team had a large carryover from the previous year and was considered sound. The only culprit, it was concluded by many, was the man behind the ball–the quarterback. (That loses sight of the fact that football is a highly organized and integrated team sport, requiring the united effort of dozens of players.) Nonetheless, in the days and months that followed the loss to Arizona State, quarterback Scott Frost was the target of substantial verbal and printed abuse.

As was observed in a previous chapter, criticism, whether warranted or not, is a fact of life in this present world. What a man or woman does in the face of such opposition becomes the measure of who he or she is. One of the greatest men of God since the writing of the New Testament was Saint Francis of Assisi, who lived during the thirteenth century. He was a man of great piety, who desired to lift up the less fortunate through a life devoted to the needs of other. Nevertheless, he had many detractors. So cruel were his tormentors that in the latter days of his life, he removed himself from the relative comfort of Assisi to dwell in a humble cottage out of town. His prayer for guidance in sorting through criticism has been a model for more than 700 years:

> Lord, Make me an instrument of your peace.
> Where there is hatred, let me sow love;
> Where there is injury, pardon;
> Where there is doubt, faith;
> Where there is despair, hope;
> Where there is darkness, light;
> And where there is sadness, joy.

> Divine Master, grant that I may not so much seek
> to be consoled as to console;
> to be understood as to understand;
> to be loved as to love;
> for it is in giving that we receive;
> it is in pardoning that we are pardoned;
> and it is in dying that we are
> born to eternal life.

Scott Frost had to shoulder the burden of public scrutiny—whether fair or not—and get on with the task at hand. Ron Brown recalled a moment with the young man from Wood River at the next practice. Scott was kneeling on one knee along the sideline during a break in the action. He had sunk to a level lower than he had ever known in his life. But he was made of sterner stuff. Quit and run was not an option for him. In a contemplative attitude, with tears in his eyes, he asked, "Coach, what happened Saturday night (referring to the ASU game)?"

"Scott," Ron responded with a hand on the quarterback's shoulder, "remember, Jesus Christ has a wonderful plan for your life."

In reflecting on that moment, Ron said, "I saw Scott like a rubber ball that had been squeezed tight, no air left in him. But he wasn't like a wad of paper–once you crumple it up, you can't do anything with it; all you can do is throw it away. I was confident Scott would bounce back."

Scott knew about the Lord and considered himself a Christian, having made a decision at an early age. At this most crucial time in his life, however, he realized he never had truly committed himself to God. Football was the centerpiece of his world. "I sat back after that game," he explained, "which athletically was the toughest week of my life because we had to bounce back from that low point and play the next Saturday. But more significantly, it was difficult personally because what I cared for most was all of a sudden pulled out from under my feet.

"As a result, I learned that if I put my faith in God, and play football for Him, and do everything else I do for Him, make Him number one in my life, no one can rip that away from me. No matter what happens, I'll always have that relationship with God. So my focus shifted to where it ought to be." He had learned in the throes of agonizing defeat that there is only one victory that matters–the victory that comes through a personal relationship with Jesus Christ.

Incredibly, as the 1996 season progressed, the Cornhuskers–setting together a string of nine straight victories–won the Northern Division of the new Big 12 and were in contention to make the New Year's trip to New Orleans after all. The only thing that stood in Nebraska's way was the first ever Big 12 Championship game in St. Louis. The University of Texas had won the Southern Division of the conference, but Nebraska was a solid favorite to take the crown. The Longhorns, however, were well prepared for the game, and the score was nip and tuck. The turning point in the game proved to be a faked punt in the fourth quarter, which, instead of giving the ball over to Nebraska, resulted in a Texas touchdown.

The 37-27 loss dropped the Huskers out of contention for the national championship and sent them instead to Miami for an Orange Bowl matchup with Virginia Tech. In winning that contest

41-21, the Big Red started a new winning streak for themselves and set their sights on a return to Miami. The 1997 National Championship game was scheduled for that same Pro Player Stadium, and the Cornhuskers were determined to be there. Alert to the possibilities, they could see beyond their present circumstances and set their sights on something higher. Just as Scott Frost refused to be wadded up as a piece of paper, the entire Husker team was popping back into shape.

In the spiritual realm, no believer should ever settle for life as it is. It is not, however, by our own strength that we pull ourselves up. Rather, as Philippians 2:13 says, "It is God who works in you to will and to act according to his good purpose." Do you—does anyone—know what marvelous things God has in store in His divine plan? If we are attentive, always yearning to be in the center of His will, sometimes He opens doors of opportunity far beyond anything we ever thought possible. We need, therefore, to be prepared whether God leads us to speak to the guttermost or the uttermost. Our message, from the heart, should always be the same. We should be in tune with Psalm 119:46: "I will speak of your statutes before kings and will not be put to shame." God, by His grace, calls all of His children to life as it ought to be, as He designs it. Such eternal hope is surely what Paul envisioned when, under the inspiration of the Spirit, he penned the words of Romans 5:1-5:

> "Therefore, since we have been justified through faith, we have peace with God through our Lord Jesus Christ, through whom we have gained access by faith into this grace in which we now stand. And we rejoice in the hope of the glory of God. Not only so, but we also rejoice in our sufferings because we know that suffering produces perseverance; perseverance, character; and character, hope. And hope does not disappoint us because God has poured out his love into our hearts by the Holy Spirit whom he has given us."

CHAPTER 21

SIGNIFICANT OPPORTUNITIES

E very Christian heart should beat with exultation that God has put us in His world for a beautiful and wonderful purpose. There is no room in the Kingdom of God for a lukewarm Christian–it is a matter of all or nothing at all. There is something invigorating about throwing oneself wholeheartedly into a particular endeavor for Christ. There are joys and thrills beyond imagination for any believer who answers God's call to immerse himself or herself unreservedly into the spiritual warfare which goes on day-by-day without abatement.

In every step of His creation, God, by speaking it, employed a divine design which He Himself classified as "good." There was no such thing as better or best, nothing comparable–only good. Everything had its function–"after its kind." When God turned to His ultimate creation, however, He handcrafted man "in His own image." To man he ascribed an eternal purpose: the joy of knowing fellowship.

Though thousands of years of disobedience have battered and marred that original design, it is still God's desire to restore it, one sinner at a time.

To accomplish this, in His divine plan God presents every believer with opportunities to be a witness to the truth about Christ. Such ordained moments may be fleeting, they may be subtle, or even obscure. The key responsibility of the child of God, therefore, is to be aware of those openings and to take advantage of them.

Kellen Knight, a high school teenager from Ogallala, Nebraska, is a sterling example of zealousness well beyond her years. She first began writing Coach Brown after the death of Brook Berringer, which dramatically affected her life, shaking her up spiritually. "She has such a heart for Jesus," Ron says. "Her letters are long and rich with Scripture, and her prayer life is deep. She has been a great encouragement to me. I've met her at FCA events out there and know she is a great young lady in the Lord.

"I want to encourage those kinds of kids, guys and girls who are in high school, to grow in their faith. I want that same zeal to be kept alive."

John Hanus, husband to Penne, Ron's ministry assistant, is an example of another kind of zeal, expressed in a quiet mode of availability. When Ron first talked to Penne about the help he needed, she explained up front that she would want her husband to be involved as well. From the first time the two couples got together, Ron said, "It seemed to be a real natural fit. Since then, as Penne makes further contact with the speaking engagements I'm able to accept, it gives me valuable time to pray about the event to see what God's heart is on the matter. John also has been an invaluable part of the team as he gives of his time willingly at events all across the state by driving me to the events and then praying during the event itself."

In his own walk of faith across the years, countless avenues have opened up for Ron Brown to share his faith. His weekly radio broadcast, "Husker Sports Report," has been the most prominent. In that forum, Ron not only highlights Christian insights in the world of sports, but also challenges listeners to make waves in their own spheres of influence.

In late 1998, during a three-week series of those broadcasts, Mark Todd, producer of the program, did the interviewing in a reversal of their normal roles. "Ron," he asked, "is there any connection between Christianity and the success of the Nebraska football program over the years?"

"I think it really depends," Ron responded, "on how you define success. I don't know how much it translates into wins and losses, as the world would normally define success. I do know that we are called as Christians to step out and live a life that is transformed radically by Jesus Christ. That means that in my coaching and in the way I do business around here it has to be for the Kingdom. So, I'm going after a much bigger win than whether we beat Colorado or win a national championship. I'm going after a win for God, and that could be taking place whether we are on top in the final score or at the back end of it."

"How do you see your role as a coach in this program?" Mark asked.

"I've often asked myself," Ron answered energetically, "why am I even here in Nebraska. I mean, I had no prior association with the state. I really believe that I was called to come here by the Lord and that He used Tom Osborne to bring me here as the receivers coach simply to remind people who Jesus Christ is. Not that I'm the only one doing it, believe me! I don't think that at all. But I'm one of the instruments God is using. Just like every person that lives in the state of Nebraska has a very similar role in terms of what we're supposed to be in Christ. We're to remind this state of who Jesus is.

"If I had a mission statement in my coaching–and everything I do–it would be one: to intimately know Jesus; and two: to intentionally make Him known. Each of us has a different gift and a different bent in the presentation of the Gospel and proclamation of it. God has given me a gift to evangelize and He has put me in opportunities to be very outspoken and very verbal about my faith. Just because a person is not in the same evangelical situation, or doesn't have the same platform as I do, doesn't mean they are any less of a committed Christian.

"Sometimes people give me credit because they hear from me a lot. But that doesn't necessarily mean I'm a great Christian. In fact, I spend probably too much time wishing I was a better man. I view my many failures too much like a player who too often worries about what the game film of his performance will look like. I've got a long, long way to go to truly be even close to what one would call 'Christ-like.' But praise God He decided to use even me. I have opportunities to share with my players–and I'm not talking about proselytizing or jamming things down their throats. But players who come up to me and say, 'Coach Brown, I heard you speak at this event, or I saw you on TV. I've watched you here for four straight years do things this way or say things this way, and I want to know what that is all about.' I've had newspaper reporters and media people come to me and say, 'I want to do a story on what it means to be born again.' These are incredible opportunities. And they're not just doing it for a story. I think a number of them are doing it for their own personal inquiry as well.

"Then, of course, I have opportunity because I'm in the media a fair amount due to the fact that the sphere of influence football around here is very large. So it's been great to work with some of the other coaches in ministry. George Darlington, who was out there long before I was here, is sharing his faith. Turner Gill, who also played for Nebraska, is a guy who really lives out his faith in Christ genuinely and consistently. Craig Bohl, who is a personal prayer partner of mine, is a man of wisdom who loves the Lord. Nelson Barnes, our rush ends coach, is a joyful Christian on our staff. Chad Stanley, one of our grad assistants, is a passionate young man of faith. Dave Gillespie has a truly quiet demeanor in Christ. And there are other people in the athletic department at the university, new Christians I'm finding out about all the time.

"We're all in this together. And combined with all the other people across the state and those in the listening audience who love the Lord Jesus Christ, we're one big team. And we need to be carrying out our individual roles every single day. Every time we back down from the Gospel, we fail as a team. But, every time we step up to the plate and take the swing we're supposed to take with the gifts God has given us, then we win for Christ as a team. I just want to do my part.

"One of the greatest prayers that I could ever utter is, 'God, open my eyes so that I see what You see.' When I look at a player who may be in a struggling situation, or even a player who has had great success and it looks like the world is adoring him, can I see beyond just what the world sees? When I look at a job opportunity that's been offered to me, that might add to my personal esteem or reputation or what have you, am I looking at it through the grid of

Scripture and God's point of view? Or am I looking at it from my own point of view? Those are the type of issues I deal with and I pray about every single day.

"It's just been neat to see people like Aaron Wills and Brook Berringer, just to name a couple out of so many guys, whose lives have been changed here in this football program and then the influence they have had.

"Psalm 119:46 declares, 'I will speak of your statutes before kings and will not be put to shame.' I'm not going to let anyone intimidate me from sharing the Gospel."

Focusing on that train of thought, Mark suggested, "Talk about some of the changed lives you've seen over the years within the Nebraska football program."

"There have been so many transformed lives, but let me begin with something exciting about the Fellowship of Christian Athletes Bible study we do in the middle of the week. In 1997, that averaged about five or six each week. In 1998, that number is up around forty on a rather regular basis. There are a number of guys whose lives have been changed and several others who are very curious, inquiring about who is this Jesus Christ? This is because of the difference they are seeing in the lives of so many others.

"Aaron Wills, whom I mentioned, is one who sticks in my mind. God has totally transformed his life–and this is after a lot of people tried a lot of different ways. Aaron confirms that they used psychology and other social strategies and none of it worked. But a newfound relationship in Jesus Christ did change his life.

"We've also heard the incredible story of Brook Berringer. Brook was a much different person than Aaron Wills. Brook was not in the world as we know it, the way Aaron was. Even though we didn't get the idea that Brook was a 'born again Christian' when he first came to Nebraska, he was a good kid, a pretty moral guy. And on the outward appearance, one might have called him a Christian. But inwardly, even he himself admitted there was something missing. And when he trusted Jesus as his Savior and Lord, little did any of us know that eight months later he would die. The kind of life he lived, the football experience he had here–the ups and downs of it, and the way he carried himself after he became a Christian, when he died in that plane crash, so many lives were moved. A lot of people began to realize, 'Hey man, I'm not indestructible. If this guy could die, I could die. And what happens when you die? And where do you go? A lot of guys on our football team had these questions. Forget all the fan applause, forget the national championships. This was something that was staring them right in the face and they had to do something about it; they couldn't put it off any longer. Numerous people across this state, including a number of our players, came to know Jesus Christ as a result of what we call a tragedy–the death of Brook Berringer.

"But really, it wasn't the tragedy; it was the life that was living inside Brook when he died–the life of Jesus Christ. Now Brook lives in heaven and now many more will have a home reserved in heaven because of what has taken place.

"And there are many other individual stories. We don't have time to talk about them all. But at the risk of sounding like we're exalting these athletes–and that's the last thing I want to do because there are too many people who do that–they are in very influential positions. In the state of Nebraska, these guys have a lot of influence, there is so much attention given to them. I don't think it's right, and I don't believe God looks down on it with enjoyment. But because of the sinful nature we have, and how we put undeserved glory on people, I think it's important to pray for these guys because they're going to be in pivotal positions. These kids get a chance to go out and share their experiences–good and bad–with kids and adults across this state. If what is coming out of their hearts and mouths is a life with Jesus Christ, that can have an enormous impact on the mood of this state. So I would be praying for the personal discipleship of the Christian athletes in this program."

"What then," Mark asked, "are some practical ways listeners can be witnesses in their own spheres of influence?"

"Every single person across this state," Ron intoned emphatically, "who has trusted Jesus as their Savior and Lord, has been sovereignly and personally placed here by God. He has an incredible role for them. Whether we like it or not, people are watching us. In a sense, we are all in the public eye. You can be certain that there is somebody who is a non-Christian who is watching you, if they know you're a Christian. If people do not know you are a Christian, then something's wrong. I'm not saying you have to stand up on the rooftop at your job and shout it out. But I think our lifestyle, the way we do business, the way we talk, the way we say things, ought to be so Christ-like that it can't be but a radical difference from what the world is used to seeing. People will eventually find out. Then we have to have the guts to speak up about what makes us different. God gave us a voice to use to glorify Him, to sing praises to Him in church, and to sing praises to Him even in a secular environment.

"I believe we can learn about performance and showcasing the abilities and talents God has given us. What these athletes do in football, we can do the same thing spiritually in the world in which we live. Ephesians 6:19 is a good verse to chew on in this regard: 'Pray also for me, that whenever I open my mouth, words may be given me so that I will fearlessly make known the mystery of the gospel.'"

"Ron," Mark observed, "you are probably as vocal as anyone in professing your faith in this entire athletic program at the University of Nebraska. How do your superiors respond to your sharing and outspokenness?"

"No one has reprimanded me on it," Ron answered forthrightly. "In fact, from time to time, I've gotten a note of appreciation from different superiors on a particular issue. I'm not necessarily saying that they buy into everything I'm saying or everything I'm doing, but within the constitutional rights I have, and by the university policy, I believe I have behaved myself in a manner that would be considered honorable. Therefore, no one has reprimanded me. Now, I have received criticism in letters from the ACLU and others. I get anonymous mail from people who don't appreciate the cause of Christ or kingdom business. And that's fine, that's part of the territory. Yet, I'm to continue on with the business at hand. I will not be intimidated. Like I've said, this is the reason I'm here. I do try to respect the authority under which God has placed me without any violation at all of God's law.

"In 1 Peter 4:16, we are challenged, 'However, if you suffer as a Christian, do not be ashamed, but praise God that you bear that name.' It is natural for a person to feel ashamed when he is being ostracized for sharing his faith or living it out. I think that every Christian who has ever done that has lived through that experience of a sense of shame. But the Bible clearly tells us to not go there, do not allow yourself to feel shameful. You're doing the right thing. God will be glorified, and He keeps perfect records. We're on the winning team!"

CHAPTER 22

MISSION NEBRASKA

I t is truly exciting that every man, woman, and child in the Kingdom of God is called upon to be prepared as His witnesses. "Always be prepared to give an answer to everyone who asks you to give the reason for the hope that you have" (1 Peter 3:15). In this, God does not demand anything beyond our ability. He does not ask us to run before we have at least learned the fundamentals of walking. His requirements are quite simple for all of His children: be prepared. Then when an opportunity presents itself, take action.

During his first eleven years as a coach for the Cornhuskers, Ron Brown had many opportunities to speak in communities across the state, often sharing the Gospel of Jesus Christ. Even though he enjoyed his speaking engagements, he knew that something was missing in his ministry. This clearly became evident to Ron while wrestling with God's will during the Tampa Bay coaching decision. "I had been praying and felt the Lord was saying that I needed to find a partner in ministry," said Ron.

He called Stan Parker to talk about the spiritual need he sensed throughout the state. Stan himself had been praying for several months about where his call to evangelism could most effectively be expressed. As the two men talked, they discovered they had a shared heart for the state and for evangelism. Over the next seven months, they continued to pray about the direction this could take. At the end of that time, they were convinced that God had called them to partner together in launching an evangelistic ministry. They founded Mission Nebraska in March 1998.

Ron believes that one of the real strengths of the two men being paired together in ministry is their dissimilarities. "Stan," he says, "is a processor and very methodical. He is very gifted in leadership and in moving others into leadership. I, on the other hand, am spontaneous and passionate. I'm a leader by example, saying 'catch me if you can.'"

Stan Parker observed from the onset of the ministry: "We've come to clarity on what we believe is at the very heart of God for this state. The way we articulate is that we believe that God wants to see Christ proclaimed across the entire state of Nebraska, giving every individual an authentic opportunity to hear and respond to the Gospel. We believe that happens as the body of Christ recaptures her call to the Great Commission, then uniting around that call, is strengthened and works together for its fulfillment. In capsule form, it is to see the whole church take the Gospel to the whole state, generation after generation."

Stan, who played tight end for the Nebraska Cornhuskers as a freshman before switching to guard in 1986, was influenced by Brad Olson, a senior who lived next door in his apartment building. That witness created in Stan a desire to search out the truth in Jesus Christ. He came face to face with the fact he was created by God, for God, and committed himself totally to the Master.

After graduation, Stan went on staff with the Fellowship of Christian Athletes, taking on the responsibility for Omaha and northeast Nebraska. After serving there for seven years, he joined the ministry of the First Evangelical Free Church in Lincoln as a co-pastor of student ministries. He and Ron were both involved in reaching out to the lost, but they were functioning in two different circles of influence. In coming together, they wanted to see a multiplication of ministry as their individual gifts were complementary to one another.

In order to get started, Ron says, "Stan and I prayed intensely about what God strategically has set in motion to reach every person in Nebraska with the Gospel. We have traveled the state, we've talked to ministry leaders and individual Christians across Nebraska, and we are seeing five points that we believe flow from God's heart. They are becoming more crystal clear than ever."

God's Passion

Stan Parker stated, "The first point, one which is clear in the Word of God and which has been clarified in our own hearts as we've prayed, is the passion of God for those who are out of relationship with Him, for those who are lost. Luke 19:41 says that when Jesus was approaching the city of Jerusalem and saw the lostness and unbelief that was there, 'He wept over it.' In Luke 13:34, Jesus had previously cried out, 'O Jerusalem, Jerusalem, you who kill the prophets and stone those sent to you, how often I have longed to gather your children together, as a hen gathers her chicks under her wings, but you were not willing!' God's heart is for those who are out of relationship with Him. He is like a father who has lost a child. The urgency level, the energy, the passion that rises within that father over that one lost child would be so great. Yet, that doesn't come close, it doesn't compare, to the energy level that we are convinced resides in the heart of God every single day over not one—even though God sees the one—but over thousands, hundreds of thousands of individuals who are lost and hurting and confused."

God's Pursuit

Ron moves on to observe, "The second truth is that with that urgency comes the pursuit of God. It's one thing to sense the urgency; it is another to actively move out, to go and find the lost. So God includes us in that plan. I'm moved by the parable of the lost sheep in Luke 15:4-6, where Jesus says:

> "'Suppose one of you has a hundred sheep and loses one of them. Does he not leave the ninety-nine in the open country and go after the lost sheep until he finds it? And when he finds it, he joyfully puts it on his shoulders and goes home. Then he calls his friends and neighbors together and says, "Rejoice with me; I have found my lost sheep." I tell you that in the same way there will be more rejoicing in

heaven over one sinner who repents than over ninety-nine righteous persons who do not need to repent.'"

"The problem is that a lot of us in the body of Christ have not left the majority, have not gotten out of our comfort zone. We have enjoyed so much, our fellowship with believers, that we have not been willing to go and find that one lost one. It is God's heart that we bring the lost one home on our shoulders, rejoicing. There is a sense of urgency in joining the pursuit of God in finding that lost one and having all of us celebrate in that glorious victory. Again, it ties into the word picture of the passion of a father who has lost one child.

"When Jesus was on the earth, He dedicated His life to pursuing the lost, and that has not changed to the present day. A gift that God gives us in this whole process is time. Second Peter 3:9 says, 'The Lord is not slow in keeping his promise as some understand slowness. He is patient with you, not wanting anyone to perish, but everyone to come to repentance.' God has given us time on this earth. Otherwise, why are we Christians still here? We should be shot to glory as soon as we become Christians. We're here to join God in the pursuit as He waits patiently for the lost He has called to come to Him. We've got to get busy."

To illustrate this concept, Stan tells of an all-out search in Florida one night for a boy who was lost near a lake. Scores of people searched around the edge of the water, calling out the name of the child. Meanwhile, a helicopter hovered overhead with a search light scanning the area. Everyone bound together in one urgent task. That is the focus of Mission Nebraska.

God's Plan

Ron Brown proceeds to tell of the third point, the plan of God. "God has a definite plan of attack for the pursuit of the lost. He gives us a strategy which is so interesting and so exciting. Romans 10:14–15 says, 'How, then, can they call on the one they have not believed in? And how can they believe in the one of whom they have not heard? And how can they hear without someone preaching to them? And how can they preach unless they are sent? As it is written, How beautiful are the feet of those who bring good news!' Amos 3:7 says, 'Surely the Sovereign Lord does nothing without revealing his plan to his servants, the prophets.'

"God could have done this whole thing by Himself. He could simply save people by Himself. And certainly the power is from Him. But incredibly He includes us in the plan! He calls *us* to preach the Gospel. He sends *us* out as called people to be ambassadors and to represent Him with words, with lifestyle, with everything we are about. It is an amazing concept that we literally can be involved in the most important process that the world could ever know: for people to come to know Jesus Christ."

In agreement, Stan adds, "How much clearer can Jesus put it than in John 20:21, when He declared to His disciples the very evening He was raised from the dead, 'Peace be with you! As the Father has sent me, I am sending you.'"

"Just from coaching football," Ron concluded, "I understand how important the concept of teamwork is. So, I have to ask myself, why am I here in Nebraska? And I think that is a question each one of us has to ask—why am I here?

"God has sovereignly placed each one of us here to accomplish His plan. It is not by accident. Ephesians 4:16 says, 'From him the whole body, joined and held together by every supporting ligament, grows and builds itself up in love, as each part does its work.' Each one of us brings something to the table. God has gifted every single one of us for His purpose. Each has a spiritual gift for knowing Him intimately and can work together in a coordinated fashion so that the world may look and see what true love in Jesus Christ is.

"So we are part of a team. We have to understand that God has brought us here to Nebraska to be part of a team of other believers. If we are going to reach every lost soul in Nebraska, it is going to be a team effort. As a coach, I know that if one position is out of whack, while the other ten positions on the field are working in sync, that team takes on a different flavor than if all eleven are working together. So each of us has a special, definite call, an endowment from God."

Lisa Hitchcock, a homemaker living in Ainsworth, Nebraska, has responded to God's call. She had been greatly helped in her spiritual growth through Christian radio. When she and her family moved to Ainsworth, which was not reached by a Christian radio station, she began to pray about what could be done to bring Christian radio to the Sandhills. She commented, "I felt so insignificant and unable to make an impact on radio in the state. Where could I begin? I didn't know anything different than anyone else."

Nonetheless, she was inspired by God to partner with a group of believers to raise $10,000 for a translator tower to project Christian radio into the Sandhills area of the state. Ron and Stan assisted them by taking part in a community event designed to help with that project, and shared Lisa's excitement when the funds were provided.

After talking with Lisa, Ron thought it was interesting that she asked the question, "Who am I?" "That's a good question," he observed. "I think that is legitimate to ask. But then let the Lord answer. Don't look for a response based on worldly standards. God says you are somebody very special whom He has endowed with gifts. The thing that is wonderful about Lisa's story is that she began to connect the dots. She joined other Christians in God's passion, pursuit, and His plan. Then the mission was accomplished."

God's Picture

Kurt Coddington of Geneva, Nebraska, through a real life experience, illustrates the fourth concept of bringing the picture into focus. Referring to a planned rally with Ron Brown speaking in his community, he said, "We got about twenty or thirty counselors for a short training session before the evening event. We talked about the process we were going to use in case someone came forward expressing a desire to receive Christ. We prayed for Ron and passed out the materials we were going to use. Then we sat and watched as the gym began to fill with about seven hundred people. Those of us who organized the event really didn't know what to expect; we were sort of like Jesus' disciples who didn't understand all that God was trying to do among them. Several of us admitted that we sat there praying, 'O Lord, at least have one or two people come forward when he gives an invitation so that people can see that this is a message with power.'

"When Ron gave the invitation for people to come down and join him in the center of the gym to pray, we sat there waiting and wondering what was going to happen. Soon we heard footsteps of people coming down the bleachers. Then the footsteps turned into a thundering sort of sound as literally hundreds of people came forward. We thought we were so well prepared in having thirty counselors, but as we looked around we knew we had under-estimated how God was going to work that night."

"Concerning the picture, then," Stan said, "Jesus gets at it in Mark 16:15, 'Go into all the world and preach the good news to all creation.' Or, in Acts 1:8, He says, 'But you will receive power when the Holy Spirit comes on you; and you will be my witnesses in Jerusalem, and in all Judea and Samaria, and to the ends of the earth.' In that regard, we believe that God is seeking to create a movement of evangelism that will sweep across the entire state of Nebraska, hitting every single individual.

"Sometimes our tendency is to hold an event or do an outreach to target people, intentionally or unintentionally, who are just like us. They are comfortable to be around. They look like us. They talk like us. But it's interesting that Jesus specifically told them to go to Samaria, people who were racially, culturally different than they. There was even an element of enmity between them. Yet, Jesus called them to go to the Samaritans."

Ron added, "I also like the words, 'to the ends of the earth.' Every nook and cranny in this state we are supposed to investigate and cover like a blanket. To see Christ proclaimed across the entire state of Nebraska, giving every individual an authentic opportunity to hear. That's the picture."

God's Power

"Matthew 9:36-38 really grabs me," Stan said. "And that was interesting, because Ron told me that there was a Scripture that had been hitting him recently. I asked him what it was and it was the same three verses:

> "When he (Jesus) saw the crowds, he had compassion on them, because they were harassed and helpless, like sheep without a shepherd. Then he said to his disciples, 'The harvest is plentiful but the workers are few. Ask the Lord of the harvest, therefore, to send out workers into his harvest field.'

In that section of Scripture, we see Jesus recognizing the need of those who were lost, seeing their condition–they were sheep without a shepherd. They were lost people. He felt compassion for them, he felt that passion of God. He realized that the plan of God was to pursue them through believers. So the direction of His prayer was that God would send workers into the harvest. But the first thing He called us to do was to pray!"

"What is so amazing also," Ron suggested, "is that so often in the body of Christ we expect the harvest to show up on our doorstep. But Jesus puts the emphasis on the workers. He says, 'Get going, workers! Get out there. Get into the harvest which is plentiful.'

"As you read John, chapter 17," Ron added, "which is the prayer Jesus offered on behalf of His disciples to His Father in heaven, in verses 20-21, He prays, 'My prayer is not for them alone. I pray also for those who will believe in me through their message, that all of them may be one, Father, just as you are in me and I am in you. May they also be in us so that the world may believe that you sent me.' It is in our unity, in our connection and our coordination as

Christians, where we really make an impact in people seeing and discovering that there is something different about these people; that Jesus truly is real as He plays out in the interaction of believers. That's why there is no way we can get around the fact that if we are going to reach the state, every lost person for Jesus Christ, and we are going to send out workers, it has to be done in a coordinated connection, connecting the dots as we have talked about so often."

"This is a God-sized thing," Stan declared. "Therefore, it has to start and finish with God. We have to be dependent on Him, seeking to fulfill His purposes, so we have to be on our knees in submission to Him. Then we have to link up arms with other believers God has put in our neighborhoods, our communities, our cities, our state. We have to hook up and come together for the purpose of the Gospel."

"When people call us," Ron concluded, "saying that they believe there is a harvest and they want to get workers out there, the first thing we tell them to do is to pray! Then, when they begin to pray, without dialogue from us for a couple of months, they begin to see things happen. They don't need us to tell them what to do. They begin to hear from God, then begin to see and discover what God has already created right in the midst of them."

Shelly Davey of Norfolk, Nebraska, has prayed for the state, county by county, for five years. "In my women's prayer group," Shelly explained, "we decided we wanted to adopt Nebraska. We took a map of the state and week by week we methodically went through each one of the different counties and prayed for the believers that they would be strengthened, that God would be relevant to them. That He would give them courage and give them a love for the people in their community. When we finished the state, we'd just start all over again."

That is at the heart of the emphasis of Mission Nebraska: developing a strategy of reaching the state of Nebraska county by county with the impact of the Gospel of Christ. It's not that the message isn't already present; rather, that the vision is to extend encouragement to every evangelistic effort, county by county.

"Shelly Davey," Ron said, "is an example of a person whose

prayer life is so advanced that she is sensitized to the voice of God. Not only that, but she seems to have her spiritual eyes opened to the circumstances around her. I think that is a very biblical thing. God wants us to take spiritual inventory across the state to see what He is doing. How can we know what He is doing unless we actually utilize 'spiritual eyesight' to see Him at work? For example, He commanded Moses to send twelve spies to investigate the land of Canaan, the promised land. He said, 'Send men to search the land of Canaan, which I give to the children of Israel.'

"We believe God wants us to see His 'fruit' across this land. Yet, there is a specific strategy. And we cannot know that strategy, we cannot join Him in that strategy unless we have a very active, very detailed prayer life where our spiritual antennae are up and we can see what God is doing and join Him in that process.

"Then when we connect with others in our community who are moving in that same direction, we break down walls and barriers which are between different churches. Two things have to be present when God comes to a community and seeks to move on that community. There has to be a prayer base functioning, and there has to be unity within the body. Mission Nebraska, in that respect, has been raised up to partner with those who are seeking what God wants to do in their community."

CHAPTER 23

1997
NATIONAL CHAMPIONSHIP

Teamwork is the single word which more than any other describes the 1997 version of the Nebraska football team as it fought against odds to an undefeated season and a third national championship in four years. This also is the emphasis of God for His children. His favorite word in this regard is "unity." It is not a unity, however, built on a false assumption that "we are all headed in the same direction." All roads may lead to Rome. But the Lord Jesus Christ said, "Small is the gate and narrow the road that leads to life, and only a few find it" (Matthew 7:13). No, the cohesiveness which God wants for His people is one which recognizes that we each have special gifts to accomplish His divine purposes. This is clearly the challenge in Ephesians 4:11-13:

> "It was he (Jesus) who gave some to be apostles, some to be prophets, some to be evangelists, and some to be pastors and teachers, to prepare God's people for works of service, so that the body of Christ may be built up until we all reach unity in the faith and in the knowledge of the Son of God and become mature, attaining to the whole measure of the fullness of Christ."

Not everyone is a leader in the Kingdom of God with high-powered gifts. Yet, each member of the team has his or her particular role to play. That portion of Scripture goes on to the challenge that we can only realize a maximum effectiveness in the body of Christ "as each part does its work" (Ephesians 4:16). A great example of teamwork took place when an insightful Christian from Oakland, Nebraska, warned Ron about doing a television

233

commercial for a particular adoption agency. The woman had just found out that the agency had placed children in homosexual homes. Ron challenged the executive director of the agency, who admitted to that action. Ron was then able to call off the public service announcement before it was aired.

In football, not many can be the coach, the quarterback, or the one who scores the winning touchdown. But everyone, including the equipment manager and the little boy with his pennant in the top row of the stadium, can be a part of the team if they realize what their part is and do it.

Certainly loyal fans have a significant, if minor, role in a football game. Cheers from the stands can give an added pump of adrenaline to a weary player. Jeers, an ignorant misunderstanding of what is happening on the playing field, have no place in competitive sports. So also it is in the church. Of all the gifts of the Spirit listed in Romans 12:6-8, the one least appropriated is that of encouragement, yet it is so vital. A kind word, a hug, a pat on the back costs nothing to the giver and can give an added boost to one who has grown weary in his or her spiritual walk.

In the church, not everyone is called of God to be out front in the battle, gaining acclaim. But every believer can and should be an active part of the body. It simply requires that they realize what their part is and do it.

The 1997 rendition of the Nebraska Cornhuskers is a striking illustration of all the factors of unity–the necessary give and take of relationships–coming together to achieve a goal. Team members worked hard in the off-season and built a cohesive spirit amongst themselves. Disappointed with their No. 6 ranking in the final poll of the previous season, they were determined to climb back to the top. The Big Red was given little credit for whipping Akron 59-14 in the opener, even though they racked up 644 yards of total offense. Then they dropped to seventh in the polls after giving up 318 passing yards to lowly regarded Central Florida, winning only 38-24.

Sadly, the polling was not the only negative from that game. Coach Tom Osborne had announced to the press in advance that he intended to get back-up quarterback Frankie London into the game in the second quarter, giving him some valuable experience while the game was still in doubt. According to plan, he did so. And Frankie, fine athlete that he is, performed well. Then, according to plan, Osborne sent Scott Frost back in. When he did so, surely one of the ugliest events ever to occur in Memorial Stadium took place: roaring boos erupted from several hundred erstwhile fans. Everyone in the stadium—and millions of others advised by the media—knew that the jeers were pointed directly at one person: Frost. Why? That is unanswerable. Who can explain unreasonable ridicule?

Nonetheless, both football fans and Christians can gain a valuable lesson from that negative incident. Scott could have allowed that ugly incident to fester inside him like a hurtful boil. Instead, he immersed himself for the next several days in the encouraging words of the tiny Book of Jude, memorizing verse 21: "Keep yourselves in God's love as you wait for the mercy of our Lord Jesus Christ to bring you to eternal life." That helped immensely, but then a couple of days before the nationally prominent game at Washington, he was introduced to another powerful verse of Scripture, Exodus 14:14: "The Lord will fight for you; you need only to be still." Scott took those words to heart. He'd keep his mouth shut and just play football. As a reminder to keep that promise always before him, he wrote the verse on his wrist bands.

In Seattle the next Saturday, not only he, but the entire team, played inspired football. In the first quarter, Frost had magnificent touchdown runs of 34 and 30 yards. Meanwhile, the defense shut down the highly-touted Washington offense. Jay Foreman and Octavious McFarlin had outstanding performances, combining for 16 tackles, while others executed four sacks on the Huskies' quarterbacks. The win was a turning point in the season for Nebraska, vaulting the Big Red to third in both national polls, setting the stage for a run at a third national title in four years.

Every believer can learn a valuable lesson from that example. Of this you can be certain in this world: boos and jeers of opposition are going to come your way from those who are not a part of the team, those who are contrary to the play of God. But we do not have to satisfy such onlookers. We are in the game of life to please our Coach. After the "game" is over, we want Him to say, "Well done!"

Two weeks after the significant win over Washington, the Huskers dominated Kansas State 56-26, and then at Waco, Texas, beat up on Baylor, 49-21. After that, Nebraska moved to the top of the polls with an impressive 29-0 victory against Texas Tech, holding the Red Raiders to just 17 yards rushing and 110 passing. At Lawrence, Kansas, the next week, the Big Red made it back-to-back shutouts with a 35-0 score against the Jayhawks.

Then, November 1, 1997, marked two significant milestones. One of the nation's premier collegiate football rivalries had been Nebraska-Oklahoma. With the creation of the Big 12 Conference, that annual event was coming to a close. The game bore little resemblance to the classic matchups of the past. The Huskers jumped to a 34-0 halftime lead, then cruised to a 69-7 victory, the most lopsided score in the 78-game competition. The game also celebrated Coach Tom Osborne's 250th win, allowing him to reach that high distinction faster than any coach in college history. The night sky lit up in splendor as a dazzling fireworks display saluted the achievement.

That, however, was nothing in comparison to the thrilling squeaker against Missouri in Columbia the following week. Many people watching by television clicked off their sets in disgust; some listening by radio turned their attention to other matters; and at the game site itself, scores of erstwhile Nebraska fans headed for the exits to get ahead of the crowd. In doing so, they all missed one of the most defining moments ever in college football that blustery afternoon. Down by seven points with just over one minute to play and no timeouts remaining, the Cornhuskers, ranked #1 in the nation, took possession of the football on their own 33-yard line.

The Missouri players and coaches had paid little attention to the pollsters. Playing before an overflowing, record-capacity crowd of nearly 67,000, the Tigers battled the Huskers aggressively as both offenses moved the ball well. Missouri fans were on their feet, sensing a stunning upset; they were ready to rush on to the field in jubilation.

Nebraska, however, had not rolled to its 7-0 record without grit and gumption. Neither the players, coaches, nor thousands of fans were ready or willing to give up. The clock was ticking and hearts were pounding.

Ron Brown, in his eleventh season as receivers coach, had always insisted that though Nebraska was recognized for its rushing offense, when Coach Tom Osborne called a passing play, his players would be ready. Quarterback Scott Frost, nimble and powerful as a runner with the option offense, always yearned for more passing opportunities; this was certainly one.

He now had a chance to showcase his hours and hours of preparation. In what seemed like lightning speed–a minute of playing time–the Cornhuskers gained 55 yards. Frost hit Kenny Cheatham for 27 yards, Matt Davison for 13, then back to Cheatham for 8 and then 7. With 12 seconds to play and the ball on the 12-yard line, there was time for only one more play to snatch victory out of the gaping jaws of defeat.

In a pressure-packed moment, with no time for a conference, and hopes for a perfect season at stake, Osborne called for 99 Double Slant. Frost challenged his teammates as they lined up in shotgun formation. Everything that defines a football team and its season was on the line.

The play was designed to go to the left with Lance Brown as the primary target. As Frost drew back to throw, Brown was wide open, but he was only barely inside the five-yard line. They needed a touchdown. Instead, with a split-second instinct, Frost drilled the ball into the right side of the end zone. It was perfectly on target to Shevin Wiggins, but a Missouri defender also arrived as the ball did. With the deflection, the ball bounced up and down off Wiggins' leg and into the arms of a diving Matt Davison, who had not given up on the play. The referee's arms flew instantly into the air, signifying a touchdown–even as Missouri fans started to stream mistakenly onto the field.

With time gone on the clock, Kris Brown unerringly kicked the extra point through the goal posts to knot the game at 38-38, forcing Nebraska's first ever overtime.

In its possession from the 25-yard line, in two quick runs of nine and four yards by Ahman Green, Nebraska moved the ball to the 12-yard line. From there Frost pounded his way to the three and went airborne with a flip of his body into the end zone for his fourth running touchdown of the day. With Kris Brown's point after, the final score was 45-38, Nebraska. Missouri was unable to score during its ensuing possession.

That brief moment in football history changed Matt Davison's life in many ways. "Everyone was now familiar with my name and my face in public," he said. "I honestly never felt that I had done something spectacular. The catch itself was not that great of a play. The timing of it is what made it so famous. There were many plays throughout the season that were integral parts of us winning a national championship, and this was just one of them. With the changes that this play brought to my life, I decided to take advantage of it. This was my opportunity to praise God for the many blessings I have received and to let everyone know that my faith is the most important thing in my life."

In reflection on that play, Ron Brown observed, "An inexperienced quarterback, or one less poised than Scott Frost, may very well have run with the ball; that's what the quarterback is instructed to do if there's no one open on the left. Lance Brown was open, but Scott did a good job in recognizing that there was nothing there. And Matt Davison was pretty well covered to start with. Scott, knowing the situation and understanding the big picture, looked back to the other side. That is a very unusual thing for a quarterback to do on this particular play. In that circumstance, it took a great amount of poise and understanding of the offense.

"I think that Scott, as a senior, has become one of the great savvy quarterbacks in the country. He has a remarkable ability to improvise, a very clever player. For example, he was the best quarterback sneaker we ever had. Not only was he big and strong, but he had a great feel for where the hole was on a quarterback sneak. Often just a little bit of a crack, just a sliver of an opening was all he needed. He had an uncanny ability to lean left or lean right and get on through there. But most importantly, on this particular play—99 Double Slant—he knew not to run."

The significance of that game for the season was that it gave the Huskers a twenty-ninth consecutive season of at least nine wins, and kept alive hopes for a national title.

Iowa State was no trouble the next Saturday. In the first quarter, Nebraska exploded for 35 points, routing the Cyclones 77-14. Colorado at Boulder the day after Thanksgiving was a different matter. Missing several opportunities to slam the door on the Buffaloes, Nebraska gave up two touchdowns in the fourth quarter, but hung on to a 27-24 victory. It wasn't pretty, but it completed a perfect 11-0 regular season, giving the Big Red its second consecutive first-place finish in the Northern Division of the Big 12.

After suffering a disappointing loss in the first Big 12 Championship game the previous year, the Huskers were determined to erase that memory in San Antonio against Texas A&M. Nebraska eliminated any possibility of an upset early, scoring on all seven first-half possessions. The 54-15 win over the Aggies also secured a return trip to the Orange Bowl, which would mark the fourth time in five seasons that the Nebraska would play in the national championship bowl game.

The Huskers' hope for the title didn't depend only on their performance, but was contingent also on the outcome of the Rose Bowl contest between front-runner Michigan and Washington State to be played a day earlier. "After practice we watched that game as a team," Ron said. "The players were disappointed that Michigan won the Rose Bowl because the sportswriters were bound to keep them in the No. 1 position. But in what I believe was his best ever team challenge, Tom Osborne very calmly yet forcefully asserted to the players that if we won big against Tennessee, we could still get the vote from the coaches' poll. He also assured the team that he felt we could beat the Volunteers convincingly."

With that assurance of their coach ringing in their ears, the Cornhuskers played an inspired game against Tennessee. It was a sterling performance on both sides of the ball. The power offense of Nebraska racked up 534 total yards. And the aggressive defense held the Volunteers' premier quarterback, Peyton Manning, to just 134 yards passing, intercepting him once and sacking him once. In addition to his superb play at quarterback, Scott Frost's passionate plea for consideration in the postgame celebration might also have swayed a couple of votes. At any rate, in the wee hours of the next morning, the results of the final coaches' poll of the year were announced. The Huskers had gained a much deserved share of the national title, the third in four years.

Such a result is only achieved by teamwork. When the children of God also come together with equal determination to win for Christ, victory is assured. The words of Paul should be taken seriously when he admonishes every believer in Philippians 2:3-5:

> "Do nothing out of selfish ambition or vain conceit, but in humility consider others better than yourselves. Each of you should look not only to your own interests, but also to the interests of others. Your attitude should be the same as that of Christ Jesus."

CHAPTER 24

THE HUSKERS MINUS OSBORNE

U nknown to most at the start of the season, 1998 was to be the end of an era, a notable transition year for Nebraska football. It marked the end of the illustrious, 25-year career of Tom Osborne, a tenure renowned in national collegiate athletics. After the Big 12 title victory over Texas A&M, Ron and other coaches fanned out across America in recruiting responsibilities. Ron was in southern California when he had a thirty-minute telephone conversation with Coach Osborne. He was surprised, but not shocked, as the man he respected more than all other coaches explained his reasons for stepping down.

The next day, after Osborne stunned Husker fans by announcing that the Orange Bowl contest would be his last as head coach, Frank Solich was named to replace him. In responding to questions about following a legend like Tom Osborne, Solich said, "I have been preparing to coach this football team for more than twenty years and I'm excited about the challenge." That answer underscored one of the key reasons for the success of the Big Red program: faithfulness of the assistant coaches. True to their form of the past, there was an important and significant carryover under Solich. The entire staff of assistant coaches remained in place. That group of men represented an incredible combined continual experience of 106 years at Nebraska.

In addition to them, Solich added another eight years of Nebraska experience by hiring Dave Gillespie as running backs coach. Gillespie had earned three letters as an I-back in the mid-1970s and had been recruiting coordinator for the Cornhuskers from 1986-1993. Speaking of the dedication of his assistants, Solich observed, "They are continually making sure that they're on the cutting edge of their position, and always open to what's new."

George Darlington, defensive backs coach, is the senior among those assistants. He served under Osborne the entire 25 years and was the 1998 recipient of the All-American Football Foundation Top Assistant Award. During those years, 18 of his players went on to compete professionally. Coach Darlington, however, has much more going for himself than mere longevity and success on the gridiron. His personal commitment to Jesus Christ is the cornerstone of his life, and he is a frequent inspirational speaker for schools, church groups, and the Fellowship of Christian Athletes.

One primary thing about him which inspires his players to reach to their ultimate limits is his dedication to them as individuals. His basic coaching philosophy is "to guide each defensive back to reach his potential as both a student and an athlete." Since four of his players have been named All-Americans and four selected as Academic All-Americans, his standard apparently works.

One of his current charges is free safety Clint Finley from Cuero, Texas. He was recruited by Coach Turner Gill as a quarterback, but then willingly made the switch to defense. Even though he had missed three games as a high school senior due to a knee bruise, he was still named the Class 3A Player of the Year in Texas. As a defensive back, Husker coaches have been impressed with his game intelligence in reading the offense and his consequent ability to put on a hit.

During his first year at Nebraska, Finley redshirted. It was in that time that he experienced his most memorable moment under Coach Darlington. He had endured highs and lows during his first few months in Lincoln. Injuries had plagued him and homesickness didn't help. "I was really excited, though," he said, "that my mother was coming up for the Baylor game. Of course, I wasn't going to play in the game, but at least my mom would see me in a Husker uniform for the first time. But because I hadn't been able to practice, I was told I wouldn't suit out for the game. I was really sick about it. But when Coach found out that my mother was coming, he told me to suit up. I'll never forget that consideration."

That kind of understanding for the needs of others should be a motivating factor for every believer, no matter who the other person might be. In fact, that is the admonition of Paul in Philippians 2:3-5:

> "Do nothing out of selfish ambition or vain conceit, but in humility consider others better than yourselves. Each of you should look not only to your own interests, but also to the interests of others. Your attitude should be the same as that of Christ Jesus."

One man who has had a tremendous impact on the football team is not on the staff of the University of Nebraska; he is on God's staff. Chris Bubak is the Lincoln representative for the Fellowship of Christian Athletes. Since he took up that position in 1994, he has applied himself diligently to the task of being a witness to both athletes and coaches. In addition to his responsibilities for guiding huddles in the junior highs, high schools, and colleges of southeast Nebraska, he devotes himself to individually counseling athletes and to leading Bible studies. When he first began, he was able to gather only a few members of the football team together for a Bible study. But as his sincerity of purpose and knowledge of the Scriptures became evident to players, the numbers began to increase. Currently about forty Cornhuskers meet with him regularly, and some weeks there have been as many as sixty.

Beyond question, a player who has his or her heart settled in regard to eternal matters is going to be better prepared to handle earthly affairs. This is the promise of Christ in Matthew 6:33: "But seek first his kingdom and his righteousness and all these things will be given to you as well."

In his first year as head coach for the Cornhuskers, Frank Solich was confronted with an awesome tradition of winning and the considerable expectations that creates. The 1997 championship team had led the nation in rushing, total offense, and scoring. That senior class had a phenomenal 49-2 record over four years (best ever in Division I football), with a perfect 25-0 home record. Lost from that team was a powerful offensive line, headlined by Aaron Taylor at guard; a striking defense with Grant Wistrom at rush end and Jason Peter at defensive tackle; and an option scoring punch with quarterback Scott Frost and I-back Ahman Green, who opted to turn pro, foregoing his senior year. Green averaged more than 156 yards a game rushing, and Frost accounted for 91 yards rushing and 103 passing.

Nonetheless, Nebraska–by good recruiting and a fabulous walk-on program–always has plenty of talent coming on to fill the gap. With I-backs Dan Alexander and DeAngelo Evans on the mend, the media focus for 1998 was on the quarterback position. Frankie London was the only returning player with much experience, seeing action in nine games in the undefeated season. Bobby Newcombe, on the other hand, to gain more playing time, had switched to wingback and specialized in punt returns. Eric Crouch received a medical hardship due to injuries and did not play in 1997; consequently, he entered the 1998 season as a freshman. As a result of spring practice, Newcombe proved himself to be No. 1; London chose to move to wingback; and Crouch, who impressed the coaches with his consistency and passing abilities, was the No. 2 quarterback.

Nebraska jumped out to a 3-0 start under Coach Solich with wins against Louisiana Tech, 56-27; UAB, 38-7; and California, 24-3. The win in Berkeley against the Bears came even though the Cornhuskers were without five starters for the second time in as many weeks. That was a harbinger of what was to occur throughout the season. Bobby Newcombe, injured in the opener, couldn't play because of lingering soreness in his knee. Then Eric Crouch, who ran for two touchdowns, aggravated a hamstring strain and was replaced by third-string quarterback senior Monte Cristo.

Nebraska extended its winning streak to 18 (45 at home), beating up on Washington, 55-7; then made it 19 straight with a 24-17 squeaker against Oklahoma State, played for the first time at Arrowhead Stadium in Kansas City.

Texas A&M avenged its 54-14 drubbing by Nebraska in the 1997 Big 12 Championship game by upsetting the No. 2-ranked

Cornhuskers 28-21 in College Station. The win streak was at an end, and a hoped-for national title in serious doubt.

The Big Red rebounded powerfully against Kansas, blanking the Jayhawks, 41-0.

Missouri then came to Lincoln on October 24, determined to make up for the 1997 loss in the game marked by "college football's play of the decade." With 1:39 left in the game, the Tigers got a chance to mirror the miracle on a Monte Cristo fumble. But it was not to be. The Huskers posted a 20-13 victory.

The unranked Texas Longhorns, Nebraska's nemesis two years earlier in the first Big 12 Championship contest, arrived in Lincoln to put a final squelch on any hopes for a national title. The 20-16 upset came on a two-yard touchdown pass with 2:47 to play, ending also a 47-game winning streak at Memorial Stadium.

The Big Red, sinking to No. 14 in the polls, came back strong to beat Iowa State 42-7, but then lost to Kansas State for the first time in thirty years, 40-30.

A 16-14 win against Colorado prevented Nebraska (9-3) from having four regular season losses for the first time since 1963, and gave the Cornhuskers at least nine victories for a thirtieth consecutive year.

Incredibly, however, Nebraska suffered a fourth loss in the post-season Holiday Bowl in San Diego, defeated by Arizona, 23-20. But a significant victory did come out of the Holiday Bowl. Ron Brown, as an assistant coach, normally leaves the locker room for the sideline about ten minutes before the team and the head coach make their grand entrance. For bowl games, he likes to get out there even earlier. It gives him a few moments alone to read a portion of God's Word from a pocket New Testament he carries.

This time, as he was on the sideline bench reading, he was interrupted by the team's bus driver. The young man asked, "Would you pray for me?"

What he actually wanted was for Ron to pray that God would give him another chance to play football at the junior college he was attending. Ron was certain, however, that God wanted to give the man a lot more than that. As he challenged the driver with Scripture, as to who he was and who Jesus is, the man admitted that he didn't know Christ as his Savior. Opening kickoff was not far off, but sensing God's guidance, Ron led the man down the Romans Road (Romans 3:23, 6:23, 10:9-13), reciting God's powerful Word to the hungry soul.

He reminded the man that without a Savior, hell is our eternal end. He pointed out the Ultimate Sacrifice of Christ, His cruel death on the cross, His glorious resurrection, and His expected return. The man's heart was melting. Referring to John 14:6, that Jesus is our only hope for eternal life, the man responded, "yes," when Ron asked him if he wanted to repent and trust Jesus. They were interrupted by the singing of the national anthem. But just before the team exploded onto the field, the two men prayed together as the driver received Jesus into his heart.

Regardless of which side you were on and the outcome of the game, there was real victory on the field that night.

To football fanatics who think that winning is everything, there is no consolation in the fact that the four 1998 losses were by a total of only 26 points, or that the outcome of the Kansas State game hinged on an amazingly-missed face mask call, or that the string of injuries to key players was incredible. Or, or, or. . . .

For the Christian, however, there is a valuable lesson to be learned from the first year of the Frank Solich era. In winning or losing, did you do your best? Did you give it your best shot? Remember what Grantland Rice, that great sportswriter of the middle half of the century, wrote: "When the Great Scorer comes to mark against your name, He'll not mark whether you won or lost, but how you played the game."

Dr. John R. Church, a contemporary of Grantland Rice, was a renowned evangelist in the southeastern United States. Church had two sons. One, a healthy teenager. The other, a handicapped, club-footed boy of eight. The preacher came home late one afternoon from riding his circuit of country churches. His horse was hot and sweaty. He was, too.

His teenage son saw him coming and hurried out of the house and down the steps. He said, "Hi, Pop. Let me take your horse to the barn. I'll unhitch him and get him a drink of water. Then I'll throw him down a load of hay and get him a helping of oats. And while he's eating, I'll give him a good rubdown with a curry comb." Tired from his day of ministry, Church stepped down from his buggy. With a smile, he laid one hand on the shoulder of his son and said, "Thank you, Son. You're the best son a man could have. I'm so very proud of you."

As he wearily climbed the steps to the house, he saw his younger son clambering through the house to greet him at the door. As he stepped inside, the boy said, "Hi, Pop. Did you have a good day? Sit down while I pump you a glass of cold water from the well outside."

Church watched as the boy laboriously went to the well and pumped and pumped until the water turned cold. In his clumsiness, as he staggered through the house to where his father was seated, water splashed out of the glass onto the floor. Proudly, he handed his dad a half-full glass of water.

Tears loomed in the father's eyes as he said, "Thank you, Son. You're the best son a man could have. I'm so very proud of you."

Undoubtedly that is the attitude God the Father has toward every one of His children; it is not based on performance. Surely a goal for every believer in being a witness for Jesus Christ is found in Colossians 3:17: "And whatever you do, whether in word or deed, do it all in the name of the Lord Jesus Christ, giving thanks to God the Father through him."

CHAPTER 25

CERTAIN NON-NEGOTIABLES

While talking about what most people in football-crazed Nebraska are interested in, Ron Brown makes certain that they know where he's coming from as he speaks to the heart of the situation. He finds that in doing so, students and teachers alike are listening, and genuine spiritual openings present themselves.

In a Paxton, Nebraska, school appearance in the fall of 1998, a sixth grader came right to the point, asking Ron about Jesus Christ in his life. When given the opportunity, children are most likely to come up with unsolicited questions from the heart. The basic problem, Ron observes, is that "adults are squeezing God out of the equation. God has made an impact on the children's lives and they want to know about Him. They're told that God isn't cool. All the more reason to preach the Word, to declare what God is doing.

"How dare we—our Supreme Court—deny the Creator of the universe, God Almighty. We have to stand strong and not allow the non-negotiables to be negotiated."

For Ron, there are several other matters closely related to the Gospel on which there can be no compromise. Having been born out of wedlock and reared for the first years of his life in a New York City foundling home, he is very keen on the pro-life issue. More than 40 million unborn babies have been murdered in America since the Supreme Court legalized abortion on demand over a quarter of a century ago. Clearly, adoption is an option. Ron gladly involves himself in public service announcements for agencies involved in helping young women avoid the trauma of abortion and in helping the placement of children in homes of loving parents.

Closely related to the abortion issue is sexual promiscuity. At the conclusion of a western Nebraska high school assembly at which Ron spoke in the spring of 1999, Stan Parker was talking with one of the students. He asked her if she was going to college after she completed her senior year in May. Her response was, "Maybe after my baby is born." In that relatively small school, it was revealed that there were 22 girls, age 19 and under, who were pregnant. No wonder students are often restless and titter when Ron speaks out boldly for chastity and moral purity. This, however should be the consistent demand of all of God's children. The Bible's instruction is clear in Ephesians 5:3: "But among you there must not be even a hint of sexual impurity, or of any kind of impurity, or of greed, because these are improper for God's holy people."

Another issue of vital concern to Nebraska's receivers coach is the lack of relations between the races. Or, looking at it from the negative perspective, the insistent demand of many for the senseless, sinful separation from others. For years, he has been a spokesman for the Fellowship of Christian Athletes on the subject. His regular column, "The Race for Glory," in FCA's official magazine publication, *Sharing the Victory*, is read by tens of thousands. Those insights have formed the basis for a new book by Coach Brown, *Teamwork*.

The ugliness of racism is a frequent focal point in what he has to say wherever he goes. Such a stand is not popular with extremists from either side. White supremacists are opposed to a black man telling them anything. And hate mail and face-to-face confrontations with black Muslims are just as vicious. Nonetheless, Ron stands firmly in the Word of God, as authoritatively expressed in Galatians 3:26-29:

> "You are all sons of God through faith in Christ Jesus, for all of you who were baptized into Christ have clothed yourselves with Christ. There is neither Jew nor Greek, slave nor free, male nor female, for you are all one in Christ Jesus. If you belong to Christ, then you are Abraham's seed, and heirs according to the promise."

In being a witness for Christ, however, every child of God must look with compassion on those who, by their lifestyle, may not exemplify the best of life in the Kingdom. We must remember that in the eyes of God, each person we meet has meaning and purpose, from the uttermost to the guttermost. In his 1995 book, *The Jesus I Never Knew*, Philip Yancey addresses this matter forcefully:

> "I feel convicted by this quality of Jesus every time I get involved in a cause I strongly believe in. How easy it is to join the politics of polarization, to find myself shouting across the picket lines at the 'enemy' on the other side. How hard it is to remember that the kingdom of God calls me to love the woman who has just emerged from the abortion clinic (and, yes, even her doctor), the promiscuous person who is dying of AIDS, the wealthy landowner who is exploiting God's creation. If I cannot show love to such people, then I must question whether I have truly understood Jesus' gospel."

CHAPTER 26

EXTEND YOURSELF

All people who are active in the Kingdom of God have one outstanding characteristic in common: they cannot keep the truth, the beauty, the glory of Christ to themselves. Ron Brown should not be considered unique in this respect. He is only fulfilling what has been the basic desire of his Heavenly Father throughout all generations: that everyone, everywhere should know Him. This was God's plan when He created Adam and Eve. It continued through the darkness of the Deluge and surfaced gloriously when He chose Abraham more than four thousand years ago. It was not His desire that Abraham be the head of a tribal religion, but that through him all mankind would learn of the One Eternal Lord. This is the intent of what God declared in Genesis 12:2-3:

> "I will make you into a great nation and I will bless you; I will make your name great, and you will be a blessing. I will bless those who bless you, and whoever curses you I will curse; and all peoples on earth will be blessed through you."

Every man, woman, and youth in the Kingdom needs to get a similar "I-you" vision from God. Abraham was not one of great significance. He was just a wandering shepherd. His distinction for the ages is that he listened to God and accepted as fundamental truth what he was told: "Abram believed the Lord, and He credited it to him as righteousness" (Genesis 15:6). The inspiration he received from God was not so much on what he was to do, but on what God would do through him. The emphasis from the Almighty always is, "I will...I will...I will–as you are willing."

God has not lost His voice. He speaks continually. The problem is that there are so few who pay attention. Those who do listen are often misunderstood in their generation, only to be venerated centuries later. The Prophet Isaiah attempted to challenge the people of Judah for more than sixty years, spanning the reign of four different kings. Many passages of his poetry are today regarded as some of the finest in all of literature. The people of his day, however, did not heed his words and the result was captivity in Babylon for the entire kingdom. The strength for his persistence did not come from within him, but from the command of God, a challenge to us all in Isaiah 43:10:

> "'You are my witnesses,' declares the Lord, 'and my servant whom I have chosen, so that you may know and believe me and understand that I am he. Before me no god was formed, nor will there be one after me.'"

God also uses the voices and pens of others to get His message of challenge into the hearts of believers. Ron Brown's life has been greatly impacted by the life and books of George Mueller, the great British saint of the nineteenth century, who, by prayer, provided for the needs of hundreds of orphans and eventually missionaries around the world.

Once we get a vision from God, seeing the world from His viewpoint, we must allow Him to internalize it so that it becomes a breathing part of us. That creates character with integrity. When we know God personally and give ourselves over to Him as a vessel for His use, the purpose of our life comes into clear perspective. One of Ron Brown's favorite Scripture verses, which he uses in witnessing and often adds to his signature when signing autographs, is John 3:16: "For God so loved the world that he gave his one and only Son, that whoever believes in him shall not perish but have eternal life." That, however, is not a slogan to glibly indicate that someone is an evangelical. Much more, it is the central truth of all history. It is the hope of mankind, to which all the pages of the Old Testament point. And it is the fulfillment of God's amazing grace, to which all the writers of the New Testament give praise.

When any man or woman takes that fact to heart, it brings about a transformation, an understanding of what is truly important in life. Most people while away their stay on earth with eating and drinking, working and playing, sleeping and talking, talking, talking. Dr. E. Stanley Jones, one of the greatest Christian witnesses of the twentieth century, said, "Whatever gets your attention gets you." For most people, that would be politics, sports, or the weather. These are popular topics in almost any situation because people can argue and debate on any of these subjects and never have to make themselves vulnerable, never commit themselves to anything of eternal significance.

What God wants to draw our attention to is His divine purpose for us all. In our busyness–using up twenty-four hours a day–we, too, often lose sight of the fact that our world is made up of souls for whom Christ died. If we allow God to share His vision with us, if we allow Him to internalize that truth within us, then we cannot help but spread it, impacting others by extending ourselves. The words of 2 Peter 3:8-9 are to the point:

> "But do not forget this one thing, dear friends: With the Lord, a day is like a thousand years, and a thousand years are like a day. The Lord is not slow in keeping his promise, as some understand slowness. He is patient with you, not wanting anyone to perish, but everyone to come to repentance."

Or, as God expressed it in similar fashion six hundred years earlier in Ezekiel 18:32, "'For I take no pleasure in the death of anyone,' declares the Sovereign Lord. 'Repent and live!'"

Lisa Hitchcock, an associate with Mission Nebraska, has observed, "God showed us that He loves and cherishes each soul in this state. When people act in ways that hurt us or seem wrong, they are broken; they may be in a battle. We need to see the unseen and recognize that God is at work in their heart. Instead of responding in a cold and unloving way, we need to love them, take the time to see their hurting hearts, and respond as Christ to them."

Ron Brown had a unique opportunity to do just that in the spring of 1999. He is frequently invited to speak to assemblies of students at public schools. His message invariably includes a powerful testimony of his faith in Jesus Christ, since that is what gives impetus to all the rest of his life. It was only after a school in the central part of the state was on his schedule that he became aware that there was a major controversy. The superintendent and principal of the school were both opposed to Ron coming because of their understanding on the issue of separation of church and state. Nonetheless, the school board met and voted unanimously to have Ron come. The principal decided to dismiss school at 2:00 p.m. so that any students who didn't want to hear him could leave.

Aware of the situation, and knowing that the enemy was at work, many people were praying that God would work for His glory. When Ron met the principal, understanding the man's apprehension, he said simply, "Thank you for tolerating me." Ignoring the uneasiness of the situation as best he could, Ron went on to address the four hundred students who stayed with his usual enthusiasm. One man in particular who listened intently was the principal. Ron, of course, had no idea what was going on in the man's life. God knew, though, that the man had no saving relationship with Him.

Again that night, Ron spoke to about 550 people at the high school, unaware that he had been used at all in the life of the principal. The next Sunday, however, the principal went to the pastor of his church with a desire to trust Christ and to be baptized.

How did Ron Brown know exactly what words to use to break through the barrier into that principal's life? He didn't. All he did was witness to the truth that is in Jesus Christ. The Holy Spirit is the one who is responsible to make the words fit into the nooks and crannies of hearts. To all outward appearances, one would conclude that the principal was an enemy, but that is not necessarily correct.

The truth is much more sinister. As believers, when confronted with opposition, we need to focus on Ephesians 6:12: "For our struggle is not against flesh and blood, but against the rulers, against the authorities, against the powers of this dark world and against the spiritual forces of evil in the heavenly realms."

None of us needs to be concerned with fashioning fancy phrases to astound listeners with what we have to say. Such pretense often is a hindrance to spreading the Gospel. Instead, the Word of God is resplendent with assurance that it is He who will speak if we but have willing lips.

"Now go, I will help you speak and will teach you what to say" (Exodus 4:12).

"The Sovereign Lord has given me an instructed tongue, to know the word that sustains the weary. He wakens me morning by morning, wakens my ear to listen like one being taught" (Isaiah 50:4).

"Therefore this is what the Lord God Almighty says: 'Because the people have spoken these words, I'll make my words in your mouth a fire, and these people the wood it consumes'" (Jeremiah 5:14).

"But when they arrest you, do not worry about what to say or how to say it. At that time you will be given what to say" (Matthew 10:19).

"For I will give you words and wisdom that none of your adversaries will be able to resist or contradict" (Luke 21:15).

"This is what we speak, not in words taught us by human wisdom, but in words taught by the Spirit, expressing spiritual truths in spiritual words" (1 Corinthians 2:13).

At the same time, God is also very clear with His warning about our responsibility to be witnesses in our spheres of influence. In Ezekiel 33:7-9, for example:

> "Son of man, I have made you a watchman for the house of Israel; so hear the word I speak and give them warning from me. When I say to the wicked, 'O wicked man, you will surely die,' and you do not speak out to dissuade him from his ways, that wicked man will die for his sin, and I will hold you accountable for his blood. But if you do warn the wicked man to turn from his ways and he does not do so, he will die for his sin, but you will have saved yourself."

The children of God often get confused in regard to what their purpose in this life is. The simple fact is that everyone is a witness. Every man, woman, and child has an influence daily on others. The question, then, is to what do we witness? Do we witness only of the truth—that is, Christ? Or do we throw in opinion, prejudice, religious jargon, and vain babbling?

Almost anyone would be willing to speak up and say a good word about Jesus if they could be certain they wouldn't be laughed at or ridiculed or be considered odd. If they could see immediate results and count another soul to their credit who "prayed to receive Christ," they wouldn't be so reticent to speak their heart.

Jesus desires that we share that glorious truth with the lost. He will take care of the seed and will see to it that some of it falls on good soil, sprouts up, and yields a harvest (Luke 8:5-15).

Harry Walls, now a pastor in Birmingham, Alabama, is an outstanding example of a believer who fearlessly lived his faith openly. He learned in his Christian walk to trust Christ, not only for his own soul but for the souls of others. Harry, as mentioned in chapters six and eight of this book, had a profound impact on Ron by the manner in which he conducted himself and his obvious dedication to Christ. It was not any word of testimony he spoke. Rather, it was Harry's consistent spirit of encouragement and walk of faith in Christ that was a key in the hand of God to unlock Ron's heart. The greater beauty of that story is that Harry had no idea that he had any influence on Ron at all. He was simply dedicated to his Savior. It was not until twenty-two years later that he would learn the result of his witness. Surely there are multitudes of Christ's faithful followers who will only be rewarded with such news when they get to heaven.

Harry had been blessed with godly parents and their nurture in a Christian home. It was quite natural, then, for him to give his heart to Christ at the tender age of six, at the end of a week-long camp meeting in southern New Jersey. "I remember that experience as clearly as if it were yesterday," he said. "Wendell Fisher, a baldheaded evangelist from North Carolina, was the preacher."

Throughout his youth, Harry had an intense desire to help people; his career focus was to be a doctor. When he went to Brown University, he began a pre-med major and was a member of the freshman football team. More significantly, however, a man by the name of Dick Scoggins began to disciple him at that time. "I had loved Christ all my life," he said, "and I was faithful in attending church and Bible study and prayer. But the discipline of being accountable to Dick—and therefore to God—transformed my life."

Before the start of his sophomore year, God used another thing to change the direction of Harry's life. During the two-a-days practice with the football team that August, he broke a finger. For a receiver, that is a major injury. He continued the conditioning program with the team, but couldn't play. Instead, he began to put into practice the discipling skills he observed in Dick Scoggins. The first person he led to Christ was a second-string center on the football team. Then two other Bruin players came to Christ. He had found a new joy in life.

Harry talked things over with his dad. With that sage assistance, he came to a two-pronged decision: he quit football, and at the end of the year transferred to Liberty University to prepare thoroughly for a lifetime of ministering the Gospel. After finishing his seminary training there, he joined the work of Dr. John McArthur at Masters

College in California, where he served as student life minister. At about the same time that Ron Brown was beginning his career at the University of Nebraska, Harry joined the staff at Shades Mountain Independent Church in Birmingham. He became senior pastor of the 1,100-member fellowship in 1995.

In February 1999, Harry attended a conference, "Disciple the Whole Nation," in Houston, Texas. At dinner one night, he was sharing about his past and that he had played football at Brown University.

Another man at the table, Mark Pomeroy from Lincoln, became very interested in the conversation. He gauged the man's age and thought maybe there could be a link between Harry and his friend Ron Brown. "Did you know Ron Brown while you were there?" Mark asked. "He's the receivers coach at the University of Nebraska."

"I knew a Ron Brown," Harry replied, thinking there was some mistake, "but he was a defensive back."

The year before, Mark had read a few pages of *I CAN* with his son every night. Now he was trying to remember details. "Yes, Ron was a defensive back in college," he recalled, "but he coaches receivers. There was a guy who was at Brown for a short time who had a tremendous influence on Ron's life–I think you might be the man."

Without details, neither man could be certain, but Mark got Harry's telephone number just in case. Harry was touched in his spirit that he might have been used of God in Ron's life, but he decided to keep it to himself until it was confirmed. One of the first things Mark did when he returned home was to find his copy of the book. Sure enough, the eighth chapter was titled, "Whatever Happened to Harry?"

In the days that followed that "chance" encounter, Harry wondered deeply, trying to remember anything he might have done or said to influence Ron Brown. He remembered the man, of course, and running sprints with him, and was especially aware–being a receiver–of the prowess of the defensive back. But in humility, he could only conclude, "I was determined in my walk with Christ to be an encourager. Ron Brown was a recipient."

A few weeks after the meeting in Houston, Ron and Harry enjoyed a reunion by telephone. The next Sunday morning, brimming with emotion in telling the story, Harry declared to his congregation, "I have just experienced a little bit of heaven!"

What if Harry had not been at Brown University to intersect his life with Ron Brown's? Would there have been someone else? Harry Walls did not do anything unusual or out of the ordinary for a child of God. He lived a life of righteousness, and that was enough! That is always enough. A person living a life of righteousness is such a contrast to life as it usually is, that it is a powerful influence to all around.

CHAPTER 27

MANY HANDS
WORKING TOGETHER

J esus Christ, the Son of God, set a very simple standard of cooperation for His disciples. In doing so, He assured them of divine blessing if they would abide by it. Today, those words in Matthew 18:19-20 reverberate with challenge: "Again, I tell you that if two of you on earth agree about anything you ask for, it will be done for you by my Father in heaven. For where two or three come together in my name, there am I with them." The only thing wrong with that promise is that not enough of God's children lay claim to it–certainly not often enough. The problem might well be that the standard Jesus set is too high: two or three have to agree.

Paul admonishes in Colossians 3:1-3, "Since, then, you have been raised with Christ, set your hearts on things above, where Christ is seated at the right hand of God. Set your minds on things above, not on earthly things. For you died, and your life is now hidden with Christ in God."

This is one thing that stands out clearly in the ministry which has developed for Ron Brown, as he has collaborated with many other hands to work together, accomplishing far more than he could ever do alone. It is the same concept that Moses' father-in-law, Jethro, gave more than four thousand years ago when he saw Moses piddling away with small matters, when God's call on his life was to specific leadership of the people (Genesis 18:13-26).

During the last decade, Ron has been blessed by many willing hands joining him in what God is calling him to do in Nebraska. Certainly the greatest help, as has been mentioned already, are the hundreds who faithfully pray, looking to God to move on the hearts of men and women and boys and girls. Nothing is of greater importance. But there is also the need for hands-on effort, for those who help with scheduling and driving and logistics. Such assistance frees Ron to focus on presenting the Gospel, often several times in one day. The coordinated effort often involves such an intricacy of relationships in which the guiding hand of God becomes most evident.

One such day in 1998 was spearheaded by Gordon Thiessen of Grand Island, Nebraska. He had helped schedule Ron to speak at Sandy Creek High School, followed by Harvard High School, concluding with an outreach meeting that evening at Harvard, organized by the Fellowship of Christian Athletes. For Ron, this would be no ordinary day, as most of these events are not; they're more of a "God thing" than a "man thing." By the way events seem to fall into place, one can normally see clearly that it is the moving Spirit of God that has shaped the day and those involved.

Ron had prayed for several months about the possibility of speaking at Harvard. It began when he first heard from Andy Leichleiter, the FCA volunteer sponsor in Harvard. During the previous fall football season, one of the players, Nick Voorhees, had been seriously injured. Though he had never met Ron, Andy called Ron to ask him not only to pray for Nick, but also to visit him in the hospital. Even though he knew neither Andy nor Nick, Ron relished the opportunity to try to bring encouragement to the young athlete. Fortunately, Nick recovered, and even had a chance to appear at the Central Nebraska FCA Banquet that November to thank Ron and many others who had been praying for his amazing recovery.

Following that incident, Andy began praying about Coach Brown coming to speak at Harvard. To facilitate that, he contacted Gordon Thiessen because of his involvement with FCA. Gordon had already planned the meeting at Sandy Creek, and when he looked at a map, he realized that it was not that far from Harvard. It would make perfect sense for Ron to speak to both groups.

As all this began to take shape, many people in both communities were actively preparing for Coach Brown's visit. The day of the event was greeted with snowy and stormy weather–a typical Nebraska winter day. As Gordon headed to Sandy Creek, he talked to Ron on his cellular phone and found out that the vehicle in which Ron was traveling was heading into the middle of a heavy snowstorm. It was questionable whether they were going to make it to the school. The two men and others in their vehicles joined in prayer over the telephone. As it turned out, the storm cleared up just enough that Ron was able to make his first appearance with only a slight delay.

Unknown to most everyone in Sandy Creek, Ron had often prayed for a chance to share there. Some of his players had played high school football in Sandy Creek. He had also watched the girls basketball team play in state title games in the Devaney Center and was impressed with the school's athletic program. Heading out there that day, he felt it was going to be a great opportunity to share with the students.

It was a packed house–Nebraska football is a definite door opener. Though he had heard Ron speak numerous times before, Gordon was touched by the powerful blending of faith and career. "He wasn't there to do any altar calls," Gordon said later, "but he certainly was there to inspire and challenge students on pertinent issues of their lives. The message was tremendous. The response was an overwhelming sense of conviction by those who listened, a realization that maybe their lives could be better if they depended on God."

Following that meeting, the entourage rushed off to Harvard. It was another large audience of several hundred students. At the conclusion of the school assemblies, many people were aware that Coach Brown would again speak at Harvard in the evening, and at that meeting he would share more of his faith and also give an altar call.

Prior to the evening meeting there was time for a break. Ron and the other volunteers spent a little time at the Leichleiter home. Ron relished the opportunity to be with Andy's kids, playing Nerf basketball in one of the bedrooms, laughing and having a great time. Although he is a man on a mission–a mission to see young people saved and come to know Christ–he's really a kid at heart.

Gordon, meanwhile, used the downtime to get acquainted with Don French. He'd heard about Don and knew he managed a restaurant in Lincoln and had come to know Christ through Ron. He was impressed by the ministry Don had in volunteering to drive Ron to his speaking engagements so he could save his strength and get back to Lincoln safely at night. During each event, the drivers and others pray for Ron while he is speaking, and afterwards as well. It's a great network of volunteers who pitch in and make things happen as Coach Brown has traveled across Nebraska the last eleven years.

An FCA group was born at Sandy Creek as a result of that meeting. Gordon had the opportunity several weeks later to meet with them to get the Huddle started, making them an active group. At Harvard, a number of people will never be the same as they met Jesus Christ for the first time. Their lives and values, even their characters have begun to shift and change to what God wants them to be.

"I suppose," Gordon said, "over the last ten years that I've known Coach Brown, I've been privileged to hear him speak probably three to four hundred times. I can recall a time when he spoke in as many as seven different locations in a single day. I was the driver, and I can remember starting out early and traveling all the way from western Nebraska to Lincoln in one day. It got a little tiring and Coach Brown often jokes about how I wore him down on some of those trips. The results are always the same: God has His way with many people by using Coach Brown. He's human, of course, but he makes himself available, he tries to be obedient to God, and he uses the gifts that he has been given. But while Coach Brown has a very special gift of speaking, that doesn't excuse us from being responsible for sharing our faith with others."

A day in the life of Ron Brown is probably different than most of our lives, yet there are some things we all have in common. One thing for sure is that Ron is challenged every day as we all are about being a steward of our time. We can all start our day with prayer and Bible study. Ron believes that he doesn't even have a fighting chance as a person, father, husband, or coach without a non-negotiable quiet time alone with God, reading his Bible, and praying. There's no doubt that his relationship with Christ is where it starts. No matter how much or little time you have in the morning, SPEND TIME WITH CHRIST. Coach Brown tries to be responsible in that area. But there are times when his mind is full of clutter as he attempts his "quiet" time. The war that rages for silence and solitude during his quiet time is fierce. Taking every thought captive takes real diligence and "daily death." Ron admits that it's a battle that he has to often fight. In the wrestling match, God blesses and helps Ron use his gifts to serve Him.

Not everyone should be involved as hands and feet with Ron Brown. But the issue isn't Ron Brown—no one is called to join Ron Brown. We're challenged to join God and allow Him to show us our point of service and our co-workers. Most assuredly, all believers should know where God wants them to minister. One of the choicest joys of human existence is reserved solely for the sons and daughters of God becoming intimately involved in prayer with one or two other of His children to claim His blessing. Once again, this is the abundant promise of the Word of God: "This is the confidence we have in approaching God: that if we ask anything according to his will, he hears us. And if we know that he hears us—whatever we ask—we know that we have what we asked of him" (1 John 5:14-15).

CHAPTER 28

A SERMON

During the course of a year, Ron Brown receives more than two hundred requests to speak. Obviously, due to his weighty obligations as a coach, husband, and father, he cannot honor all of those invitations; he must be selective. On one occasion, June 5, 1999, he was one of the speakers at the Omaha Men's Conference held at Westside Church. His message was to be on "Preparing to Go to Work." At the conclusion of his message, Tony Lambert, senior pastor of the 4,000-member church, interrupted the proceedings to say, "I think that this, possibly, is the greatest message that has ever been given in this pulpit. And I'm fully aware that when I make that statement, I am covering a lot of ground, a lot of godly men through a lot of years." He then called the men to their knees in commitment.

Here is that message:

"I was assigned the topic for this morning of 'Preparing to Go to Work,' but to me, what I do is not work—I enjoy it so much. But sometimes you do get burned out a little bit with it. I'm at one of those stages right now. I just spent most of the month of May recruiting the top senior athletes for next year from everywhere around the country, especially in the western part. Then my high school basketball team was honored back on the east coast, so I had to fly there last weekend. So it has really been a jet lag kind of deal for me.

"In thinking about 'Preparing to Go to Work,' I really had to try to understand that concept of work. So many times I thought of it this way, that we are called as Christian men to be spiritual scientists. What I mean by that is, a scientist gets all this credit for creating things. But scientists don't create; they discover what's already been created. As I think about being a spiritual scientist, my role is to discover what God has created and where He's at work and join Him in that process. If you've done any reading in *Experiencing God* by Henry Blackaby, that's a concept he continues to nail, which I believe is very biblical.

"My role is to discover God and join Him at my workplace because God has already gone before me. I came to the University of Nebraska thirteen years ago, without knowing what God had in store. I didn't create anything. God had prepared the way and asked me to join Him with the particular gifts and talents that He's given to me. That applies to every single one of us here.

"That's the first thing I need to understand about work. It isn't about work that I can conjure up for God. God is doing a work among you—at your workplace, with people, with circumstances. My job, your job, is to discover what God is doing and join Him there. Therefore, I need to know my mission, my position, what God wants me to bring to the table. The Bible clearly talks about spiritual gifting, a packaging of gifting to every single person who comes to Christ as Savior and Lord, and joins God's family. And that is the only way you can join God's family—through Christ. You've been given some type of spiritual gift or gifting. Perhaps it's multiple, perhaps it's one. But everyone has been given a gift, including the natural abilities of singing or mechanical, you name it.

"Imagine a football player not knowing his position. I see it all the time with players we recruit. At some point they want to know, 'How do you want to use me, Coach? What position am I?' Can you imagine an offensive guard wanting to line up at wide receiver? I mean, it wouldn't make sense! Let's say he's six-foot-five and three hundred pounds. And he shows up in my meeting, thinking he's a receiver. If you look around the body of Christ, how many of us know our position? If somebody were to ask you, what are your gifts, what are your talents, what do you bring to the table? Do you really know?

"It seems to me that after we became Christians, in our

American way of discipleship–and I know this happened to me–no one ever explained to me or I never really got schooled in the intricacies of Scripture, regarding what God wanted me to bring to the table and what position I was to play. I think that it's crucial to have a purpose, a position, a mission. As I've thought about it, I've asked, 'God, what is my mission?' Because just as I can't begin to show up for work unprepared on Sunday afternoon when we get ready for another football camp for high school students, I really can't do the Kingdom business without understanding my purpose, without understanding in what it is God has asked me specifically to join Him.

"God is big. He's doing all sorts of things. I can't do it all. You can't, either. But there is some specific mission He has for us. So I thought about a mission statement. Is it to help us win a national championship? I tell you what. That's not good enough. We've only done it three times in the thirteen years I've been here. That's not very good. In a mission statement, we should be getting that done every year–of course, there are a lot of fans out there who believe that, too.

"At any rate, I sorted through all the outward stuff because coaching is just a disguise for me, it's a drawing card, a worm on the hook to get to the real thing. My mission statement is to intimately know Jesus Christ and to intentionally make Him known. I really believe that is why God called me to the state of Nebraska. I really believe that is why I have breath in my body. There is no other reason that's good enough, other than that. If anything else gets in the way of that, then I have problems.

"So my mission statement can't center on my career or my job. When I have time after football, then I can work on this mission statement. That's got to be it. That's the core. Then the career and everything else centers on that, what God has called me to do: to intimately know Jesus and to intentionally make Him known. And I put the stress on intimate and intentionally. It is an act of the will in obedience to the Lord Jesus.

"There are three portions of Scripture I want to hit with you rather quickly. Acts 20:24, where the Apostle Paul, in a sense, gives his mission statement—a great verse. In the midst of danger, Paul says, 'However, I consider my life worth nothing to me, if only I may finish the race and complete the task the Lord Jesus has given me, the task of testifying to the gospel of God's grace.' Paul understood his purpose. That's why, in any circumstance, no matter what it was looking like with his career, his climb up the ladder of success, and all these things that we put so much weight on—it didn't matter. Paul knew that in every situation, whether he was in a dungeon, in a jail, or thriving with the applause of people praising him for the message he just gave, it didn't matter. Paul was focused on a mission.

"Second Timothy 2:3-4 gives us the context of that mission: 'Endure hardship with us like a good soldier of Christ Jesus. No one serving as a soldier gets involved in civilian affairs—he wants to please his commanding officer.' Paul talks in the context of a war. We are in a war! It appears, at times, that we have peace. You go into your job and you don't necessarily feel this war, you don't sense that there is trauma all around you, danger all around you. That is because our lives are so limited. When you begin to see the unseen because of an intimate relationship with Christ, you begin to see the warfare around you, that it is a spiritual battle, that Satan is negotiating for your soul. He wants to take you down, and the battle rages on.

"Verse 4 goes on to say that 'he wants to please his commanding officer.' There are basically two types of people. There are those who do something, who work for something for the applause of men and women; and there are those seeking only the applause of God. You fall into one of those two categories at every moment of the day, with every decision and every thought. And I do, too.

"In the third portion of Scripture I want to hit, we get right to the crux of matter—and I want to talk on this one for a little bit—Luke chapter 4. There are three accounts in Scripture about Jesus' temptation. I like Luke here for this particular message because I want to accentuate in Luke's version the second temptation of Christ. Remember, He was led by the Spirit to the wilderness on the top of a mountain to be tempted. Understand this: We know He was God and could have resorted to His godly faculties at any time, but chose to suffer and live as a man, fully God and fully man. He allowed Himself to be tempted by the devil.

"Now, you all know what it is to be tempted by the devil as I do. Jesus was tempted the same way. But look at the second temptation in verses 5 and 6. 'The devil led him up to a high place and showed him in an instant all the kingdoms of the world. And he said to him, "I will give you all their authority and splendor, for it has been given to me, and I can give it to anyone I want to."' Isn't it interesting–and I hear it all the time from Christians–when you get a call from your boss or from someone else outside your workplace and they ask you to join them for a promotion. They want to promote you, in the eyes of the world, from your financial base, job prestige, status, the number of people working underneath you. And we say, 'God has blessed me!' We don't even think about it sometimes in terms of the fact that Satan gives these same promotions. We don't even consider sometimes who's giving the promotion. We automatically assume that you must take the promotion.

"People have said to me, for example, since I've been here in Nebraska, 'Why have you stayed here for twelve years? You've had job offers to go and to leave here for more money, more prestige. You can climb that ladder and have a better chance to be a head coach'–as if that is necessarily God's will for me. It's not even considered that maybe Satan is offering this thing.

"I mean, think about it a minute. Satan offers some good stuff. It's not just bad stuff that he offers. He offered Eve great knowledge, godly knowledge of good and evil. God had specifically told Adam and Eve, 'Eat from this tree, stay away from that tree.' Yet Satan said, 'Naw, this is a good thing.' Somehow we have justified these 'good things' and gone after them and chased after them.

"How about the battle cry back in 1876? Have you heard it? Maybe you've seen depictions on TV or you've read books about him–General George Custer. That battle cry he heard, just before he engaged in the Battle of the Little Big Horn in Montana. He saw a few Indians running down there in the bottom of the valley. Custer, a man of great ego, historians say, a man who was on track perhaps to be president of the United States of America. He had a lot of things going for him. He was a national hero. And without really thinking through the ambush that was about to befall him, he galloped after these few Indians with banners waving. And many men followed him, galloping along under his leadership.

"Then, with the perfect orchestration of strategy, Crazy Horse and Sitting Bull ambushed and killed the cavalry troop and General Custer–a man who rode to his destruction.

"That's how Satan works so many times. A promotion–Custer could see it from the hill–glory! And many of us think the same way on our jobs: if I could do this, if I could do that, if I could pull the right strings, if I elbow this guy enough and knock him down, if I can please my boss enough and do a few little goody things for him, if I can make the right contacts and write this little guy a card over here he'll remember me one day–and I'll get that promotion in life, forgetting that God Almighty is the God of promotion, the promotion that counts.

"I often think about the man who was possessed by devils. Jesus rebuked the devils and they came out of the man and they asked to go and reside in something. They pointed to some pigs on the hill and Jesus sent them to reside in the pigs. The pigs had just been grazing along, minding their own business. When Satan's army got into those pigs, what did they do? They all galloped together like the cavalry troop running down the hillside, off the cliff and into the water to drown. And that's many of us in the body of Christ as we pick up on promotions Satan is offering, not thoroughly considering it or understanding who is giving the promotion, and we gallop to our destruction.

"So the question I have to ask myself every day when I go to work: How much is it going to take to buy me off? When God gives me a nudging and an urging inside to go in a direction, how much money would it take to get me off just a little bit? How much of a job promotion would it take? How many people can work under me? How much prestige and national acclaim will it take for me to come off just a little bit? After all, I deserve better; I've been on track for this, prepared my life for it.

"When am I going to understand that it's not *my* life? It's not my life anymore! My life has been bought and paid for with a huge price! I can't look at that promotion the way *I* want to!

"One of the guys on our football team that really, I think, best demonstrated this focus, this intensity for a singular cause without being swayed, was a guy named Tommie Frazier, a great quarterback for us. The thing I really appreciated about Frazier was that when he walked into the huddle, he took charge. The huddle sometimes would be very chaotic, nobody paying attention. When Frazier got in that huddle as a freshman, in practice one day he told everybody, 'SHUT UP! I'm in the huddle! Nobody talks!'

"Freshmen quarterbacks don't talk like that. Frazier didn't care; he knew he had the play from Coach Osborne. He knew what he had to run. He didn't care what anyone in that huddle thought of him. So many of the other young quarterbacks would blend right into the huddle, become just like the huddle. You couldn't tell the difference between them and the huddle; it was chaotic. When Frazier got into the huddle, the huddle became like him.

"We men have been called to leadership, to walk into the huddles of our culture and to change the huddle for Christ. We've got the right play! We know what to do! Now we have to stay focused. But because everyone else around us is dipping a little bit to the left, or dipping a little bit to the right, we kind of sway with them because we like the popular vote. And it takes a real man and a real leader to say, 'You know, I don't care what they're offering me. I don't care what the rest of the huddle says. The huddle is going to become like me because I'm becoming like Christ.' As Paul says, 'Be imitators of me as I imitate Christ.'

"That's what I appreciated about Frazier. Yet, we drop the ball in many issues in our lives that affect our work for God. Alcohol– there are many of us here who have had to deal with that issue, I'm sure. I don't know you personally, but that's an issue in our culture and certainly among men. And our culture, basically, the huddle, says it's a cool thing for men. Turn on the TV, a nationally televised Nebraska game even, and you'll see numerous commercials where the huddle makes alcohol look like a great thing.

"I'm not here to tell you how much to drink. I can't do that. I've decided not to drink alcohol simply because I had to ask this question: 'What good has it done? What eternal benefit is this?' When I pick up the newspaper, concerning alcohol, there are people dying, people smashing up their cars. Satan will even use the good fellowship you see in these commercials, the time to relax and let you hair down a little bit. Let me ask you this. If you were about to get brain surgery tomorrow and your surgeon came up to you just before the operation and said, 'You know, I need a little calming effect here. Do you mind if I have a martini before we do this? How about a couple of brews? Would that be all right?' I don't think that would go over real good with you. You want that guy to be in the strongest state, the most godly condition he could be in–the way God made him.

"How about sex? This is an area we really struggle in. This is an area that's a problem at the workplace. A number of us probably work in a place where there are those of the opposite sex, and we can get off skew just a little bit. In a recent poll–and I call it the definition of sexcess–Americans were asked to list the most influential popular figures regarding sex and the influence of sex in this country. Here is what the listing was: Number one, Madonna; number two, Ellen DeGeneres; number three, Hugh Heffner; number four, Pat Johnson; number five, Dr. Ruth Westheimer. No wonder we're all screwed up! I mean, look at that list. That list has nothing to do with what it says in this Word about sex, how God says it is a beautiful, wonderful act for procreation and marital pleasure, a symbol of union between Christ and His church for us men to engage in with a wife. And yet we have decided to pervert it. We lust in our hearts.

"I recently had a pastor friend of mine tell me that during a pastors conference at a hotel, he was trying to witness to one of the hotel clerks. The man said to him, 'Get out of here with that witnessing stuff. This Jesus stuff doesn't mean anything to me. Do you realize this is a pastors conference and there are only pastors in this hotel for this week, and yet fifty percent of the pastors here have ordered X-rated films to come to the TV sets in their rooms? I don't have any confidence at all in you people.'

"Pastors struggle with this. Christian men struggle with pornography–a $10 billion per year industry–an addictive, horrifying sin. America won't blush anymore about a little clothing on TV or in books. And many of us may find ourselves in the grip of pornography.

"The violence in abortion. The huddle endorses it while we men look the other way in that issue. We've walked away from it– Christian men–many of us. It's mainly women who are fighting the battle. How can we walk away from forty million babies screaming for their lives since 1973? How can we walk away from that? What does this have to do with the workplace?–the devaluing of life. If you can't appreciate the life of a baby on the other side of that birth canal, how can you appreciate someone at your job? How can you really love them the way Christ loves them?

"Race and class is another issue how we separate into our little hierarchies. I recently read something on the *Titanic*. There were three times more first-class men that survived on that ship than third-class children. What that means was, there were a whole lot of guys on first class who were jumping in those life boats to save themselves. And third-class children on the bottom of that ship perished because of the hierarchy we have; we won't bend and reach over and pull others up.

"So I've really had to ask myself, 'God, am I just about being a football coach, just showing up at the office and getting things done, trying to win another game?' If that's all there is for me, somebody put me on top of a tall building and just push me off, because I'm ready for glory. I don't want it. It's nothing, nothing. I want some eternal significance, something that will last. I want a purpose.

"Now, it's painful, fellas. It's really painful to think that you're on track for something in your career. I came out of the Ivy League, people thought I was a smart guy. I rose very quickly in the profession in the eyes of the world: an assistant at Nebraska at thirty years of age, not much older than some of the players. People think I'm on track, man! I'm on track to be a head coach, to be a nationally known guy.

"You know, early on in my Christian life, I was buying into that. I was thinking, yeah, I'm going to give glory to God as I walk this line. I'm going to press all the right buttons. I'm going to visit all these pro camps and I'm going to write notes to this guy and I'm going to pat these people on the back and I'm doing things so that people will notice me, so that men will promote me.

"But God was speaking to me. And He was nailing me on some things. And each time a so-called promotion would come along to leave Nebraska, to fatten up that resumé, God would say, 'You can go. But I tell you, I have something better for you. If you're willing to die, die to your reputation, die to your career; I've got an eternal weight of glory for you.'

"I had to ask myself—and it was a struggle and it was painful— each time I have decided to do it what I believe is God's way. I'm not saying you don't ever accept a promotion. I think of guys like Craig Bohl and Turner Gill on our staff—great Christian guys—it looks like God has them on track. And I say to myself, 'You know, I'm just a little bit older than those guys.' That was me. I was on track. I turned down a pro offer in 1994. Boy! That would have been a great move. Christians were telling me, 'Man, that is a great move. You get to work for a Christian guy. You get to be in the NFL, a lifelong dream for you.' I mean, I've been tracked for this. I've worked hard for this. This is my career. And God, I knew it, was leading me somewhere else. Inside, He was saying, 'I'm not done with you in Nebraska yet. You can go if you want. But I'm not done with you in Nebraska yet. How much is it going to take to buy you out? How much is it going to take? Is it going to be pro? Is it going to be more money? Is it going to be prestige? What will it take?'

"I really thought about what God had gifted me in. He has given me a platform to preach the Gospel across the state. I get a chance to walk into public schools all over Nebraska and share about Jesus. I have the ACLU running down my back right now. But that's all right, that's all right. What I'm trying to say, fellas, I'm not trying to exalt myself. All I'm saying is that it's painful when you've been gripping something for so long and God says, 'Will you let that go? Will you let that go? Will you let that go?' It hurts. It hurts as He pulls those fingers apart.

"I went back home and my friends asked me, 'When are you going to be a head coach? We expected it by now. It's time!' Many of them are worldly, and even some of them who are Christians don't understand that God has a great plan for me, for me to join Him with.

"Some of you are going through that, these sacrifices you have made, and you wonder, 'Man, was I dumb? Ten years ago I could have been this, I could have been that, I could have been doing this.' I go through that all the time. I look back and I say, 'Man, God!' But then I'm reminded. I was reminded when I went to Hastings last night and spoke to people who were walking in an American Cancer Society Relay for Life, who are ready to die, many of them. And I get to share the Gospel with them and see the look of hope in their eyes afterwards. Then I'm reminded, 'Man, this is where it's at!' There is something far greater than some worldly promotion in life.

"So, what's it going to take to get our full attention on God and doing it His way? Just think if you had a Scrooge experience tonight. Remember Ebeneezer Scrooge, that man who was so bad around Christmas time? He had that dream that night before Christmas Day, and the angel took him to all those places, and he saw people he had mistreated. And he saw how hard these people worked and how good these people were, and he was convicted, and he began to treat them in a whole different manner.

"Just think if God gave you a similar experience. He could take you to heaven tonight in some kind of a dream or revelation. You could see streets of gold up there and people who are praising God forever and ever and ever, people sitting at the feet of Jesus, worshipping Him. No more injury and illness and disease; people loving God. And you'd say, 'This is where I want to be. That's what it's all about!'

"But God says, 'We're not done yet. You haven't seen it all yet.' Then you would take a trip to hell. You would see in hell people burning in a lake of fire because it is real. Jesus talked more about hell than He did about heaven. You would hear people screaming! The Bible says there is 'weeping and wailing,' people screaming at the top of their lungs for ever and ever and ever. It's like being tortured and never dying–forever. It will be a place of outer darkness and loneliness.

"Some of you are lonely today. You don't know what loneliness is until you see what is in hell. Eternal fire. These regrets. Why didn't I listen? You'd see people there that you'd loved, but your work got in the way of sharing the Gospel with them. You had to go get another promotion. You had to give up this career that God wanted you to get into to bring Him glory because you had to go get the dollars and success. After all, that is what you were tracked for.

"You'd be very disillusioned, very disappointed. You'd say, 'God, I want to get out of here!'

"'We're not done yet,' God would say.

"He would take you to the Garden of Gethsemane where Jesus was on His knees and He was praying so profusely that the sweat coming out of His head was as if it were blood coming down, knowing that He was going to the cross, knowing that He was sacrificing everything. And you would feel guilty for what you and I have not sacrificed for Him.

"God would say, 'No, we're not done yet.'

"Then we'd go to the front row, and you would see on the big screen up top, Isaiah 52:14, where it paraphrased that Jesus was beaten like no man had ever been beaten before. Then you'd realize and witness for yourself the replay of the ugly scourging before Christ hit the cross, where they literally tore open His flesh, and His body and His bones were revealed. Historians say that between the eighteenth and twenty-fifth lash, you could begin to see a man's bones. If you read Psalm 22, the prophecy of Christ's crucifixion before He died, you'll realize that His bones were exposed. He was brutalized. He was punched out. He was unrecognizable. He was fully God; He could have gotten out of it like that. But He chose to suffer as a man. Perhaps in metabolic shock, dehydration, with a cross on His back of a hundred or a hundred-twenty-five pounds, trudging up the hill to Golgotha, collapsing and falling, getting back up with the help of another.

"Keeping His eyes focused, and not letting the huddle change Him, He didn't give it up. He kept going straight ahead. He had a singular purpose in mind, and that was to go to the cross for every single one of us. And then to allow the nails to come pounding through the hand area, in excruciating pain. The ankles crossed, the driving spike went through. Hoisted up on a cross. If you read the fifteenth chapter of Mark, you realize He hung on the cross for six hours in incredible agony and pain. He was separated from His Father. Everybody else left Him; so many left, even those who had known His intimate love.

"You and I are guilty. First of all, in our sin. But even after coming to Christ, we're guilty for leaving behind the purpose for which God has placed us here: to intimately know Him and to intentionally make Him known. To allow Him to pick and choose our lives.

"So, I'm moved by a soldier of a different sort. I'd like for you to hear about this soldier. I just want to read an excerpt briefly, regarding a young woman from Columbine High School named Cassie Bernalt. I had the opportunity just a couple of weeks ago to sit on an airplane next to Cassie Bernalt's Mary Kay representative, a woman who went to church with Bernalt. I heard some amazing things. But here's something that might interest you:

"Among those who were killed at Columbine High School was Cassie Bernalt. It was Cassie who made the dramatic decision I just described, fitting for a person whose favorite movie was 'Braveheart,' in which the hero dies a martyr's death.

"Cassie was a seventeen-year-old junior with long blond hair, hair she wanted to have cut off and made into wigs for cancer patients who had lost their hair through chemotherapy. She was active in her youth group at Westpool Community Church and was known for carrying her Bible to school.

"Cassie was in the school library, reading her Bible, when the two young killers burst in. According to witnesses, one of the killers pointed his gun at Cassie and asked, 'Do you believe in God?'

"Cassie paused and then answered, 'Yes, I believe in God.'

"The gunman asked, 'Why?'

"Cassie did not have a chance to respond. The gunman had already shot her dead.

"As her classmate, Micki Cain, told Larry King on CNN, 'She completely stood up for God. When the killers asked her if there was anyone who had faith in Christ, she spoke up and they shot her for it.'"

"You know, when those killers went in that day, they were looking for categories of people. One of them was athletes, which I can relate to. But those athletes were under the tables, hiding. Why? Athletics isn't worth dying for, that's why! There isn't anything about athletics in itself that's eternal! Why would you die for athletics? That's why they went running and hiding.

"But, when they asked for someone who believed in God, there was somebody in there: a young seventeen-year-old who knew that God was something to die for! That was the work that God had called her to, nothing less! And she stood up, knowing she was going to get shot.

"The woman who sat next to me on the airplane said she believed Cassie, because of her evil deeds in the past before she came to Christ, knew these killers, and they knew she was a Christian. And they sought her out. And she was willing to stand up and die for her faith.

"I've often thought since reading and listening to that, 'Man, God! It took You to take a seventeen-year-old girl to teach us how to be a man for Christ. How to really be a man, how to really be a champion. Because she was willing to stand up and die.' Yet we're not even ready to die to our careers, to our reputations, to our egos, let alone our lives. We're just strung off in all kinds of diversions.

"You don't have the right to take a second look at a young girl walking down the street who looks good. You've been bought! What's it going to take to sell you and me out? Picking up a magazine or turning on the TV to things that we should not be looking at? You don't have the right! What's it going to take? Half nudity, full nudity, someone approaching you, someone making it so easy and so convenient for you that you couldn't turn it down? What are you going to sell out for? On your jobs? Outside of your jobs? With your families? With Christ?

"What are you willing to die for? Are you willing to stay singular for Christ? That's the question I have to ask myself every day. I have to die daily, as Paul said. And it hurts! It hurts to do that. You may listen to me talk and encourage others on the radio, but there are many times in my life while I'm doing it that I'm hurting inside. I'm letting go of some things that I could have had; 'God, why are You holding me back?'

"He's not holding me back. He's accentuating every single time. So basically, I've come up with a math equation of how to live life for Christ. Simply, it is my responsibility, it is your responsibility, to divide God's Word every day, rightly divide God's Word. Gentlemen, there is no way that we can understand what position we're going to play, there's no way we can understand the big picture without knowing the Playbook of Life. A football player can't possibly go out there and really be a great player without understanding the playbook, understanding the context of the team, how it functions and how that person's position specifically coincides with other people's positions.

"I suggest to you, and to myself as well, to get into this Book regularly. Begin to read often, if you haven't, about spiritual gifting, wherever you've been called. God has called me to be a public exhorter and an evangelist. If I were to go somewhere and be a head coach right now, I guarantee you they'll try to put the squeeze to me. I could take that promotion, and Satan would be clapping in applause, saying, 'Go for it, Baby! I'm going to shut you up. And that's how I'm going to do it. I'm going to get you so politically entangled that you can't open your mouth the same way you do now.' I know Bill McCartney went through that rub.

"Some people are not evangelists. They can kind of fit into these spots that maybe I can't fit into. But God has created each one of us for a purpose. That's why you can't compare yourself with others. So we are to rightly divide the Word. Then we have to subtract the flesh. That is our job, to subtract every day the flesh, the ego. The Bible says in Romans 12:2, 'Do not conform any longer to the pattern of this world, but be transformed by the renewing of your mind. Then you will be able to test and approve what God's will is —his good, pleasing, and perfect will.' You have to subtract! John the Baptist said, 'I must decrease and He must increase.' No self-esteem building yourself up. Subtract the self, and God enters in, and He leads you to great and mighty things.

"Then it's God's job to add and to multiply. Peter said, 'Lord, we have left all and have followed you.' And Jesus said, 'Anyone that will leave behind all of these things, will get them back in this life—and life eternal, with persecutions.' What He means by that is, in my leaving behind these job promotions and all these things, I've gained a whole new family here in Nebraska. I have brothers and sisters all over the state of Nebraska, whom I get out across the state and see.

"While I'm preaching and sharing about the Good News of Jesus Christ, I'm able to fellowship. And it's been a wonderful experience. God has added and multiplied in my life, and He has put others around me to build me up in Christ, stronger men and women than me, to encourage me along. And there have been persecutions. Whether it be the ACLU or any other force that is out there, there will be persecutions. 'I can do all things through Christ, who gives me strength.'

"So, that's my admonishment to you today, guys. On your job, I can't tell you how to do your job and run your job. But I can tell you this, though, that God has a master plan. He has an ulterior motive for your job. It is really a disguise, it is an entry point to get in with the Gospel. I think that if we strategically see how God has created us with the gifts and talents spiritually He has given us, combined with the natural talents He has given us on our jobs; and you see the spiritual packaging together; and you dedicate that over to God and you lay it before Him every day; and you die to yourself and allow Him full play—that's when the power really steps out. That's when you are really powerful in Christ."

The fact that Ron found ultimate satisfaction in Jesus Christ was not an end in itself but a beginning. In fact, Ron, even though he's on the winning team—the body of Christ—still has to do battle every day. The most significant point of this book is that true success is not measured by wins and losses on the field, nor by human acclaim or status in any other endeavor. More than being successful, the role God has in life for every man, woman, and child is to be faithful to His eternal purpose.

In reflecting on his thirteen years with the Cornhuskers, Ron said, "I believe God called me to Nebraska to remind people of who Jesus is and He used football as a medium. It's not that people hadn't heard before or that the message is unique. But the platform of football was so big that it opened the door." By means of radio, television, printed media, and speaking engagements, Coach Brown has some awesome opportunities.

In similar fashion, every person who reads this book has his or her own spheres of influence. It may be a mother whose primary touch is on three children and a husband. But she also has a responsibility to the checkout clerk at the grocery store, the gas station attendant, the woman next door, etc.

The student reader has a great range of influence to a number of other students, teachers, brothers, sisters, and parents.

The man who thinks his life is a humdrum affair of eight hours daily of repetitive work needs to allow God to awaken him to the fields that are "ready for harvest" all around him, all the way to the halls of Congress.

In short, it is hoped that everyone will catch their own fresh vision from God and know that "I can do this. Indeed, I must!"